Starting a Small Business in Connecticut

Managing Editor   **John S. Purtill, Jr., CPA**

Sponsors   **Community Accounting Aid Services, Inc.**

Connecticut Small Business Development Center

United States Small Business Administration

ISBN 0-9639309-3-1

This material is based on work supported by the United States Small Business Administration under cooperative Agreement Number 4-7770-0007-13. Any opinions, findings, conclusions or recommendations expressed in this publications are those of the authors and do not necessarily reflect the views of the United States Small Business Administration.

This publication is designed to provide practical and useful guidance about the subject matter covered. In publishing this book, neither the authors, the editor, the sponsors nor the publisher are providing accounting, legal or other professional services. They cannot and will not assure that your business will be successful as a result of implementing any advice contained in this book. For accounting, legal or any other expert advice, you should consult with a qualified professional.

EDITORIAL STAFF

Managing Editor

John S. Purtill, Jr., CPA   Purtill & Company PC, Cheshire

Assistant Editor

John S. Purtill, III   Purtill & Company PC, Cheshire

Contributing Authors

Steven K. Carter, CPA	Carter, Hayes, and Associates, PC, New Haven
A. Donald Cooper, CPA	Cooper & Company, Ltd., Waterford
John L. Evanich, Jr., CPA	Haggett, Longobardi & Company, LLC., Glastonbury
John K. Jepsen, Jr.	UPC Capital Business Credit, Hartford
Susan K. Krell, JD	Jackson Lewis LLP, Hartford
Paul A. McMahon, CPA, FLMI	Consultant, Bristol
Andrea Obston	Obston Marketing Communications, LLC, Bloomfield
John J. Palmeri, JD, CPA	Attorney-at-law, Cheshire
Anthony J. Switajewski, CPA	Deloitte & Touche, Hartford
Lynette Vallecorsa	Paychex, Wethersfield

Editorial Advisors

Lori Budnik, CPA	Blum Shapiro & Company, West Hartford
Lucia M. Chubet, CPA	Purtill & Company, PC, Cheshire
John Ertlmaier, CPA	Westport
Charles J. Frago, CPA	KPMG, LLP, Hartford
Vernette D. Gray, CPA	Purtill & Company, PC, Cheshire
Pat McMahon, CPA	Fulco, DiTommaso, McMahon & Co. PC, Newington
Thomas J. Mortimer	Avon
Dan O'Mara, CPA	O'Mara & Rehrman, Hamden
Danny A. Pannese, CPA	Trumbull
Ernest E. Pierson, CPA	Fairfield
Anabella Pinho-Cerdeira, CPA	CIGNA, Bloomfield
Wayne Stanforth, CPA	Southington
William D. Zeidenberg, CPA	ILZ Group, Woodbridge

Cover Design

Betty Standish   Standish Associates, Wethersfield

ABOUT OUR AUTHORS

Without the efforts and knowhow of our authors, this book would not exist, and we would be without the resources needed to help small business owners. We're proud of them and would like you to know a little more about them.

John S. Purtill, Jr., CPA is Managing Partner and a management specialist with Purtill & Company, Cheshire. His experience includes financial and general management assignments in two major corporations. His firm provides services to small businesses including business and tax planning, accounting and business systems. He is author of several education courses sold to CPAs throughout the United States.

Steven K. Carter, CPA is a Partner in Carter Hayes and Associates, PC, New Haven. He has a comprehensive background in not-for-profit organizations and closely-held businesses.

A. Donald Cooper, CPA, is a Partner in Cooper & Company, Ltd., Waterford. Mr. Cooper directs the firm's Management Advisory Services Department, which offers planning and consulting services to small businesses in addition to traditional accounting and tax services.

John L. Evanich, Jr., CPA is a Principal with Haggett Longobardi & Company, LLC, Glastonbury. Hspecializes in tax research and consultation.

John K. Jepsen, Jr. is Vice President and Commercial Loan Officer in UPS Capital Business Credit, Hartford, specializing in commercial lending.

Susan K. Krell, JD is a partner and employment law specialist in the Hartford office of the national employment and labor law firm of Jackson Lewis LLP. She represents clients before government agencies and in court, conducts employment law training, and has been voted by her professional colleagues to be in Best Lawyers in America since 1991.

Paul A. McMahon, CPA, FLMI, is a retired insurance systems and productivity consultant from IBM and Digital Equipment Corporation. He operates a Bristol-based management consulting firm.

Andrea Obston is the president of Obston Marketing Communications, LLC, Bloomfield, specializing in public relations and special events.

John J. Palmeri, JD, CPA is an attorney-at-law in Cheshire. He is a frequent speaker and author on tax topics.

Betty Standish is a graphics designer at Standish Associates, Wethersfield, a full-service advertising, marketing and public relations agency specializing in business-to-business communications.

Anthony J. Switajewski, CPA, is a Senior Manager in the tax department of Deloitte & Touche in Hartford. He specializes in tax planning for individuals and small to medium size businesses.

Lynette Vallecorsa is sales manager for Paychex, the Wethersfield payroll processing firm.

FOREWORD

Throughout its history, Connecticut has depended on its many small companies to create products, services and jobs. The creative spark for these companies comes from individual entrepreneurs who take personal risks to implement their business ideas. Sometimes, their risks bring financial rewards. But always, the risks bring the personal rewards of ideas born, people served, products manufactured and jobs created. Supporting these entrepreneurs is a cadre of advisers and service providers who enable small business owners to launch their ideas, bring them to market and make their companies prosper.

This book is dedicated to these entrepreneurs and their advisers. It was written for people who are going into business for the first time, but many parts of it will be valuable information resources for experienced company owners. It is made available through Community Accounting Aid and Services, Inc. and the Connecticut Small Business Development Center. Every year, business counsellors from CAAS and CSBDC spend thousands of hours helping entrepreneurs through the challenges of starting their own companies. This has been one of their handbooks. Thousands of copies of earlier editions can be found in successful companies throughout the state.

We designed the content of this edition by asking two questions: *What topics do our clients most often ask about?* and *What topics give small companies the most difficulty?* We then enlisted some of Connecticut's leading business advisors as authors. They drew on their extensive experience to put complex business concepts into practical, useful terms, and added many examples to illustrate their ideas.

Like many publications, this was the work of many people and was supported by many organizations. We gratefully acknowledge the contributions of the many sponsoring organizations, advisors, copyreaders, technical reviewers, administrators and others who made the book possible. The list, as complete as we could make it, appears below.

Connecticut Society of Certified Public Accountants
United States Small Business Administration
Connecticut Small Business Development Center
Connecticut Economic Resource Center, Inc
University of Connecticut School of Business Administration
John J. Collins, Community Accounting Aid Services
Dennis Gruell, Connecticut Small Business Development Center
Mark Zampino, Connecticut Society of Certified Public Accountants
EPS Printing, Inc.

TABLE OF CONTENTS

TABLE OF CONTENTS

TABLE OF CONTENTS

INTRODUCTION

At first glance, the Connecticut business climate seems to favor large companies. After all, many of the five hundred industrial giants on Fortune Magazine's annual company list have their headquarters or operations in Connecticut. But, Connecticut's history of innovation also makes it a breeding ground for small businesses, even during tough economic times. The state boasts thousands of small businesses and thousands of new ones start up every year. Not all of those new businesses are successful. In fact, 75% of all businesses fail in their first year of operation. We want your business to be part of the 25% that succeed!

Starting a successful business means more than having a good idea for a product or service. The idea must be planned, financed and brought to market. Then, if you want your company to remain successful, you must have an information system that allows you to make good business decisions. And, you must comply with many tax, record-keeping and employment rules. If you fail to do these things, you may make poor business decisions and you may also have to pay extra taxes and penalties.

The purpose of this book is to help you to go from a good idea to a good business. It draws on the expertise of some of Connecticut's leading experts in business planning, accounting and taxes. These authors have used their experience in helping small businesses to bring you useful, practical advice on how to start up and run your business.

The material in the book is arranged in the order in which you'll use it to start your business, starting with writing a business plan. It takes you through deciding on the type of business, setting up business records, paying payrolls, dealing with employees and finally, paying income taxes.

ORGANIZATION OF CHAPTER

This chapter discusses the following topics:

- Starting up a business.
- Why do people start small businesses?
- Are you ready to run a small business?
- Getting free help for your business.

STARTING UP A BUSINESS

The Appendix at the end of this chapter has a checklist that shows the process you'll need to follow in setting up your business, once you've decided on what the business will be. Although it does not cover every possible situation, it is a good starting point.

This checklist emphasizes the six important success factors for small businesses:

■ Develop a business plan to guide you.

■ Have enough money available to start your business and to carry you through the start-up phase.

■ Select the right form of business organization and get it formed correctly.

■ Market your company effectively.

■ Keep good business records.

■ Handle your tax obligations without paying too much or too little tax.

WHY DO PEOPLE START SMALL BUSINESSES?

Everyone has a reason, but more than any other reason, people start small businesses because they want the autonomy that goes with it. A recent survey finds that business owners have both financial and nonfinancial reasons for business startups and the nonfinancial reasons are the most compelling.

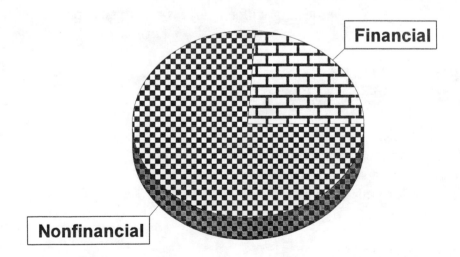

The proportions are summarized in the following table.

- Financial reasons include earning more income and building personal wealth.   24%

- Nonfinancial reasons include being self employed, being independent, seeking   76%
  personal challenge, pursuing an idea, using skills, meeting personal expectations, building an organization, gaining respect or recognition, contributing to
  society, living in an area of choice or other reasons.

- Total   <u>100%</u>

ARE YOU READY TO RUN A SMALL BUSINESS?

Should you start up a small business? Maybe not, because running a small business isn't for everyone. If small business isn't for you, one of the best things this book can do for you is to suggest you stay out of it. Successful small businesses demand much from their owners, and many of them fail because their owners don't have the right personality traits for the small business environment. This is a list of some of the personality traits the Small Business Administration says are important for small business owners:

Experienced	Having a management or supervisory background in the type of business being started.
Farsighted	Able to set goals and plan ahead.
Leader	Able to direct the activities of others and accept responsibility for the results.
Organizer	Able to develop and establish routines and procedures for efficient execution of plans.
Decision maker	Able to make decisions quickly and act on them.
Disciplined	Able to get things done on time.
Hard working	Willing to work long hours.
Motivated	Able to be a self-starter, without someone else to initiate actions.
Healthy	Having the stamina and energy to do everything that is required in the business.
Personable	Able to work with customers, employees and suppliers.
Adaptable	Willing to learn new techniques and procedures.

GETTING FREE HELP FOR YOUR BUSINESS

Two of the sponsors of this book, Community Accounting Aid Services, Inc. (CAAS), and the Connecticut Small Business Development Center (CSBDC) provide free start-up services for small business owners. We urge you to take advantage of these services.

CAAS is a not-for-profit organization supported by the accounting profession, CSBDC and by several Connecticut companies. It consists of a full-time executive director and a network of CPAs and accountants who offer education services to all businesses and free professional services to *disadvantaged* businesses. There are three ways to take advantage of CAAS services:

Education services	CAAS professionals conduct seminars throughout the state, in conjunction with the CSBDC and local adult education programs. Contact CAAS, CSBDC or the local board of education for a schedule. There is a small charge for these seminars.
Accounting assistance	CAAS professionals provide a full range of accounting assistance, except for financial statement audits, to eligible disadvantaged businesses. To be eligible for this free service, a CAAS client must have less than $25,000 in net income or be a not-for-profit organization with an annual budget less than $100,000.
Workshops	CAAS professionals conduct free tax workshops and clinics. To find out about them, contact the CAAS office.

CSBDC is a cooperative venture of the United States Small Business Administration and the University of Connecticut, which operates a network of consulting offices in Connecticut.

This book is a CAAS/CSBDC service to small business, too. Study it carefully and use it for reference. It was written by CPAs, lawyers and other business people who run successful companies and who help others to do so. It explains the many steps you must take to get started in business and to run your business. You must be prepared to take these steps if you want to be successful.

 NOTE The Appendix in this chapter contains a list of Connecticut organizations that provide accounting, management and finance support to small business owners.

Appendix

Business Startup Checklist

Business plan creation

_____Establish business and personal goals
_____Assess your strengths and weaknesses
_____Do market research
_____Identify your customers
_____Identify your competitors
_____Develop a marketing plan
_____Assess your financial resources
_____Identify the financial risks
_____Determine start-up costs
_____Assess financial feasibility
_____Cash flow projection
_____Projected income statements
_____Write the business plan

Find a location

_____Decide on your business location
_____Building permit
_____Building codes
_____Zoning codes
_____Environmental regulations
_____Obtain a lease
_____Get furniture and equipment
_____Get signs

Utility service

_____Telephone
_____Electric
_____Water
_____Sewer
_____Internet

Create your business

_____Decide on business name
_____Decide on legal structure
_____ Sole proprietorship
_____ LLC, SMLLC
_____ Partnership, LLP
_____ Corporation: "S", "C"
_____Form entity
_____File "S" corporation election within 75 days
_____Register with state if necessary

_____Register your business name
_____Reserve Web domain name

Support services
_____Select a CPA   Name _____
_____Select a lawyer   Name _____
_____Line up suppliers

Register for business taxes
_____Discuss federal state and local tax issues, as applicable
_____Federal tax ID number
_____State tax ID number
_____Local tax ID number (if necessary)
_____Federal income taxes
_____State income taxes
_____Self-employment taxes
_____Business property taxes
_____Estimated federal tax payments

Necessary business licenses and/or permits
_____Sales tax permit
_____Trade permit
_____Health/food permit

Banking services
_____Select a bank   Name_____
_____Set up a business checking account
_____Set up a investment account for surplus funds
_____Apply for business loans (if applicable)
_____Establish a line of credit (even if loans not needed)
_____Loan amortization schedule for business plan

Accounting
_____Choose a tax year
_____Choose your accounting method
_____Choose accounting software
_____Chart of accounts (account categories for income and expenses)
_____Cash disbursements and payroll records and procedures
_____Cash receipts and receivables records and procedures
_____Inventory records and procedures
_____Set budget up on accounting system
_____Monthly close-out procedures

Insurance

_____Select an insurance agent   Name _____

_____Obtain business insurance

_____   Business liability

_____   Business casualty

_____   Business interruption

_____   Product liability

_____   Directors' and officers' liability

_____   Vehicle liability/casualty

Miscellaneous first steps

_____Get business cards

_____Get office stationery and supplies

_____Join a professional organization

_____Set a starting date

Do you have employees?

_____Unemployment tax ID number

_____Payroll service or software

_____Form W-4, employee's withholding allowance certificate

_____Form I-9, Immigration and Naturalization Service employment eligibility verification

_____Workers compensation insurance

_____Group medical, life and disability benefits

_____Minimum wage

_____Overtime laws

_____Child labor laws

_____Occupational Safety and Health Administration

Followup appointments with CPA

_____1st quarter

_____2nd quarter

_____3rd quarter

_____Pre year end

_____End of year

Connecticut organizations that offer small business management assistance

Accounting

Community Accounting Aid & Services, Inc.
1800 Asylum Avenue, 4th Floor
West Hartford, CT 06117
(860) 570-9113

General business

Connecticut Small Business Development Center. For closest office:

University of Connecticut
School of Business Administration
2100 Hillside Road, Unit 1094
Storrs, CT 06269-1094
(860) 486-4135

Business Outreach Centers. For service office information, contact:

Connecticut Economic Resource Center
(800) 392-2122

Set-aside Program (For minority vendors)
(860) 713-5236

Hartford Economic Development Corporation
15 Lewis Street
Hartford, CT 06103
(860) 527-1301

Financing

Connecticut Development Authority
999 West Street
Rocky Hill, CT 06067
(860) 258-7800

U.S. Small Business Administration
330 Main Street
Hartford, CT 06106
(800) 729-1779

Connecticut Innovations, Inc.
999 West Street
Rocky Hill, CT 06067
(888) 337-5454

Community Economic Development Fund
(800) 656-4613

Service Core of Retired Executives (SCORE)
Business Information Center
330 Main Street
Hartford, CT 06103
(860) 251-7000

INTRODUCTION

This chapter discusses marketing topics from the perspective of small start-up companies. Like their counterparts in large companies, managers of small ones must use the two main tools of marketing: research and planning. However, they have the advantage of being closer to their customers, and they should exploit that advantage.

The biggest challenge entrepreneurs face is their own enthusiasm. Their businesses are their children and it is hard to be objective about them. "Of course," they reason, "any sensible person would jump at the prospect of buying my product…it's simply the best." Unfortunately, most customers do not share that excitement. They must be told how and why a product or service meets their needs, and persuaded to change their buying habits to accommodate it. That means researching customers' needs and planning ways to meet those needs.

ORGANIZATION OF CHAPTER

This chapter discusses the following topics:

■ Defining the customer.
■ Getting information about the market.
■ Estimating market size.
■ Differentiating a company from competitors.
■ Choosing a retail location.
■ Setting selling prices.
■ Advertising.
■ Sales promotion.
■ Keeping customers satisfied.
■ Increasing sales.

The techniques discussed in this chapter apply to both of the major marketing fields: *consumer marketing*, where the retail customer is the target and *business-to-business marketing*, where business customers are the target. Many of the marketing concepts and strategies used for each are similar, but the seller must use separate marketing programs for each customer group. The chapter follows the development of effective marketing, from identifying the customer to developing strategies to increase sales.

DEFINING THE CUSTOMER

The purpose of marketing is to position your product or service to meet the needs of the target audience. This starts with a clear understanding of the customer. Without exception, programs that focus on customer needs are more successful than those that emphasize the strengths of a product or service.

The customer definition process can take the form of questions, the more the better. The goal is to identify the target customer and learn what's important to that customer. Examples of questions are:

- Who are the people who have a need for your product or service?
- What need does the product or service meet and why?
- How much are the customers willing to spend on a product or service similar to yours?
- Where do the customers live or work (depending upon the buying process for the product or service)?
- How old are they?
- What are their occupations?
- Are they married or single?
- Do they have children? How many?
- What are their shopping habits?
- What are their likes and dislikes?
- Where do they go for information on such a product or service?
- How important is cost to them?
- How important is quality? Timeliness?
- Why would they use my product or service instead of a competitor's?

> **NOTE** — To make the most of these questions, you must ask a significant number of people who represent your target market. Here's a critical point: most often the target customers are **not** like you. This bears repeating: chances are the business owner is not a good representation of the needs of the company's target market. If the business is designed to meet the owners needs, it may not meet the needs of the target market.

Ask these questions in the same way (phone survey, written questionnaire or e-mail survey) to a significant number of potential customers or clients. Compile the data in a consistent manner and then look for trends. In general, you are looking for:

- Groups of similar consumers (your target market segments.)
- Solutions to their problems that your product can provide.
- Ways to communicate with them using the media they already trust.

GETTING INFORMATION ABOUT THE MARKET

Once the customer is defined, the next step is to get more information. For this objective, there is no substitute for market research, which replaces hopes and opinions with facts. The research gathers information about three broad areas:

- Market size, behavior, location and potential market share.
  - Where are these customers found?
  - How do they make their purchase decisions?
  - What is the total market size for the products or services?
  - How much market share is realistically attainable?

- Competition.
  - What competitors are trying to attract the same customers?
  - What are the competitors' strategies in pricing, packaging, and location?
  - What are the competitors' market shares and trends in the marketplace?
  - What are the competitors' strengths and weaknesses?

■   Competitive positioning.
  •   What percentage of the market is available for capture?
  •   Is the business well-located?
  •   Is the product or service priced correctly?
  •   Does the packaging or method of delivery suit the customer's needs?

Fortunately, most of this market research can be done by the business owner without the help of paid professionals. Business schools have tremendous libraries that are free for the taking. State governments often have small business development programs aimed at making successes of small businesses. And, of course, there is the Internet, which offers vast amounts of data, often too much data. A good rule of thumb for Internet research is to verify that it comes from credible sources.

While a Web site may contain information that looks credible, the information may be slanted or even false. So, look for university or government-based sites and verify them. There are professional market research firms, but most are too expensive for the average start-up business owner.

Formal Sources of Information

There are several sources of reliable, current market information. These include the following:

Trade associations	These organizations represent specific industries and are a good source of information and support. Most trade associations publish data on their industries and make that data available to members. The names of trade associations can be found in a library. Two publications include the *Encyclopedia of Trade Associations* and the *Connecticut State Register and Manual*. Both are updated annually.
Chambers of commerce and local economic development officers	Local chamber offices can provide local population information, zoning regulations, maps and lists of other local business. In addition, they can lead to other information resources.
U. S. Census Bureau and Connecticut's Department of Economic Development	Both agencies publish great quantities of economic data. Besides population data, the Census Bureau publishes specific trade and industry data. This information is available through local public libraries, the Connecticut Small Business Development Center (CSBDC), or the U.S. Dept. of Commerce, Bureau of the Census, Washington DC. 20230.
Public libraries	Many books, magazines, and government publications are available in the public library along with assistance in locating available resources.
Newspapers	Local and regional newspapers are an excellent source of information on local business news, town planning and zoning issues, local economic conditions and of course, a chance to study advertising placed by the competition.
Yellow Pages	This is a good source for competitive information, because most competitors are listed, and many take out display ads telling more about themselves.

The Appendix contains a list of government sponsored market data resources.

Informal Sources of Information

One effective way to get good market information is to communicate directly with potential customers or with others who either know the market or represent the market. These sources can give invaluable insight into customer attitudes, market conditions and competition. And, they are inexpensive sources of market information. Some of these sources are:

Customers	This is where small business owners have an advantage over their large company counterparts. They are closer to customers and are better able to get market information from them. As the company grows, the best strategy for a small company manager is to remain close to the customers.
Suppliers	Suppliers communicate with many competitors and also with customers. They are an excellent source of information about business conditions, customers, market trends and competitors.
Competitors	Surprisingly, competitors are very willing to share information about market and product developments. This is especially true of companies that are close, but not direct, competitors.
Employees	Customers often say things to employees that they would not dare say to company managers or owners. Employees should be encouraged to become friendly with customers and seek information about the company's performance and competitive actions.
Business owners	These non-competing business operators are excellent sources of information about general business conditions. The chamber of commerce is the best place to meet them.
Businesses in other markets	Suppliers and trade associations are quite willing to help business owners to network with their counterparts in other states. A successful counterpart is one of the best sources of ideas to improve business operations.

The drawback of all these sources is that they're not objective. All their information contains some degree of bias that has to be filtered out. Here are two examples of this bias:

- *Customers may complain about prices if they think their complaints can influence prices.* However, price may not be a significant consideration in the customer's purchasing decision compared to others such as quality, delivery and other factors the customers take for granted.

- *Suppliers may add their own slant to market trend information.* They may exaggerate estimates of demand in hopes of influencing a customer to increase purchases.

One way this information is gathered is by formal surveys. However, this is one area of research that shouldn't be a do-it-yourself project. It is best left to professionals who have been trained in the research techniques used in this highly specialized field. Questionnaire writing is much more complex than it looks. The way a question is worded, which questions are asked - and even which questions are not asked - can influence the answers and produce information that is worthless or misleading and may lead to poor business decisions. Done properly, however, surveys can generate information needed for the business and can be the best source of information available.

NOTE — Research isn't just for new businesses, and should be used periodically by established businesses as well. It can answer many questions when business is not going well, when a new competing product is introduced into the market, or when a new competitor comes into the market. It will keep existing businesses on target with their marketing plan and in tune with changing customer needs.

ESTIMATING MARKET SIZE

One of the biggest mistakes a business manager can make is to misjudge the size of a market. Estimate too high and there isn't enough sales volume to stay in business; estimate too low and customers are dissatisfied when they can't get service. To avoid these predicaments, all business managers must answer this critical question: "How many customers are out there who will want my product or service?" The answer to this question can come from careful research.

In judging markets, three concepts are important: potential market, served market and market share.

- *Potential market* is the total number of customers who could possibly become customers for a product. This is an interesting but misleading piece of information. Many people who plan business operations rely too much on their estimates of the potential market. In their optimism, they think that every customer in a market is a real customer, but, it's not true. The fact is that many potential customers in a market just aren't going to buy from any source at any price.

- *Served market* is the number of customers who are real buyers in a market or market segment. This is the most meaningful statistic for market planning, because it represents real customers.

- *Market share* is the percentage of the customers in the served market who do business with a company or who can reasonably be expected to do business. This is a measure of the extent of competition, and the company's success in competing. Market share is never 100%, unless the company enjoys a monopoly.

  EXAMPLE
  To illustrate, assume you publish a newspaper in a town that has 20,000 families. Of them, 5,000 families don't subscribe to any newspaper, 5,000 subscribe to your newspaper, and only a very few subscribe to more than one newspaper. In this case, the *potential market* size is 20,000, the *served market* size is 15,000 (20,000 families minus the 5,000 who don't subscribe to any newspaper). You have a *market share* of 33⅓% (your 5,000 divided by the 15,000 served market).

In developing the business plan, served market and market share are critical success factors. In planning the entry into a market, the first step is to estimate the served market. The second is to figure how, and how soon, the company's market share can advance from zero to an acceptable level.

In business planning, market share is figured from the company's sales and the size of the served market. So, the first step is to figure the size of the served market. Rough estimates of the served market are adequate. So are estimates that are expressed as a high and low range.

There are three methods to estimate the size of a served market:

- Guesses, hunches or personal experience.
- Published information sources.
- Customer surveys.

Guesses or hunches or personal experience

This is the least scientific method to forecasting the size of a market, but it can be a reliable method if it's done by an expert, and every field has its experts. These are people who thoroughly understand the demographics of the market and have first-hand experience in the market. They can be hired from universities or companies in the industry, and there are many who operate as free-lance consultants. Most of them can be located through trade associations, trade conventions, and advertising or articles in trade magazines.

Besides market size information, an expert can provide this information:

- Where to locate.
- The geographic definition of the market.
- The distance a customer will travel to make a purchase.
- The distance the owner can travel to sell or support a product.

 NOTE Once the served market is identified, the company is structured to fit into it and the development of the marketing strategy continues.

Published Information Sources

This involves using information that is available to the public. The benefit of these sources is that they are accurate and free. Most of this economic data covers total markets, so it has to be adjusted before it can be used as an estimate of the served market.

Surveys

For business-to-business marketing, published data isn't as pinpointed as survey data. Normally, the best approach is to ask customers about their buying habits and other information needed for market planning. Either telephone surveys or mail surveys are effective. The limitations of surveys for planning were discussed earlier. The data is likely to be unreliable unless the survey is done carefully.

NOTE When the market size data is assembled and evaluated it's time for a serious question: "Considering served market size and competitors, is it feasible to continue?" The answer is "Yes" if the market is large enough, the competitive situation allows for another competitor and the product or service is needed. If the answer is "Yes," the next step is to determine how to compete in the market.

DIFFERENTIATING A COMPANY FROM COMPETITORS

It is crucial that a product or service stand out from the crowd. Without that, it gets lost in the clutter. The average consumer is exposed to 1800 to 2000 advertising messages every single day, and ignores most of them. Leading marketing authorities say one of the most effective competitive strategies for standing out from the competition is for a company to *differentiate* itself. This means finding things that make the company different from its competitors and to point out the differences to customers.

There are four basic rules for differentiation:

■   *The more similar a product is to that of a competitor, the more important differentiation becomes.* The goal is to turn a commodity into a unique product that is more desirable than those of competitors.

■   *If the company's goal is to get into a particular market, the product should be differentiated for that market.* This implies that no other product is suitable for the market.

■   *The first competitor that claims a feature gains an advantage.* If you claim your product has a special feature, a competitor would be making a mistake merely to claim the same feature. The competitor must now claim an additional feature to even the score. That may not be possible without revamping the product.

■   *Service providers, most of all, must differentiate themselves.* This is because a service is an intangible, which can't be seen, and it is difficult for customers to tell the difference from competitors' services.

Thus, provided the product or service can deliver on its promises, you can make a claim that is unique. Below are some examples found in everyday advertising and promotion. In each case, the product or service is a generic one, and the company uses the claim of uniqueness to generate attention from consumers.

■   A gasoline manufacturer claims its gas burns cleaner, even though it comes from the same refinery as other manufacturers' gas.

■   An apparel manufacturer advertises its products are made in the USA, even though many others are, too.

■   A floppy disk manufacturer claims its product is *for government or educational use only*, even though it's identical to those sold for other markets.

■   An insurance company claims you're in good hands, implying you're not in good hands with other insurance companies.

Now imagine that your product or service is truly unique. A differentiation based on truly unique features is much more powerful than one based upon mere words. Differentiation strategies are limited only by the imagination. The process is to position the product in the mind of its target audience in a way that satisfies their needs. The following table shows some ways this can be done. The references to products in this table also apply to services.

Differentiation Opportunities	
Quality	Offer highest quality. Provide higher performance.
Service	Offer fast service. Offer free delivery.
Custom offering	Vary product to give customers choice of colors, brands, styles, sizes. Offer customization of the product. Bundle another product with basic product for same price or 1¢ more. Include more product at the same price as the regular sized product. Use a different product package or display.
Location	Use different distribution channels to move the product to the market.
Price	Discounting, coupons, volume discounts.
Advertising	Use advertising to point out product differences. Use different advertising media.

CHOOSING A RETAIL LOCATION

Marketing professionals say there are three truly important factors for retail stores: location, location and location. In other words, where you put your store can make or break you. The choices cover a broad range:

- Central business district, or downtown area.
- Mall.
- Regional shopping center.
- Small shopping strip.
- Area heavily concentrated with a combination of shopping and commercial activity.

The major difference among these choices is the *traffic count*, or number of customers that travel through, and *type of traffic*, or the number of travelers who have the potential to be customers.

Both are important factors in deciding on the location.

> *EXAMPLE*
> Large numbers of cars and pedestrians pass through downtown areas, but many of them are traveling to work or school and may not be prospective customers. But, of the many people who go to shopping malls, most are customers, because they have come to the mall to make purchases.

Deciding on the location is primarily a matter of trading off between several factors:

- *Traffic counts and rents.* As a rule, high traffic counts translate into high rents.

- *Competitors.* Having a competitor close by can be an advantage or disadvantage. The nearby competitor will divert business, but it will also draw likely customers.

- *Complementary stores.* These are stores that draw traffic for each other. Today's customers want *one stop* shopping, where they can park and do all their shopping or errands in one location, without driving to another. Examples of complementary businesses are dry cleaner, gas station, liquor mart, drug store, convenience store and supermarket. All can be on someone's Saturday errand list, so a stop at one could lead to a stop at others.

Retailers can judge a particular store's effectiveness by looking at four indicators:

- Number of people passing by on an average day.
- Percentage who enter stores.
- Percentage who buy something.
- Average amount spent per sale.

A store that is doing poorly might be in a poorly trafficked location, or not have enough drop-in traffic, or too many drop-ins who browse but do not buy, or do not buy very much. Each problem can be remedied. Traffic is remedied by a better location. Drop-ins are increased by better window displays and sale announcements; the number buying and amount purchased depend on employee sales skills, merchandise quality and prices.

SETTING SELLING PRICES

Pricing a product or service is another crucial step for the business. Price too high and no one will buy. Price too low and there won't be enough profit to support the business in the long run. For large companies, product pricing is a major preoccupation. It should be for small companies, too. However, experience shows that small company managers don't take advantage of opportunities to improve pricing strategy and profits. Some of them are listed in the following table.

- *Avoid relying too much on competitors to set selling prices.* Too often managers ask what prices their competitors are asking and set prices at the same - or lower - levels. This may not be the best strategy. For one thing, competitors may have different costs. For another, following the competition ignores the opportunity to practice differentiation. It may be a good idea to set prices higher than the competitors to differentiate from them.

- *Don't confuse profit and markup percentages.* Markup and profit are one and the same: the amount added to cost to arrive at a selling price. However, as a percentage, markup is measured against cost while profit is measured against selling price.

  EXAMPLE
  A scarf costs $3.00 and sells for $5.00. Both the markup and the profit are $2.00. The markup percent is $66\frac{2}{3}\%$ ($2.00 ÷ $3.00) and the profit percent is only 40% ($2.00 ÷ $5.00). The confusing custom of using two different bases to figure the same profit can lead to bad decisions. If the goal were to earn a 40% profit, it would be a mistake to add 40% on top of cost. That would give a profit of $1.20 (40% X $3.00), less than was needed. The table below compares common markup and gross profit percentages:

Markup %	Profit %
200%	66⅔%
100%	50%
50%	33⅓%
25%	20%
11%	10%

■ *Avoid pricing strictly on cost.* Cost may not be the best basis for deciding on prices. One basis for pricing is demand. The higher the demand, the higher the price should be. Determine which products are selling and see if they are underpriced.

■ *Learn which products are price-sensitive.* Products that affect the customer's budget, like food, or are highly visible, like gasoline, are price sensitive. That is, customers will decide not to buy them if prices are raised even a small amount. A company that sells price-sensitive products has two options:

• Watch prices carefully and avoid getting too far ahead of the market price.
• Differentiate the product, so the customer is able to recognize its value.

Avoid thinking that lower prices equal more sales. By positioning your product as the low-priced competitor, you may be shutting out a significant market segment that expects high cost to equal high quality. There are many consumers who still believe the old maxim, "You get what you pay for" so don't underprice for this market.

ADVERTISING

The formal definition of advertising is: any paid form of non-personal presentation of ideas, goods or services by an identified sponsor using mass communications media. A good ad has three attributes:

■ It emphasizes benefits rather than features.
■ It targets one response only.
■ It excludes extraneous information.

 You must pick both the message and the medium that best reaches your target audience if you want your ad to be effective.

Effective advertising helps you stand-out among the clutter of all information, positions your competitive advantages as the answer to your customers needs and differentiates you from your competitors. Most importantly, it inspires action, not just reaction. A really memorable ad that does not cause the consumer to buy is worthless.

Every company must make three decisions about advertising:

- How much money to spend.
- Where to spend the money.
- What to say in the advertisements.

Budgeting Advertising Dollars

Dollars are generally a scarce commodity in a new business, and budgeting them carefully helps ensure that advertising dollars are spent effectively. The idea of budgeting is to set aside a fixed annual sum for advertising and spread that amount - no more, no less - over the year. The budget helps remove some of the temptation to make impulse advertising purchases. A sure way to overspend on advertising is to leap at every chance to place an ad.

There are three ways advertising budgets are figured:

Percentage of sales The company allocates a percentage of annual sales to advertising. As sales increase, the ad budget is also increased.

Unit of sales The company sets aside a fixed sum for each unit of product or service sold.

Judgement The owner decides how much to spend based on knowledge, experience or intuition.

One disadvantage of the first two methods is that advertising is cut when sales drop. But when sales levels fall, advertising should probably be increased, not decreased, to get sales back on track. A cut in advertising may lead to further reductions in sales, producing a downward trend for the company.

The percentage of sales method is the most popular for small companies. The general rule of thumb is to allot 2-3% of sales to advertising, but it is best to base your figures on the amount spent by similar businesses. Industry statistics on advertising spending vary by size of the business and can be found in trade magazines and independent data reports. One popular source is the Almanac of Business & Industry Ratios which publishes summary data by standard industrial classification (SIC code) to use for comparison. Below are a few examples of advertising expenditures, expressed as a percentage of sales, from the Almanac:

Store category	Sales budget
General merchandise	2.6 - 3.4%
Hardware & garden store	1.0%
Apparel & accessory store	2.5 - 6.0%
Contractors/developers	0.5%
Restaurants	2.0 - 4.0%
Personal service companies	2.0 - 5.0%

Deciding where to spend advertising money

There is a wide range of advertising mediums, and a wide range of prices, too. Pick the wrong medium, and the advertising money is likely wasted. The challenge is to select the right medium for the company. Each medium has its advantages and disadvantages; some work well for one type of customer or product but not for others. Some experimentation may be necessary to find the best advertising mix. The key to measuring success is to track the results and spend advertising dollars on those programs that seem to work.

When evaluating a medium, look at its reach and frequency. That is, who uses it for information and how often does it reach them. To be effective, you must reach your target audience and you must do it repeatedly. Purchasers respond to repeated reinforcement of a message they find relevant. Like the proverbial mule, they must be "hit upside the head" at least three times before they even pay attention. So, if you have the choice of media to reach your target audience, pick the one with a cost that allows you to run your ad several times over. Media buyers call that a "flight" and it's better to have a smaller ad that runs in a flight than one big ad that only gets to your target audience once. Remember the mule.

Here are some of the media that are available:

■   Radio and television.
■   Newspapers.
■   Cable.
■   Yellow pages.
■   Internet.

Public Relations

Small business owners often overlook public relations as a tool for business development. PR adds credibility and substance to even the smallest venture; it highlights the company's specialties; best of all, it's free.

> The formal definition of public relations is any form of unpaid public exposure through mass media. The practical definition is "doing good and getting credit for it."

Public relations efforts wind up in the body of a newspaper or newscast as part of the news, not as advertising. When a company official is quoted, an organization profiled or a specific stance on an issue highlighted in print or over the airways, chances are that the information had its genesis in public relations. In fact, 85 percent of the stories in the average daily newspaper start with PR efforts to help a company or a product weather a storm, advance a company position on an issue or position a company official as an expert on a topic.

Public relations has both good and bad aspects. On the good side is media attention and credibility. In fact, research shows PR getting three times the credibility of advertising. Even better, PR space is free. On the bad side, the company has no control of what part of its PR is used or even if it's used at all.

The most effective public relations involves earning credibility with people in the media by consistently delivering usable, quotable information over a long period of time. Below are some ways to create effective public relations:

- Don't threaten to pull your advertising in order to get a PR piece printed.
- Give the newspaper news, not puffery.
- Avoid superlatives or the word "announce." This material gets thrown away.
- Concentrate on earning respect from reporters; not making friends.

If a PR piece isn't readily accepted by a reporter, drop it. Don't bug or harass the reporter. Many companies use public relations professionals, but you can do your own public relations. Figure out what makes your business, product, situation, or viewpoint newsworthy and you are half-way there. Start with your competitive advantage. What do you do, create, or have access to that no one else does in the same way? Next, look at the company through the eyes of a journalist:

- What business trends are the company caught up in?
- What is the impact of national news on the company?
- What expertise do company's employees have?
- What advice or self-help information do you have to offer?

 After these positions are determined, mail letters to reporters that list the company resources and offer yourself and your staff as resources for interviews.

A well-managed, constantly maintained public relations program should remind customers, potential customers and competitors about the company and its activities. It will position your company as the source of information. It will tell the world your side of an issue. Most of all, it will position your company as a winner. And people like to do business with winners.

SALES PROMOTION

Sales promotion, also known as collateral, includes those marketing activities, other than personal selling, advertising and public relations that stimulate consumer purchasing and sales force effectiveness. Among them are: logos, brochures, direct mail, displays, websites, trade show participation and exhibitions. The possibilities for these activities are endless and would make up an entire book. The two sales promotion techniques most used by small companies are brochures and logos.

Brochures

A brochure is an essential marketing tool for situations where the customer must be given something to refer to after the sales call, and can be expected to refer to it after the sales call. In many sales situations, the customer expects to receive something after a sales encounter and feels under-served if nothing is delivered. However, in many situations, an expensive brochure winds up being discarded after the sales call and represents wasted money.

Many business owners think they must have a brochure before they can consider themselves to be truly in business and invest vast sums in professionally-produced brochures. The truth is that many businesses, in fact most, can and should survive initially without a brochure. The exceptions are catalogue companies and businesses in which competitors are already relying heavily on brochures. One reason is that small companies often reposition themselves after they encounter the competitive environment. Another is that they find their customers are the best source of input about the form and content of the brochure. To reduce the risk of getting stuck with obsolete brochures, startup companies should keep initial print quantities low. Today's desktop publishing environment makes it easy to revise and reprint brochures.

Logos

A logo is the visible mark of a company that identifies it to the world. A logo can be either a symbol or the consistent use of a specific type-style. Whatever its form, it should be:

- Consistent with your strategic planning.
- Able to function as the visual symbol of what you do and your competitive edge.
- Simple and clean.
- Easy to reproduce.
- Capable of working in black and white so it can be photocopied.
- Used consistently, such as in the same place on the page.
- The same color every time it is used.

Having a logo designed by a professional graphic designer is worth the cost because it creates a visual presence with customers, prospects, employees and vendors and it needs to have the look that can be provided by a professional. An amateurish logo is often worse than having none at all.

When creating the logo, the designer should also suggest how it should be used on the page and the color it should be. The designer should provide both a *mechanical* - the final artwork that goes to the printer for reproduction and a *file* - the logo in a standard data format that can be sent to a printer for reproduction or used to create a mechanical.

After you've chosen it, guard its integrity to make sure it is reproduced consistently:

- Retain one clean copy of the mechanical and a backup copy of the logo-on-file.
- Make a note of the PMS number. PMS, or Pantone Matching System, is the universal ink-matching system which expresses colors as recipes, and insures consistent reproduction regardless of which printer uses it.

KEEPING CUSTOMERS SATISFIED

Most owners want their companies and profits to grow. For this to happen, sales must increase. To many, this means they must get new customers while retaining their old customers. And, they feel they must then aggressively seek out new customers. However, experience shows the opposite is true: ample growth can come just from the existing customer base.

 NOTE To successful companies, the best customer is a repeat customer. *They find that an overwhelming part of their growth is from existing customers and only a very small part is from new customers.*

So, the best growth strategy seems to be the one that concentrates on existing customers. This includes these actions:

- *Stress quality.* A strategy of quality improvement aims at increasing the functional performance of the product or service - its durability, reliability, speed, taste, etc. A small business owner can often overtake the competition by launching a new and improved product or service. The strategy is effective to the extent that the quality is improved and buyers accept the claim of improved quality.

- *Emphasize service.* Many successful companies today have shifted their emphasis from sales to *sales and service.* Customer service has become an integral part of the sales package. The front line employees in these companies are trained to sell the product and also to support the customer. A satisfied customer is a repeat customer.

- *Handle complaints properly.* The best advertising is word of mouth. Studies show that if a complaining customer is handled properly, the customer will go on to tell an average of five other customers about the positive experience. And a dissatisfied customer will tell up to <u>fourteen</u> potential customers about the unpleasant experience! These actions can turn a dissatisfied customer into a cooperative one:
  - Let the customer fully air the complaint.
  - Don't interrupt or argue with the customer.
  - Ask how the problem can be resolved.
  - Take prompt action.
  - If possible, over-serve the customer the next time around.

INCREASING SALES

The previous section discussed ways to grow by servicing existing customers. For many successful companies, that is the sole growth strategy. But what if that's not enough growth? That means getting many more new customers. And a somewhat different strategy.

First, remember that bigger doesn't always mean better, often it just means bigger. Before starting a strong burst of growth, ask if the growth is both justified and manageable. During the 1980s, many small service companies grew for the sake of growth. They suffered for the growth by having to shrink or go out of business in the 1990s.

Some good reasons to expand a small business include these:
- Provide career opportunities for employees.
- Improve customer service levels.
- Retain customers who demand a broader range of products and services.
- Improve personal income and net worth.

The expansion strategies for the 2000s are expected to be much different from those that worked during the 1980s and 1990s. That's because the customer base has become more wary and more conservative. For the next decade, these strategies show the most promise:

- *Specialize.* Experts predict that the business winners in the 21st century will be those that specialize. The business successes of tomorrow will be smaller companies that have highly skilled workers, who can always find ways to improve their product and production. They will serve narrow market niches and produce high-quality products.

■ *Remain flexible.* The chief characteristic of a successful company will be (and always has been) flexibility. Market segmentation demands agility to keep pace with the market niche. Smaller companies are proving that small size allows them to make changes quickly to respond. Competition will come from entrepreneurs that are niche marketers, seeing a product or service market that is not well served and going after it quickly.

■ *Continue to think small.* Direct new product programs to small businesses. Don't launch a product or service by trying to sell big-name customers. Big companies take too long to make decisions, particularly about new or innovative products or services. Evidence shows that smaller companies make decisions more quickly, because they have fewer levels of management.

■ *Make everyone a sales person.* Start selling at the reception desk. Many low-level employees, such as the receptionist, have close, regular customer contact. They are in an excellent position to spot needs and suggest products. However, they are often handicapped by lack of product knowledge, so they miss opportunities. So, all employees should receive product and sales training and they should be recognized and rewarded for their sales efforts.

■ *Use modern sales tools.* Four important methods for increasing sales efficiently are the Internet, telemarketing, direct mail and trade shows.

Internet

The Internet represents an excellent opportunity for small-business owners to showcase their companies, get wide recognition, and in some cases appear much larger than they really are. Thus, the Internet is a great business equalizer because the viewer of a Web site doesn't know the size of a Web page sponsor unless the sponsor chooses to divulge the information. This allows small companies to gain the same level of attention normally granted only to large companies.

Once considered an expensive luxury, an Internet site is now very affordable for small companies. Two attractive aspects of the Internet site hosting and online sales.

■ Practically all Internet service providers now provide some form of low-cost site hosting for small business. Creating the site normally costs a flat fee of less than $1000. Monthly site host fees are as little as $25 per month.

■ Creating and online sales site to sell your products over the Internet requires only that you establish a link from your Web site to one of the many Internet store providers. One example is Yahoo store, which can be reached at www.yahoo.com. The cost of these services is normally a small setup fee and a monthly charge. Some charge a commission instead of a service fee. All provide credit card collections.

Telemarketing

Telemarketing is a service to can be used to make fast market share gains, launch new products, and get a company's sales off to a fast start. Unlike other techniques discussed in this section, telemarketing is a costly technique. A small business could use it on a limited basis, by direct calling a select list of carefully-screened target prospects, or on a wider basis, by using a telemarketing service firm to make sales contact calls to a large number of prospective customers.

One reason to use a service firm is that a telemarketing campaign requires large amount of resources for a short period of time, and most small companies just don't have the personnel available to make the calls. Another is that telemarketing involves a great deal of rejection; most of the people you talk to on the phone will say, "No!" Trained telemarketers can handle this rejection more easily than can be owners of small start-up businesses.

Direct Mail

Direct Mail enables you to talk directly to your consumer. To make it work you must have:

■   A package that speaks to the needs of your prospects, in a personalized manner. It must explain that your product is the answer to their problems and give them an easy way to respond.

■   A quality list that contains only the members of your target audience. This list must be current. You may develop your own or purchase one from a list house that is reputable, stands behind its work and develops its lists through sound and ongoing research.

Response levels improve when direct mail and telemarketing are combined with special offers, such as:
■   Free trial.
■   Money back guarantee.
■   Free gift.
■   Sweepstakes or contest.

Trade shows

Trade shows are a growing sales opportunity. They reduce both selling and purchasing costs by allowing buyers and sellers to have many more contacts in a very short time. These shows can produce immediate sales, although they aren't intended for that purpose. They're designed to facilitate contacts that will be followed up after the show.

CONCLUSION

This section has been a brief overview of marketing, and each topic covered here could be the title of a full college level course. Do your research before undertaking any of them, and, remember to start with a plan before you put your dollars into any marketing effort. Stick to the plan and suppress the urge to grab at any new marketing tool that comes along without seeing if it fits into the plan.

Marketing is the business function that identifies unfulfilled needs and wants. It defines and measures their magnitudes and determines which target markets the company can best serve. It also pinpoints the appropriate products, services, and programs to serve these markets. In the end, the companies that best satisfy their customers will be winners.

Appendix

Connecticut market data sources on the Web

Connecticut Market Data
www.ct.gov/ecd/
Over 200 tables of Connecticut data covering markets, government, transportation, demographics, labor force, personal income, economic profile, exports, education, housing and geographic regions. Also available in printed form.

Links to Economic Data Sites
www.state.ct.us/ecd/links.htm
A huge listing of other economic sites, including those managed by economic development regions, towns and universities.

Connecticut Economic Information System - in development
www.state.ct.us/ecd/research/ceis/index.html
A database of Connecticut data of all types for research, much of it updated monthly. Public access will be through this internet site.

INTRODUCTION

This chapter discusses the process of business planning and shows a practical approach to business planning for small companies. The chapter contains an adaptation for small companies of techniques that are effective in large companies. Large companies devote considerable time to formal business planning. Their managers know they will not succeed unless they make ambitious plans and carry them out. Small companies owners should do formal business planning, too, if they want their companies to survive and prosper.

The most important time for business planning is before starting up. This planning allows the owners to make many crucial business decisions, including the decision of whether or not to go into business. A written business plan is essential when the owner must get financing to start in business because banks and investors will not advance money to a company without first studying its business plan. The plan is equally important for company owners who *do not* need financing, because it helps them decide if their money will be well spent and if they will have enough money to start up.

The techniques discussed in this chapter have been used by all types of companies for many years. They are used by CPA firms, the Small Business Administration (SBA), the Connecticut Small Business Development Center (CSBDC) and other consultants that advise small companies. The chapter also contains an example of a business plan to illustrate the plan elements. Very likely, some lenders and investors will ask for more information than this one contains, because most of them have their own requirements for business plans. So, it is a good idea, before starting to work on a business plan for lenders and investors, to discuss the contents with them.

The power of a good business plan for obtaining financing is well established. During the Internet expansion days in the late 1990s, all that was required for an Internet startup company - one of the many dot-coms - to get millions in financing was a good business plan.

ORGANIZATION OF CHAPTER

This chapter discusses the following topics:

- Background of business planning.
- Time frames for business plans.
- Narrative part.
- Financial part.

In addition, the chapter contains an example of a business plan and checklists for deciding the financial resources required and available for starting a business.

BACKGROUND OF BUSINESS PLANNING

Recent decades of business turbulence have proved the value of business planning. Before that, the owners of small companies relied on their instincts when making business decisions. They did not stray far from their basic lines of business, and the business climate was stable, so instinct worked well. However, modern managers have found they have to use business planning techniques to manage through the dramatic shifts and rapid changes that have occurred lately.

Some business owners can still rely on their instincts, if their companies are very well established and very stable. The rest of us have to devote more time to planning in order to keep pace with change.

The business plan, with its focus on strategy, has grown to be accepted and demanded by private investors, banks, governmental agencies, venture capitalists and others. They use it to measure the viability of existing or new ventures. But, the common perception that the prime purpose of a business plan is to get loans and investments is false. The real purpose is to help in making strategic business decisions.

Goals of Business Planning

Good business planning is an essential tool for success. Experience shows a strong connection between business planning and success.

 NOTE Good business planning allows management to:

- Figure the amount of money needed to start up and continue in operation.
- Estimate the company's future profits.
- Decide on marketing strategies.
- Identify opportunities to improve the business.

Unfortunately, many small business operators don't get around to developing business plans unless they are pushed to do so by their bankers or by prospective investors. For these operators, there is one additional goal: persuade investors or bankers to advance money to the company. Without this persuasion, they will not advance money.

Business Plan Contents

Most business plans consist of three parts:

Narrative This part covers the company's purpose and descriptions of the various operating functions, (marketing, sales, organization & management, competition), followed by a summary.

Financial This part presents balance sheets, operating and cash flow projections for at least one, but normally three to five years.

Appendix This part contains statistical and reference material to support the first two parts. It also includes the resumes of the owners and top managers.

These three parts are the minimum content for a business plan. When it is used to support a financing request, the business plan is a sales tool. It also might include photographs, charts, graphs, product samples and other items to make the reader comfortable with the company and its plan.

TIME FRAMES FOR BUSINESS PLANS

A business plan should carry the reader about three years into the future. A one year plan isn't enough, especially for a startup company, because the first year cannot be considered a normal operating year. A five year plan is desirable, but difficult to predict for a startup operation. A typical plan might cover three different periods:

First Year   A one year outlook showing monthly financial detail for the first year of operation. Includes start-up costs and actions to achieve goals in the following years.

Next Two   A two or three year picture showing the effect of plans to achieve success as the company matures.

Later   A broad overview, in discussion form of general plans for the future. Includes dealing with the changing economy, introduction of new products and services, etc.

NOTE — The first three years are the *make-or-break* years. If a company gets past them, its prospects are very good. The next three to five years determine whether a company has true staying power. If so, it can weather recessions, management changes, market changes and other adversity.

NARRATIVE PART

The narrative part is a brief description of the overall plan. It is important to strike a balance between too much and too little detail. If there is too much detail, nobody will read it. If the business plan is only an outline, a reader will think the owners haven't done enough planning. The language should be precise and the writing should flow easily from section to section.

A suggested structure for the narrative part is shown in the following table. A discussion of the subsections follows the table.

Section	Description
Introduction	Background of company, owners, products, industry.
Business Purpose	Description of company's product or service.
Marketing	Demographics of customers; approaches to selling; location of business; analysis of competition.
Organization	Company structure; assigned responsibilities; personnel needs.
Summary	Overview showing company's long term viability.

The entire business plan for a small business should be about eight to twelve pages, especially when it is to be used to obtain financing. Experience shows that loan officers and investors begin to form their opinions about a business in the first page of the business plan. If the plan drags on too long or contains too much detail, they begin to find things they don't like or lose interest in the business venture.

It's also a good idea to include a table of contents. An example appears on the facing page.

Springdale Computer Consignment, LLC
Business Plan
Table of Contents

    *   Not included in this example due to space limitations.

Introduction Section

Entrepreneurs must recognize that many companies fail because the owners lack the experience and planning to implement their visions. Owners must be comfortable with their experience in the chosen business. This experience can come from various sources in several forms: the proposed line of business; related business fields; handling people (customers and employees); financial skills.

> **NOTE** Most lenders and investors receive many business plans to read, and don't have time to study each one closely. In some business plans, these decision-makers never get past the introduction. If the purpose of the business plan is to raise money, the introduction must convince the reader that the plan is worth reading in full.

For new businesses, the introduction should tell why the owner decided to start the company. For mature companies, the introduction should tell a brief history. For all companies, the introduction should influence the reader to read the rest of the plan.

Springdale Computer Consignment, LLC **Page 2**

Business Plan

Introduction

Springdale Computer Consignment is a development stage computer resale consignment shop, which will also offer repair services and computer training, located in a recently completed strip mall in Springdale, Connecticut. The owner is an experienced computer technician and manager, who has worked in retail computer sales for eight years and managed sales departments for six years. In fact, in this position, the owner has managed a highly successful department that has won the regional award for highest sales for the last two years. The owner has many skills for this business, including:

- Product knowledge.
- Management experience.
- Technical knowledge.
- Marketing knowledge.

Initially, the owner intends to keep the current job, with reduced hours, in order to maintain a steady stream of cash flows.

The location for this business is ideal. It has a high traffic volume and easy highway access. The town only recently began development of the land for retail use, so there is little competition. The strip mall includes two solid anchor stores; the remaining stores include a pharmacy, bagel shop, and several specialty stores. Initially, the owner plans to offer previously owned computers and accessories, and repair services. Later, the owner plans to add training courses in the evening hours as interest increases.

The total funds needed for this business will be $125,000, including security deposits, inventory and fixture acquisitions, and start-up costs. It will be provided as follows:

Owner's investment	25,000
SBA/Bank financing	100,000
Total cost	125,000

In developing this plan, the owner has consulted with a CPA, an attorney, and the Springdale town planner over the past two months. The following is an approximate timetable of events leading up to starting operations:

Complete business plan	January 31
Financing in place	May 1
Closing on lease	May 15
Start store setup	June 15
Complete store setup	October 30
Initial opening	November 15
Grand opening	December 1

Business Purpose Section

For new companies, this section should broadly describe the company's products or services and the market to which they will be offered.

Sometimes, it's helpful to describe the business using the North American Industrial Classification System (NAICS) code number. That's because many bank loan officers use published NAICS data to validate information presented in a company's business plan. All companies fall into a NAICS classification. For example, the NAICS group for *Retail Computer and Software Stores* is *44312*. The NAICS code number is used to classify statistical data on companies, including sales volume, numbers of companies and financial performance ratios.

> **NOTE** This published information starts with *your* business income tax return, which contains a space to enter the company's NAICS number. The IRS summarizes the data from income tax returns using the NAICS number and publishes it in a form that professionals can use for analysis. You can download this data from the IRS's tax statistics Web site:
>
> www.fedstats.gov

The competitive market should be considered and identified. In every industry, there are markets that are defined by a *quality-price-service* relationship. For example, the clothing industry has at least three competitive segments: high, medium and low. Some retailers occupy the high quality, high price and excellent personal service segment. Others compete at the intermediate level. Still others sell lower quality, lower price goods. The positioning within these markets is constantly being refined as competitors battle for customers and profits. *It is possible for a well-managed company to be successful in any one of the markets it chooses to occupy.*

For mature companies, the business purpose section of the narrative should discuss the company's history, considering changes in the economic environment, shifts in population, shifts in the customer base, shifts in the "quality-price-service" market and organizational problems.

Background

This business is really three businesses in one: a computer sales showroom, a computer repair department, and a training course classroom. It offers expansion opportunities, too.

The computer sales showroom will feature computers and peripheral equipment (printers, scanners, etc.) received on consignment from individuals and businesses. In addition, the store will carry the accessories needed to make these items work (cables, connectors, etc). The owner has extensive computer assembly and repair experience, so offering repairs to local individuals and businesses is a logical offshoot of the sales business. This will also allow the owner to include a short term warranty on equipment sold, since the owner can do all repairs. The owner has also determined that there is a shortage of inexpensive, quality computer software training courses. By outfitting the computers in inventory with software packages, the floor models can be used in training courses that can be offered when deemed profitable.

This combination of businesses at one location should appeal to two types of customers: business owners either on a tight budget or not in need of the higher power machines that would be purchased new, and local residents.

Since the town has only recently begun to develop the area where the store will be located for retail purposes, a large volume of traffic by the location is expected. Further, residents of the surrounding towns do not have many retail stores available to them, so shoppers from surrounding towns can be expected as well. Lastly, the solid anchor stores and pharmacy will attract a steady stream of customers, and the bagel shop will ensure local business people stopping for their morning coffee will see the business in their travels.

Marketing Section

Realistically speaking, small businesses rarely create new wants or needs. They normally fill existing wants and needs. Therefore, the first step in market planning is to define those in need of the product or service. This section of the plan is data-oriented, and owners should plan to get a solid command of the market numbers. These include:

■   Demographics of market, including size, description, location, growth rates, affluence, trends, etc.

■   Competition, including names, sizes, location, products, strategies, strengths, weaknesses, trends, etc.

> **NOTE** The marketing section of the plan should be very specific about this market data. Being specific helps the owner to make better, more informed decisions. It also shows lenders and investors that the company is not relying on hunches, intuition, dreams or limited observations but rather depending on confirmed facts.

There are two main types of market data:

Retail The demographics for local areas or regions are available at chambers of commerce, the Connecticut Development Authority, CSBDC and other state departments. These demographic reports give a detailed composition of the population across several categories, such as education, sex, age, and income.

Wholesale The demographic data for companies is arranged by Standard Industrial Classification numbers and can be secured from local, state, and national trade associations, regional and local chambers, state economic development offices and the United States Department of Commerce.

Springdale Computer Consignment, LLC   **Page 4**

Marketing

In planning this enterprise, we have studied three factors:

- Local market.
- Marketing plans.
- Competition.

The market *hook* is the consignment. Because of rapid technology advancement, many business owners are turning their PCs over after two years. These machines have several more years left in them, but there is no practical way to sell them so the owners end up giving them away to employees or charities. This store will allow those who want to turn their computers into cash to do so without risk.

Local Market

Town planners have estimated the total traffic volume through the area at 75,000 vehicles per day. In addition, there are approximately 15,000 people living within 5 miles of the proposed location. The residents in the surrounding towns commute elsewhere to work and shop, because there are few local employers or retail stores. Therefore, we believe these residents are potential customers.

An estimate of the sales and profit factors for the first year of business appears in the projected income statement. As the sales plan shows, it is anticipated that both computer sales and repairs will increase on a monthly basis as more and more people become aware of the store, and its reputation for quality begins to spread amongst the surrounding area. It is anticipated that the training courses will begin by the end of the first year, but only a small number of courses should be offered during the first year.

The profit margins have been determined by the historical experience of the owner. To keep prices low, only a 30% margin is expected for the first year on consignment computer sales. Repairs should generate a higher percentage of 40%, and the courses should generate an estimated gross margin of 43-50%.

Marketing Plans

The owner has decided to model the marketing plan on other small businesses in the area, as well as the successful copy and ads used by the owner's current employers. After an initial rollout, which is included in the estimate of start-up costs, we will place regular advertisements in the *Shoppers World* free weekly paper, and the daily *Springdale Gazette*. The owner also plans to distribute flyers on cars in parking lots and at public places. The flyers will be generated by the owner on colored paper directly, helping to keep the cost down. These flyers will carry discounts on repairs, a description of several of the computers and peripherals currently in inventory, and an offer to sell computers on consignment.

Armed with the definition of the target market, management must develop plans to capture market attention. Generally, these plans include three items:

■ Type of sales organization (employees or agents).

■ Advertising plans, including company awareness and product advertising.

■ Promotion plans, including use of media for sales and promotional events.

> **NOTE** The company's location is a key element of the market plan. The business plan should list the reason the company's location was chosen. Location should depend on the demographics of the target market and the nature of the product or service. Different factors are important for different types of companies. For a retail business, customer travel convenience and parking are key factors. For manufacturing companies, raw material supply, transportation, labor supply and customer locations are the major factors to be considered in site selection.

The final aspect of the market summary is the competitive analysis. All companies operate in a competitive marketplace. Competitive planning requires research on, and personal observation of, current and potential competitors. The competitive analysis should clearly define:

■ Total market potential for products or services.

■ Segment of market in which the company will operate.

■ Strategy to be used to penetrate the market.

■ Competitors.

■ Extent of market penetration projected for each year in the business plan, either in units or sales dollars.

New companies must consider all of these factors in developing their marketing program. However, existing companies need to be cautioned that past practices need to be reviewed in light of today's, not yesterday's, environment. Failure to make such a review leads to the ultimate failure of the planning process.

Springdale Computer Consignment, LLC   **Page 5**

Competition

Computer sales is a competitive market, with technology driving down cost of new products, and the availability of computers at so many different types of stores. However, there are no other consignment stores in the area. The extremely low prices of previously used equipment also opens the doors to many different types of customers. Therefore, we expect to hold a reasonable market share. In addition, the downside to many stores selling computers is poor performance in repair services for computers. The owner feels a real opportunity exists for an experienced, quality repair shop for computers already in the marketplace, and intends to fill that niche.

The proposed location has superior visibility from one Interstate because it sits at the top of an overpass. A normal sign can be seen from well before each exit ramp. From the other Interstate, we will need to use billboard advertising to capture customers. We do not plan to use billboards at this time. We also expect that the traffic the anchor stores bring in will be enough to generate additional sales.

Sales plan

	Computer Sales			Repairs			Training		
	Sales	Profit	Profit	Sales	Profit %	Profit	Students	Price	Amount
Jan	5,500	0.30	1,650	2,500	0.55	1,375	0	50.00	0
Feb	6,500	0.30	1,950	2,750	0.55	1,512	0	50.00	0
Mar	6,500	0.30	1,950	2,850	0.55	1,568	0	50.00	0
Apr	7,000	0.30	2,100	3,000	0.55	1,650	0	50.00	0
May	7,500	0.30	2,250	3,300	0.55	1,815	0	50.00	0
Jun	7,900	0.30	2,370	3,500	0.55	1,925	0	50.00	0
Jul	8,250	0.30	2,475	4,000	0.55	2,200	0	50.00	0
Aug	8,500	0.30	2,550	4,100	0.55	2,255	0	50.00	0
Sep	9,000	0.30	2,700	4,300	0.55	2,365	0	50.00	0
Oct	9,300	0.30	2,790	4,600	0.55	2,530	5	50.00	250
Nov	9,900	0.30	2,970	5,000	0.55	2,750	7	50.00	350
Dec	10,000	0.30	3,000	5,100	0.55	2,805	11	50.00	550
Total	95,850		28,755	45,000		24,750	23		1,150

Organization Section

This section discusses the company's legal structure, management assignments and similar issues.

The legal structure depends on tax, ownership and legal protection questions. The business plan should explain what structure was chosen and why. There are eight ownership forms, which are discussed in the chapter Choosing the Right Legal Organization:

- Sole Proprietorship.
- Single Member Limited Liability Company.
- Partnership.
- Limited Partnership.
- Limited Liability Partnership.
- Limited Liability Company.
- "C" Corporation.
- "S" Corporation.

> **NOTE** The right choice of business organization depends on many factors, including the type of business, owners' financial situation, legal liability and plans for the future. The selection of a form of ownership should not be made casually. This important decision should be made only after consulting with both a CPA and an attorney.

The other organization issue is organizing the people. In small, owner-dominated companies, there is little doubt who is in charge. As the company grows, and needs more money, lenders and investors need to see that it has depth in personnel, and that the company could survive if the founder were not around. Thus, business plans for some companies should clearly define the top leadership positions and the responsibilities for each position.

To show the people in the organization, the business plan might also include a simple organization chart and brief descriptions of the employees' jobs. The job descriptions are especially helpful if the jobs are unusual. They also can be helpful in managing the business, and dealing with employees who need a lot of structure in their jobs. Conversely, they can be a handicap to an owner who wants an open, informal business atmosphere.

Springdale Computer Consignment, LLC   **Page 6**

Business Organization

Because of the tax advantages during start-up, the company will be a Limited Liability Company (LLC) and the owner will own all the shares. However, as the company grows and prospers, shares will be transferred to the owner's spouse and children. Practically all similar companies are organized as LLCs, because of the need for legal and environmental protection.

Personnel

The owner's resume is enclosed. Pat Washington is well qualified to manage this business because of the extensive experience as listed below:

- Total experience of 8 years.
- Management experience of 6 years.
- Won departmental regional award for highest sales for 2 years.
- Product knowledge.
- Management experience.
- Technical experience.
- Marketing knowledge.

The owner plans on initially having the store open Monday through Friday, from 9:30 a.m. until 6:00 p.m., and Saturday from 9:30 a.m. until 12:00 p.m.. The owner has been able to manipulate the schedule of hours worked elsewhere without giving up that job, so only a part time employee will be required to assist in running the store.. The owner will be available to work from 3:00 p.m. until closing Monday through Friday, and on Saturdays. An employee will be used to keep the store open between the hours of 9:30 a.m. and 3:00 p.m.

There are two aspects of organization that owners of start-up companies neglect: training and expansion. If new employees have to be trained, the business plan should say so and the company budget should include money for the training. Even on-the-job training costs money, because the people are getting paid when they aren't fully productive. If the business plan calls for growth, it should also plan for more people to handle the growth. The plan should identify the points at which new employees will have to be added to handle the anticipated business.

The owner of a small company should consider the benefits of an advisory board. This is a panel of outside experts who serve as mentors, analysts, aides and sounding-boards. They advise on strategy and problem-solving. The advisors should be people whom the owner respects and can rely on to be open and candid, not "yes" people. Company owners should check with their trade associations for support, too. Many of them run support groups that meet regularly for discussion.

A final aspect of the company's organization is the source of its professional services. It is common for owners to rely on outside experts to guide them through regulatory and financial complexities. These would include lawyers, CPAs, environmental specialists and others. They should be named in the business plan. They should also be given copies of the complete plan for future reference.

Summary Section

The summary statement bridges the narrative and financial parts of a business plan when it is being submitted with a financing request. Typical themes for the summary include the following:

Market   Size of the total market, size of the company's target segment and projected growth. Information about basis for the projections.

Financial   Income, cash flow and balance sheet projections condensed and combined into a summary table. A possible format for the income summary is shown on the facing page.

NOTE It is not unusual for a start-up business to lose money the first year, because of the one-time expenses of starting in operations, such as stationery, start-up advertising, initial inefficiency of employees and slack sales. If a business plan shows the company will make a profit from the start, some skeptical readers might not believe it.

The example plan, on the opposite page, shows a typical start-up loss followed by two years of profit. The profit enables the owner to begin taking out a salary.

Springdale Computer Consignment, LLC   **Page 7**

Summary

Springdale Computer Consignment, LLC presents an excellent opportunity to provide inexpensive computers and quality repair services to an area that has neither. The combination of an experienced owner/manager, outstanding location and solid marketing combine to give excellent chances of success.

Overview Of Financial Projections

Because the company is a Limited Liability Company, where the owners are taxed on their individual income tax returns, no provision for income taxes is included in the financial projections.

	2004	2005	2006
Sales	142,000	200,000	220,000
Direct Costs	87,845	120,100	133,200
Gross Profit	54,155	79,900	86,800
Operating Expenses	55,110	77,790	85,250
Income from Operations	(955)	2,110	1,550

The apparent decline in profit from 2002 to 2003 is the result of the owner taking a greater amount of salary as the business becomes more successful. The amounts are as follows:

2004	2005	2006
0	30,000	35,000

FINANCIAL PART

Bankers, investors and business owners use financial statements and accounting records to present information on operating results and as the basis for their business decisions. This chapter discusses them from a business planning point of view. A more detailed discussion appears in the Paying Employees chapter.

> **NOTE** — Financial statements are the tools used by the financial community to measure a company's financial health and viability. They are a major part of every business plan. Business owners need to understand them in order to communicate with bankers and investors and to chart the company's future.

The source records are not a formal part of the business plan. But, because they are the source of data for the statements, they have to be accurate. The quality of source records is a strong indicator of how well a business is run. Poor records usually mean poor management. Experienced investors know enough to look at a company's source records in order to form an opinion of how well it is being run.

The business plan should contain balance sheets, operating and cash flow statements. For a start-up company, they should show at least three future years. For a mature company, they should show two to three past years and five future years. For all companies, the first of the three years should be broken down into monthly periods. That is because the first year of a business plan has many fluctuations that do not show up in an annual statement. For illustration purposes, the examples in the next few sections present three year projections, without the monthly detail for the first year.

Proposed Funding

A good starting point for making a lender or investor understand a business venture is to express the amount of funds needed and to explain how they will be used. The table on the facing page is an example of how this is done.

Springdale Computer Consignment, LLC   **Page 8**

Sources and uses of funds

This business requires a modest investment, largely because the only inventory the company must buy will be a small amount of repair parts. The rest of the inventory will be paid for by the computer owners who consign their equipment to us for sale. The table below shows the required investments and how they will be funded.

Sources	
Owner's investment	25,000
SBA loan	100,000
Total	125,000
Uses	
Security deposits (rent, utilities, etc.)	3,000
Inventory (for sale and repair supplies)	25,000
Furnishings and fixtures	20,000
Start-up costs	10,000
Reserve for emergencies	67,000
Total	125,000

Projected Balance Sheets

The balance sheet reflects a company's financial condition at a specific moment in time by reporting what it owns, or assets, and what it owes, or liabilities. The term *balance sheet* refers to the fact that its two main components *balance*. The company's total assets equal the sum of its liabilities and its net worth. The table below defines the components.

Assets	Assets are the company's property, such as cash, inventory, furniture, motor vehicles, machines, computers and amounts receivable from customers. An asset is classified as *current* or *noncurrent* depending on whether it is converted into cash during the company's normal business operations cycle (usually one year). The company's inventories are current assets because they are sold to customers who pay for them in cash. Its furniture is a noncurrent asset, because it is normally not sold.
Liabilities	Liabilities are what the company owes to others, such as its unpaid bills, installment notes, unpaid payroll taxes and temporary advances from the owners. Like assets, liabilities are classified into current and noncurrent categories, but for liabilities, a strict time frame is used. Current liabilities are those payable in less than one year from the date of the balance sheet. Noncurrent, or long term liabilities, are those payable after one year.
Net Worth	The company's net worth, or *equity,* is the balance left over after the liabilities are subtracted from the assets. This is the amount of the owners' investment in the company.

The format for the projected balance sheet in a business plan is similar to that of the usual balance sheet described in the record keeping chapter. The main differences are the number of time periods and the amount of detail presented in the business plan. The business plan statement presents three to five future years but in less detail than the normal company balance sheet.

The example on the facing page shows a projected balance sheet for our example, Springdale Computer Consignment, LLC. This example shows the beginning position plus three yearly columns after that, but the owners could present any number of periods they choose.

Springdale Computer Consignment, LLC   **Page 9**

Projected Balance Sheet

	Beginning	2004	2005	2006
Assets				
Cash	67,000	61,045	59,655	57,305
Inventory	25,000	35,000	40,000	45,000
Equipment & fixtures	20,000	20,000	20,000	20,000
Less: accumulated depreciation	0	(4,000)	(8,000)	(12,000)
Organization costs	10,000	10,000	10,000	10,000
Less: accumulated amortization	0	(2,000)	(4,000)	(6,000)
Security deposits	3,000	3,000	3,000	3,000
Total Assets	125,000	123,045	120,655	117,305
Liabilities				
Accounts payable	0	5,000	6,500	8,000
SBA loan	100,000	94,000	88,000	82,000
Total Liabilities	100,000	99,000	94,500	90,000
Net Worth	25,000	24,045	26,155	27,305
Total Liabilities and Net Worth	125,000	123,045	120,655	117,305

Note: This statement is included to illustrate the general principles of a balance sheet. A professionally-prepared statement is likely to contain more detail, more classification of amounts and extensive supplementary detail.

Projected Income Statements

Income statements report the company's revenue and expenses, and the amount left over after expenses and income taxes is the company's *net income*. It isn't unusual for a company to lose money in the first year of start-up. This is because of start-up expenses and the fact that a newly-organized company is less efficient than a mature one.

The income statement projection in the example shows a one part presentation where all income and expenses are combined on a single page. The income statement can also be presented in two parts: a summarized basic statement and a supporting schedule. The supporting schedule would present the details of operating and administrative expenses.

The projected income statement should be kept simple and clean. Investors and lenders need to be able to refer quickly to the basic financial information. This means moving the detail out of the main statement and into supporting schedules. If the Springdale Computer Consignment business plan needed to cover more details, such as a marketing plan or employment plan, it might include schedules with those details. These plans cover the major elements of the income statement and show that the owner has done the necessary homework.

The projected statement of income, as well as other financial projections, is an excellent computer application. The planner who has access to a personal computer and simple software can try out different combinations to arrive at the best combinations. Available software includes commercial spreadsheet software such as Excel or Lotus 1-2-3. Software products designed specifically for business planning include Strategy Planner, Venture, Up Your Cash Flow and many others. The statement on the next page is an example of a projected income statement for a business plan that was prepared using a computer and spreadsheet.

The *Depreciation and amortization* expense category is an annual charge for long term business expenditures. These expenditures must be paid at one time but provide a business benefit over several years.

- **Depreciation.** The annual charge for investments in business equipment, based on the estimated useful life of the equipment. For example, a copy machine costing $800 is expected to last 5 years. The company would record $160 per year as depreciation until the entire $800 is used up.

- **Amortization.** The annual charge for expenses that have a future benefit. For example, Springdale Computer Consignment must spend $10,000 in bank fees and professional services to get started in business. The IRS allows a five year amortization of this expense, so Springdale's owners have also chosen five years for the business plan.

Springdale Computer Consignment, LLC **Page 10**

Projected Income Statement

	2004	2005	2006
Sales and services	142,000	200,000	220,000
Costs	87,845	120,100	133,600
Gross profit	54,155	79,900	86,400
Operating Expenses:			
Owner salary	0	30,000	35,000
Employee salary	10,000	10,000	12,000
Payroll taxes	1,210	1,210	1,450
Rent	6,000	6,000	6,000
Insurance	1,200	1,200	1,200
Advertising	7,500	4,200	4,200
Supplies	5,500	1,000	1,000
Professional	2,000	2,000	2,000
Credit card fee	2,000	3,080	4,000
Depreciation and amortization	6,000	6,000	6,000
Communications	2,000	2,000	2,000
Travel and entertainment	1,000	1,000	1,000
Miscellaneous	1,000	1,000	1,000
Interest	9,700	9,100	8,400
Total Expenses	55,110	77,790	85,250
Profit before tax	(955)	2,110	1,150

Notes:
1. This simplified income statement has been included to illustrate the general principles of an income statement. A professionally-prepared income statement is likely to have different categorizations and details. The Company is an LLC, where the owners pay the company's share of taxes on their personal tax returns, so no provision for income taxes has been included.

2. Some expenses shown for 2004 include one-time expenditures. For more on these, see the section on start-up expenses.

Projected Cash Flow Statements

Balance sheets and income statements show only two parts of the company's financial picture. Their limitation is that they don't present a complete cash picture. They do not provide information concerning the varying cash needs of the company. Cash flow statements were designed to fill that void.

The cash flow statement presents the flow of funds needed to support the business. It projects the receipts and payments, adds them to the opening cash balance and projects the closing cash balance. This statement tells the owners whether they need to borrow or invest more money to stay in business.

If the cash flow projection shows a shortage, the business plan must show how the shortage will be covered. If there is surplus cash, the plan should show it being invested in the business or paid back to lenders and investors.

The example on the opposite page shows an example of a three year cash flow projection. This simplified cash flow statement has been included to illustrate the general principles of a cash flow statement. A professionally-prepared statement is likely to contain considerably more detail.

> **NOTE** — The example also shows a considerable amount of cash. It's a good idea to have a heathy bank balance, but when the company also owes money to a bank, it is really borrowing the cash balance from the bank. The company would save on interest cost by using any excess cash balance to pay off the bank loan.

Assumptions

In order to prepare financial projections, we have to make assumptions about inflation, tax rates, population and many other items. The business plan should present these assumptions in a summarized form to help the reader understand the plan better, and believe it. The table shows the typical assumptions that would have to be made in order to prepare a business plan.

Springdale Computer Consignment, LLC   **Page 11**

Cash Flow Projection

	2004	2005	2006
Net income after tax	(955)	2,110	1,150
Add: depreciation and amortization	6,000	6,000	6,000
Less: increase in inventory	(10,000)	(5,000)	(5,000)
Add: increase in accounts payable	5,000	1,500	1,500
Cash flow from operations	45	4,610	3,650
Less: SBA loan payments	(6,000)	(6,000)	(6,000)
Opening cash balance	67,000	61,045	59,655
Ending cash balance	61,045	59,655	57,305

Summary of Planning Assumptions

	2004	2005	2006
Depreciation life - Equipment and fixtures	5	5	5
Inventory turns per year	4	4.5	5
Payable turns per year	12	12	12
Term length - SBA loan (months)	120	120	120
Interest rate % - SBA loan	10.00%	10.00%	10.00%
State income tax rate % - Note 2	0.00%	0.00%	0.00%
Federal income tax rate % - Note 2	0.00%	0.00%	0.00%

Notes:

1.   No projection for inflation has been included in any part of this business plan.

2.   Because the company is a Limited Liability Company, where the owners are taxed on their individual income tax returns, no provision for income taxes is included.

Start-up Expenses

Before a company can even open its doors, it has to buy furniture and equipment, make security deposits and go through a period when there are expenses but no revenues. These costs have to be figured in the business plan, but many small business owners either forget them or underestimate them. One way to get a list of the equipment needs is to take a mental walk through the office, store or factory, listing everything in sight. Another is to consult with financial advisors and others who have started their own companies. A third way is to use a checklist, such as those in the Appendix to the Financial chapter.

NOTE Startup expenses come in two forms, those that are treated as business expenses in the year incurred and those that have a lasting value and must be spread over several years' business expenses as amortization. For a more complete discussion see the chapter entitled, Business Income Taxes.

CONCLUSION

Business planning is not just for big companies. A business plan, and the business planning process, are essential to *any* company's success. The process is detailed, but it pays off in better chances for success.

The business plan consists of a combination of written material and analytical data. A good business plan covers all aspects of running the business: product, service, customers, market, competition, type of business organization, personnel and financing. This broad coverage, and the discipline of preparing the plan, stimulates the owner to decide on business strategies and to be realistic about financing needs and growth prospects.

INTRODUCTION

The title of this book, and much of its content, implies that the main way to get into business is to start from scratch. If marketing a unique skill or product is the reason for going into business, there may not be any alternative to starting a new company. Sometimes, though, the reasons for going into business have more to do with being independent or having more control over daily activities. In that case, the alternative, purchasing an existing business, is very attractive, because it reduces some of the risk of failure.

ORGANIZATION OF CHAPTER

This chapter discusses the following topics:

■   Deciding whether to buy or start-up.

■   How to find a business to buy.

■   How to buy a franchise.

In addition, the chapter contains a checklist to use in evaluating business purchase situations.

DECIDING WHETHER TO BUY OR START-UP

Many business owners choose to get into business for themselves by purchasing an existing business. Because there is an active market for companies for sale, they find plenty of companies to choose among. And, if they shop carefully, they may be better off than if they started new companies.

There are five main advantages of purchasing someone's company:

■   *Start-up cost savings.* The business owner who starts up a new business has to pay the costs of getting into business including advertising, training employees, developing suppliers, experimenting with product lines, design, decorating and signs. By far the biggest cost is the many mistakes an owner makes during start-up. The owner who buys an existing business doesn't normally have to incur any of these expenses.

■   *Become profitable faster.* A start-up can take from six months to several years before it starts producing profits. By purchasing a profitable operation, the purchaser starts off in a profitable position.

■   *Better chances of success.* Unless the success of a business is totally dependent upon the personality or skill of the former owner, a going business should continue to prosper.

■   *Easier to finance.* Because there is a less risk, lenders will be more willing to finance the purchase of an existing business.

- *Seller training.* Normally, the seller is required to stay on for a while to make the transition easier for customers and to train the new owner. This reduces the amount of previous experience the new owner needs to have.

- *Reduce competition.* If an owner starts up a new business, and there are similar businesses in the area, competition becomes more fierce. If, instead, the owner buys one of the competitors, competition remains unchanged.

Of course, there are a few negative aspects to buying a business, too.

- *Higher cost.* The initial cost may be a lot higher than starting a new business. Somebody else has taken a lot of the risk and spent years building a business; the former owner will want to be compensated for both the risk-taking and the time spent. Also, when owners decide to sell the business they have built, they tend to overestimate its value.

- *Business may not be suitable.* Many business purchasers find the operation is very different from what they expected. The new owner ends up undoing the previous owner's operating methods and procedures. To avoid this, prospective owners should spend time at the company, even working there, before making a final purchase.

- *May not be able to manage like the previous owner.* Small companies reflect their owners' management styles and skills. After running their companies for many years, owners make it look easy. A new owner might not have the necessary skills to handle the former owner's job.

- *Need higher profits to justify cost of purchase.* When a company is sold to new owners, they take on debt or reduce their savings to pay for it. The cost of this debt reduces the company's profits until it is paid off, often taking as many as five to seven years.

- *Business may have been misrepresented.* This is one of the biggest, and most common, risks of buying a business. Sometimes the owner of a failing business alters the records in order to make it look more attractive to a potential buyer. Or, the owner makes a profitable company look even more profitable. To guard against this, all buyers must make exhaustive studies of companies they plan to buy.

The decision to buy a business rather than start from scratch brings up another important decision: what form the purchase will take. Many purchasers think only of buying an entire operating business. That thinking limits their options. There really are four main alternatives:

- Outright purchase of a going business.
- Outright purchase of a failed business.
- Purchasing part of a business.
- Purchasing a franchise.

One overlooked alternative is that of buying just *part* of the assets of a company. Finding a company for sale, a buyer is free to make an offer to buy only part of it: one store of a group, one product line, or the distribution operations of a company that both manufactures and distributes products. Even if a company isn't for sale, the owners may be willing to sell off part of it. There's never any harm in asking.

HOW TO FIND A BUSINESS TO BUY

The first step to take in buying a business is to *find* one. This means extensive prospecting through many sources, just to find something for sale. There are many sources of information about businesses for sale:

■　*Newspaper business opportunity section.* The local Sunday newspaper or the Friday edition of the *Wall Street Journal* are excellent sources. So are specialized newspapers such as *The Business Opportunity Journal.* The local library can point out others.

■　*Trade magazines.* There is a trade association, usually at both the state and national level, for almost every industry. These associations usually publish magazines and newsletters to communicate with their members. The classified advertisements of these publications are a good source of information about companies that are for sale.

■　*Business brokers.* Brokers normally work for business owners on a commission basis to sell businesses. But, brokers also are willing to search for businesses that are for sale. You can find a broker near you by searching the web site of the International Business Brokers Association at www.ibba.org or call them toll-free at (888) 686-4222.

■　*Networking.* Suppliers, vendors, distributors and trade associations are all excellent sources of information for industry-specific businesses as are customers and competitors. One strategy is to ask the owner of a business if it is for sale. Even if the answer is "no," the owner may be able to suggest a company that *is* for sale.

■　*CPAs and attorneys.* These business professionals often know of businesses for sale. So do insurance agents, real estate brokers and venture capitalists. Banks can also be a good source; ask local banks if they have listings of businesses for sale. Your banker may be able to recommend a newsletter if the bank doesn't publish one of its own

■　*The Internet.* The Internet can be a good way to access listings of businesses for sale. Classified ads by region, state and local web sites, and specific trade associations may all provide this resource. The International Business Brokers Association maintains a searchable data base of over 3,000 businesses for sale. You can specify geographic region, type of business and range of revenue. Individual business brokers with web sites may post listings of available businesses.

Investigating a Business

When the search has narrowed down to one or more potential prospects, it's important to make a *thorough* investigation. Some experts say that buyers should expect to spend at least a year finding a business, evaluating its potential and analyzing its marketplace. That's a long time in most situations, but the point these experts make is that the investigation process isn't a quick task. A *quickie* checkup is destined to result in a bad purchase; a more thorough one will uncover the true strengths and weaknesses of a business.

Using a Checklist

The checklist in the Appendix is a useful tool for this analysis. The extent of the checklist should suggest how thorough the investigation has to be. Professional help from a CPA and a lawyer is suggested. A CPA is a good resource for investigating the financial and operating health of a business and a lawyer can help examine the legal risks associated with a particular business and assist in drafting agreements.

Part of this review is to look at internal documents that show the company's health and past performance. The seller should be willing to talk to the buyer's representative, to provide back tax returns and financial statements, and to permit complete access to all business records. If the seller is not willing to cooperate with a thorough investigation of the financial history and condition of the business, the buyer must BEWARE. Besides internal records, buyers need to talk to customers, the company's landlord, major suppliers and municipal officials. It's a good idea to do a credit check, too.

Finding Out Why the Seller Wants to Sell

An important part of evaluating a business is to learn the *real* reason the owner wants to sell. This is hard to do sometimes, because owners aren't forthright about their reasons. It's essential to find out the real reason because it could affect the purchase price of the company and the structure of an offer. For example, an owner who wants to retire may entertain an offer that includes a retirement income factor. Or, an owner who is getting out because of overwork or burnout may welcome an opportunity to sell part of the company now, remain for a few years, and then sell the rest. Some of the common reasons for selling a business include:

- Retirement.
- Burnout.
- Escape debts.
- Dump losing business.
- Need money for personal expenses.
- No longer capable of managing.
- Need money for expansion.
- Interested in a different business or career change.
- Poor health.
- Change in marital status.
- Need to move to a different area.

It's also a good idea to be suspicious about an owner's motives for selling. When the owner gives an explanation, be sure to ask follow-up questions to verify the explanation. The goal is to search for hidden hazards.

> **NOTE** — A business owner claims to be selling a company and planning to retire. That may be true. Or, the company might be in trouble, it might be running out of cash or a competitor might be planning to open a store down the street. The follow-up questions should confirm the owner's plans. The questions should be conversational:
> - "Where are you retiring to?"
> - "How are you going to spend retirement?"
> - "Was the business able to provide you the funds for retirement?"

The list below contains examples of hidden hazards to look for. Experience shows that business owners either conceal or downplay these factors when they sell their companies.

■ *Customer base* - Will changes over which you have no control impact it? Is there one major customer whose loss would be catastrophic?

■ *Accounts receivable* - How current are they? Should some be written off?

■ *Employees* - Will they remain? Do you want them to?

■ *Supply sources* - Will they continue?

■ *Inventory* - How old and how saleable is it?

■ *Possible competition* - Is a new super store about to break ground? Are there already too many competitors in the market?

■ *Possible industry change* - Is a better, faster, cheaper alternative becoming available which makes your product/service obsolete?

■ *Environmental regulations and compliance* - Is there contamination on the company's property?

■ *Zoning regulations* - Are they about to change?

■ *Landlord* - Who owns the property? Will the present terms be continued? Will you be locked into staying?

■ *Liabilities* - Are there any that will carry over to you?

Negotiating the Purchase

When the number of possibilities is narrowed to one or two, the next step is to negotiate the purchase. The offer should be in writing, should allow time for a more detailed study of the business and provide for cancellation if the business is not right for any reason.

> **NOTE** — Many experienced CPAs and attorneys have developed standard offer forms for this purpose and they should be consulted prior to taking action.

The offer should always include a deposit; the deposit shows that the buyer is serious and it can sometimes prevent the seller from entertaining other offers.

Settling on a Price

One problem that buyers typically encounter is the seller who holds out for an unrealistic price. This happens when the seller has been given an unrealistic value by a business broker or when the seller isn't able to look objectively at the company. If the buyer and seller are having trouble coming to terms, one solution is to meet the seller's asking price but get the seller to improve the terms or include other things in the sale. Examples of such seller enhancements are:

- Seller to finance the purchase.
- Seller to work in the company for up to a year.
- Seller to guarantee the company's profit for a year.
- Seller to include assets that weren't originally included in the sale.

Letter of Intent

Once the buyer and the seller have agreed on a preliminary purchase price, they should write a letter of intent to get the owner to take the business off the market. The letter of intent spells out the terms of the sale. A letter of intent is essentially an agreement to write an agreement. It lists the major points of agreement, and is used by the lawyers as the basis of the final agreement. Without a letter of intent, the deal remains unsettled until the final purchase contract is signed. After the letter of intent is signed, the buyer should seek professional help to investigate tax issues to decide on the form of business and many other issues.

When both parties are ready to complete the sale, the final purchase agreement should be drawn up by an attorney. The attorney should also provide advice about other necessary documents and agreements. Most purchase agreements include some form of a *covenant not to compete* where the former owner agrees not to compete with the buyer for some period of time or within some physical distance. A CPA will help allocate the purchase price into its various components (real estate, if any, fixed assets, and intangibles) as required by the Internal Revenue Service.

 NOTE The agreement should also include an indemnification provision where the owner will be responsible for "hidden" liabilities such as environmental contamination.

HOW TO BUY A FRANCHISE

In many fields, there is yet another way to get into business. Instead of buying a business and operating it independently, some people prefer to operate within a franchise chain. Franchises provide the wisdom, experience and existing business of a corporate parent while providing local business operations the freedom of independent operations. A franchise is a unique partnership between the franchise company and its local outlets. Every chain structures its franchise differently from other chains. Some franchise sellers (called franchisers), such as McDonalds® and Burger King®, have prospered and, at the same time, made their franchise holders (called a franchisee) wealthy.

How Franchises Operate

Franchise operations are almost always retail operations involving product or service sales, but a few involve business-to-business sales.

There are hundreds of different fields available; the list in the Appendix is just a sample. One reason to buy a franchise is the industry's track record for success. According to a 1992 survey, nearly 97% of franchisee-owned businesses that opened in the previous five years were still in operation and nearly 86% were owned by the original franchisee. They are definitely worth a careful look.

In a franchise agreement, the business owner and the franchise company make mutual business commitments. The buyer purchases a franchise and enters into a franchise agreement with the franchisor which defines rights and obligations, for example:

- Purchase of supplies from franchisor company.
- Pay a monthly franchise fee, usually a percent of sales.
- Use the franchisor's name and logo in advertising.
- Receive local and national advertising support.
- Meet the franchisor's quality standards.
- Receive a protected territory.
- Receive training and management support.
- Purchase start-up inventory.
- Make a required contribution to an advertising fund.
- Make regular operational and financial reports to the franchise company.

How to Find a Franchise

Several sites on the Internet maintain extensive searchable data bases. The resource list in the Appendix to this chapter lists a few of them. Of course all of the franchisers have web sites of their own if you know which ones you are interested in. If you don't know, enter the word "Franchise" in your browser and go from there. In addition to the methods described above for finding other businesses for sale, there are four others for potential franchise owners:

- Networking with successful franchise owners.
- Franchise fairs.
- Entrepreneurial magazine ads.
- Consultants and sales agents.

Whenever a seller offers a franchise, the Federal Trade Commission requires it to furnish the buyer an *offering statement*, a document which discloses the risk factors of the franchise. A buyer should ask for this document, read it and have a CPA and lawyer review it, too.

Franchise Cost Considerations

A franchise operator has to pay many of the same start-up costs as for any other start-up business. In addition, the owner has to pay other costs:

- A franchise fee, which ranges from hundreds to thousands of dollars.
- Advertising costs, including signs and logos, required by the franchiser.
- Training programs required by the franchiser.

NOTE Owning a franchise means giving up some of the autonomy that is cherished by most independent small business operators. Most franchisers insist that their franchisees follow their programs rigidly and set rigid standards for cleanliness, quality, and service. These standards protect the value of the franchise. Even brokers offering franchises for sale advise, "If you can't follow somebody else, don't buy a franchise because your life will be miserable and the franchiser's life will be miserable."

CONCLUSION

By purchasing an ongoing business or a franchise an owner reduces the risks associated with a business start-up, may increase the likelihood of it becoming profitable faster and reduces the amount of experience needed to go into business. But buying a business means paying a premium to the person who started the business. The premium may be worth paying, provided it is a reasonable one.

The most important aspect of buying a business, and the one most often overlooked, is that of making a thorough investigation of the company being acquired. This takes time and costs money, but the effort should pay off in reduced risk.

Appendix

Examples of franchise opportunities

Adult daycare

Airport parking

Auto service and repair

Auto sales

Bakeries

Beverage sales

Bookkeeping services

Bookkeeping systems

Building materials sales

Carpet cleaning

Cleaning

Computer graphics

Computer sales

Computerized bookkeeping

Convenience store sales

Copying

Cosmetics sales

Dance studio

Day care

Dog walking

Drain cleaning

Drug store sales

Dry cleaning

Electronics parts sales

Employment agencies

Eyeglass sales

Fast food

Financial products sales

Gasoline sales

Gyms

Hair cutting and styling

Health clubs

Home appraisal

Home remodeling

Home evaluation

House cleaning services

House painter

Ice cream sales

In-home healthcare

Limousine service

Mail forwarding

Mechanics tool sales

Medical appliances

Motels and hotels

Nail care

Oil changing

Paging and message services

Payroll preparation

Pest control

Pet sales

Pet grooming

Photo finishing

Printing

Real estate

Restaurants

Retail sales

Security alarm monitoring

Siding installation

Tax preparation

Telephone answering

Training, languages

Training, computer

Training, accounting

Video rentals

Business purchase checklist

Note: This checklist should be used as a starting point to supplement a buyer's judgement and initiative. It was drawn from several sources including the author's experience and is somewhat generic. Don't use it without customizing it for the circumstances.

1.   General considerations

1.   Description of the company
       Company history
       What is for sale - Entire company, part of it, partial interest?
       Why is company for sale?
       Evaluation of industry and growth potential
       Status of company within its industry
       Capital structure

2.   Markets and competitors
       Markets served
       Potential new markets
       Growing, mature or declining market?
       Proposed new products
       Principal competitors
       Effects of economic developments, tax changes or legislation

3.   Capital requirements

4.   Location and facilities

5.   Evaluation of:
              Management
              Production
              Work force

6.   Sales and marketing - Analysis of current and potential
              Sales promotion methods
       Relationship between company and its customers
       Sales:
              By product
              By major customer
              By market
       Particulars of any major open contracts
       Any fixed price or long-term contracts?
       Any controls on selling prices by government, etc.?

Business purchase checklist   **Continued**

2.   Legal considerations

    1.   Corporate, statutory and regulatory documents

    2.   Contractual obligations, other than management or labor
        Loan agreements
        Government and/or long-term contracts
        Leases
        Licenses
        Franchises
        Mortgages
        Insurance policies
        Are contracts assignable?

    3.   Management/labor obligations

    4.   Pension, profit sharing, and other employee benefits

    5.   Property titles and liens
        Intangible personal property (patents, trademarks, etc.)
        Existing liens
        Pending legislation

3.   Accounting considerations

    1.   Accounting policies - Compliance with accounting standards

    2.   Financial statements
        Assets
            Accounts receivable and bad debt reserve
                Aging schedule, concentrations, any pledged as collateral
            Inventory
                Inventory turnover, basis of valuation
                Methods for slow-moving and obsolete inventory
            Building and equipment
                Real and personal property taxes
                Relation of cost to appraisal value and market value
                Depreciation rates
                Replacement policy
                Assumable mortgage
                Adequate insurance
            Intangible assets
                Patents, trademarks, designs
                Goodwill
            Investments

Business purchase checklist

Liabilities
- Bank and other Debt
  - Amounts
  - Dates of repayment
  - Interest rates
  - Security
- Availability of further financing
- Leasing agreements
- Guarantees
- Contingent liabilities
- Discounted bills
- Litigation pending
- Arrangements for company cars

Income statement
- Gross profit ratio
- Comparison with other companies
- Operating profit ratio
- Do expenses include personal items of owners?
- Nonrecurring income and expenses
- Analysis of executive salaries and bonuses
- Explanation of fluctuations in income or expense
- Sales
  - Trends
  - Back orders
- Cost of sales and expenses
  - Percentage margin on sales
  - Method of spreading profit on long term contracts
  - Interest and costs of borrowing
  - General and administrative expenses

Sources and uses of cash

Adequacy of working capital

Relationship with bankers

Other considerations
- Insured values
- Any material purchase commitments?
- Deferred pension plan costs, if any?
- Non-qualified pension agreements - Extent of liability
- Agreements, written or unwritten, regarding expenses

Taxes
- Adequacy of income tax liability
- Possible additional taxes for prior years
- Any years closed by IRS?
- Any audits in progress with IRS or state?
- Details of loss carry forwards

Resource list

Franchise Opportunity Superstore
www.franchise.com
An exhaustive site, searchable by category, locale or company which also offers a wealth of information about selecting, buying and starting a franchise.

The Franchise Handbook
www.franchise1.com

Offers more directories as well as articles and a bulletin board

Franchise Direct
www.franchisedirect.com
A searchable directory, first person articles, a guide to franchising and a free monthly E-mail newsletter

The American Franchise Association
53 West Jackson Blvd, Suite 205
Chicago, IL 60604
(800) 334-4252

Entrepreneurs' Guide to Franchise and Business Opportunity
Entrepreneur Media, Inc.
2392 Morris Ave.
Irvine, CA 92714
(714) 261-2325

Entrepreneurs Magazine Group business start-up guides
Each one on a particular business and how to operate and what to look out for. Can be ordered by phone from Entrepreneur magazine at (800) 333-3700

INTRODUCTION

One of the first decisions an owner must make is to choose the type of business organization for the company. This choice must be made with care because the initial choice is sometimes hard to change. Even changing the company name to add or drop the word "Incorporated," involves added printing cost. In some cases, companies lose the benefit of tax write-offs when changing business form. In some cases, it may take the help of a CPA or lawyer to make the change. So, a poor decision about the type of business organization can cost money in administration, income taxes and professional fees.

This chapter discusses issues the owner must consider in selecting the right legal organization for the company. It covers the pros and cons of a number of different forms including: sole proprietorship, single member limited liability company, partnership, limited partnership, limited liability partnership, limited liability company, "C" corporation, and "S" corporation. The business form decision affects the way the company is owned, the way ownership is transferred, the form of its name, legal protection and income tax payments.

CONTENTS OF THIS CHAPTER

This chapter discusses the following topics:

- Overview of the types of business organization.
- Fiscal years.
- Analysis of each business form with tax and legal implications.
- Setting up a company in Connecticut.
- Applying for tax numbers.
- Getting permission to do business.
- Insurance.

The chapter also discusses the mechanics of setting up the company, including deciding on accounting periods and accounting methods, registering with federal and state agencies and getting licenses to do business. It includes checklists for forming a business organization and a list of names, addresses and Web sites for important government offices.

TYPES OF BUSINESS ORGANIZATION

Before starting in business, the owner has to select a form of business organization for the company. The types, together with their rights and protection, are defined by Connecticut law. The way the company pays income taxes is defined by the Internal Revenue Code and Connecticut tax law. Within limits, the owner can change the type of business organization at any time, but the easiest time to do so is at the beginning of the *fiscal year*, discussed in the next section.

There are eight basic types of business organization:
- Sole proprietorship.
- Single member limited liability company.
- Partnership.
- Limited partnership.
- Limited liability partnership.
- Limited liability company.
- "C" corporation.
- "S" corporation.

This section provides an overview of these basic organization types.

Sole proprietorship

A sole proprietorship is the simplest form of business. It is owned and operated by one person and is not a separate legal entity. A sole proprietorship does not involve creating a new legal entity or transferring ownership of assets. Rather, the owner simply segregates a group of assets and dedicates them to the business. All of the taxes of the business are paid by the owner and the owner has unlimited personal liability for the debts of the business.

✱ Single member limited liability company

A single member limited liability company (SMLLC) is a hybrid entity that combines the simplicity of the sole proprietorship for tax purposes and the benefits of limited liability for the owner, or *member* as the owner of an SMLLC is called. The SMLLC is a separate legal entity from its owner.

Partnership

A partnership, also called a general partnership, is generally the simplest way to do business when there is more than one owner. The partnership is a separate legal entity. Each partner contributes money, skills, labor, property and/or other capital to the partnership and shares in the profits and losses. Every partner is an agent of the partnership and can take actions that obligate the partnership and the other partners. Partners, like sole proprietors, are responsible for their shares of the company's taxes and have unlimited personal liability for business debts.

Limited partnership

One form of partnership, the limited partnership (LP), allows some partners to limit their liabilities to the amount of their capital contribution to the partnership. For this limited liability protection, the partners are denied the right to participate in the management of the business. This form of partnership is not common for small businesses, but may apply in some cases. It is especially helpful in including a business owner's estate planning into his or her business plans. The limited partnership is a separate legal entity.

Limited liability partnership

A limited liability partnership (LLP) is a type of general partnership that offers liability protection to its owners in most circumstances. Used most commonly in professional practices, it gives the owner/partners the same rights to participate in the management of the business. The LLP is a separate legal entity.

Limited liability company

A limited liability company (LLC) with more than one member is a hybrid entity that combines a partnership's tax advantages and the corporate benefit of limited liability for its owners. The LLC is a separate legal entity from its owners.

Corporations

There are two main types of corporations for tax purposes, "C" and "S." Both are types of business wherein shareholders form a separate legal entity. The difference between "C" and "S" lies in the way they are taxed, and the letters come from the chapters of the Internal Revenue Code that define how they are taxed. Shareholders of both types of corporation have the advantage of limiting their personal liability for business obligations.

■   **"C" Corporation** - A "C" corporation pays federal and state income taxes on its earnings. When the earnings are distributed to the "C" corporation's shareholders as dividends, they are taxed again. This double taxation is one of the big drawbacks of the "C" corporation.

■   **"S" Corporation** - An "S" corporation has the same legal attributes as a "C" corporation. However, an "S" corporation generally does not have to pay federal income taxes; its shareholders pay taxes on their share of income on their personal tax returns. This allows it to escape the double taxation of a "C" corporation. Connecticut has special rules for "S" corporations.

CHOICE OF FISCAL YEAR

When a company chooses its business type, it must at the same time choose its *fiscal year*. A fiscal year is the company's business year, the span of time over which it keeps its records, measures its profits and pays its income taxes. This time span can start at the beginning of any month and it must end twelve months later. It can never be more than a year in length.

Although a great many companies use the calendar year as their fiscal year, it is possible and often a good idea to use a different year. For example, government organizations normally choose fiscal years that end in June. This is partly due to a tradition and legal requirement, but by ending their business years at a time other than December, they are spared the massive workload that would result if they tried to handle their year-end accounting tasks at the same time they were also handling their annual tax collection tasks.

Companies also can benefit from using a fiscal year that ends in a month other than December, and most of the reasons have to do with paying taxes:

■   Retailers often choose January or February year ends so they can finish post-holiday discount sales. The losses from these sales reduce their taxable income and income tax bills.

■   Corporation owners often end their fiscal years during the first half of the year. Thus, if the business has a highly profitable year, it can pay big bonuses to the owners, who can put off the individual income tax effect until the following April 15th.

Because many business owners select their fiscal years so as to reduce income taxes, the Internal Revenue Service has narrowed the range of choice, as discussed in this chapter. Some businesses are required to have the same tax years as their owners. Others are allowed to have different tax years, but must make *equalizing payments* to the IRS. Because of the tax implications of having a fiscal year, it is a good idea to consult a professional about the choice.

When you apply for a taxpayer identification number, you make a tentative selection of a tax year. However, the official fiscal year choice is made at the end of the first fiscal year by the act of filing a tax return for the year. Thereafter, you have to use that fiscal year unless you receive permission from the IRS to make a change.

SOLE PROPRIETORSHIP AND SMLLC

The sole proprietorship and single member limited liability company (SMLLC) are businesses that are owned by a single person, who is free to make decisions and do business wherever and whenever permitted. These simple business forms involve very limited administration; the only restrictions placed on the owner's operational flexibility are licensing and fictitious name statutes.

An SMLLC is a form of business organization that brings together the simplicity of the sole proprietorship with the liability protection that most small business owners want.

> **NOTE** Originally, a limited liability company (LLC) had to have two or more owners and they were called *members* to point out their unique ownership status as a group of owners. Later, the LLC law was changed to allow a single person to form a SMLLC, but the term member stuck despite the fact there is obviously only one owner.

The table on the following page summarizes the characteristics of sole proprietorships and SMLLCs.

Characteristics of Sole Proprietorship and SMLLC	
Personal liability	• *Sole Proprietorship*: Unlimited liability for obligations of the company; personal and business assets are subject to claims of business and personal creditors. • *SMLLC*: No liability for obligations of the company; only business assets are subject to claims of business creditors.
Separate legal entity	• *Sole Proprietorship*: Not a distinct legal entity apart from the owner. • *SMLLC*: Distinct legal entity; can own property in its own name and can sue and be sued by itself.
Management and control	• *Sole Proprietorship*: Free to make business decisions and engage in any legal business with few state registration requirements. • *SMLLC*: Owner should always use the LLC designation in business dealings.
Continuity of existence	• *Sole Proprietorship*: Ends with death of owner; many business rights (such as franchise fees) also end on death of owner and cannot be transferred to heirs. • *SMLLC*: Has continuity of existence and is not dissolved upon death of the owner.
Transferability of interests	• *Sole Proprietorship* and *SMLLC*: Free to sell or transfer any portion or all of the company.
Expense and formality of organization	• *Sole Proprietorship*: No required filing or documentation to begin business; if using fictitious name, must file an inexpensive Trade Name Certificate with local town clerk. • *SMLLC*: Must file articles of organization with Connecticut Secretary of State and pay a small registration fee.
Record keeping	• *Sole Proprietorship* and *SMLLC*: No tax consequences when forming, but owner should keep separate records for business and personal finances.
Income taxes	• *Sole Proprietorship* and *SMLLC*: Business is not a separate taxpayer; all taxes are paid by owner on Form 1040, Schedule C; income is considered owner's "salary;" owner pays self-employment tax instead of Social Security and Medicare taxes on Form 1040, Schedule SE.
Deductibility of losses	• *Sole Proprietorship* and *SMLLC*: Owner may usually offset business losses against other personal income; consult CPA for loss limitations.
Tax year	• *Sole Proprietorship* and *SMLLC*: Must have same tax year as owner.
Sale of an interest	• *Sole Proprietorship* and *SMLLC*: Gain or loss on sale is treated as sale of each individual asset because the business is not considered separate entity; some of the gain or loss is then "ordinary" and some are "capital gain" type items; ordinary income is generally taxed at higher rates.

Conclusion - Sole Proprietorship and SMLLC

A sole proprietorship is indeed the simplest form in which to do business. But that doesn't mean it is the right form of business for the company. If the owner likes most of the attributes of the sole proprietorship, but is concerned about personal liability, the sole proprietorship is probably not the right way to go.

An SMLLC is the simplest form of business organization that provides liability protection to its single "member." It might be the ideal choice for the owner if simplicity and liability protection are important objectives.

PARTNERSHIP, LP and LLP

A partnership is the simplest form of doing business for two or more business owners. One of the most important aspects of a partnership is the partnership agreement, which defines partners' rights and obligations. Personal conflicts between partners can cause problems, which can result in a dissolution, so it is important that the partnership agreement be complete. An individual, a corporation, a trust, an estate, and even another partnership may be a partner in a partnership.

The limited partnership (LP) and the limited liability partnership (LLP) forms of business organization provide some protection from personal liability for their owners. General partners in a limited partnership are treated as partners in a regular partnership. A limited partnership must have at least one general partner. The limited partners, and the members of an LLP, are provided protection from personal liability. The limited partnership and LLP offer this protection and also provide the tax advantages of a regular partnership. The operations of both entities are usually governed by a written partnership agreement, or in absence of one, by the Connecticut uniform limited partnership act. When there are business investors who don't participate in management, the best arrangement is often a limited partnership or an LLP.

> **NOTE** Most professional firms, such as those of engineers or doctors, used to be set up as partnerships. These professionals can't avoid taking personal liability for their acts as professionals, so they don't need a business form - like a corporation - that provides liability protection. But, in a partnership, all the partners share liability, so one partner's actions affect all the rest - personally! Then the LLP came into being, a boon to professionals. Now, they can do business in a simple form - the partnership - and get some meaningful protection. The partnership still assumes responsibility for the actions of the partners, but the liability stops there. A partner's actions affect that partner and the firm, but not other partners.

The following table summarizes the characteristics of partnerships, LPs and LLPs.

Characteristics of Partnership, LP and LLP

Record keeping	• *All*: Must keep separate records from personal records of the owners.
Personal liability	• *Partnership*: All owners have unlimited personal liability for actions of the partnership. • *LP*: General partner (must have one) has unlimited personal liability for actions of the partnership; limited partners not personally liable unless expressly guaranteed to creditors by the partner. • *LLP*: Partners not personally liable unless they sign guarantee of business debts.
Separate legal entity	• *All*: Separate legal entities in Connecticut that can own property, sue, and be sued in entity's name
Management and control	• *Partnership and LLP*: Unless provided in a written agreement, business affairs are governed by vote of the majority of voting partners. • *LP*: Controlled by general partner, which can be a person or another company.
Continuity of existence	• *Partnership*: Upon death of a partner unless the remaining partners agree to continue partnership, or on a predetermined termination date. • *LP*: Must state date of termination of agreement. • *LLP*: Not required to state termination date in its partnership agreement, but if an LLP drops to a single owner it is deemed dissolved.
Transferability of interests	• *Partnership*: Cannot without consent of partners, unless agreement allows it. • *LP and LLP*: Interest is considered personal property that can be sold or transferred, under the rules set up in original formation agreement.
Expense and formality of organization	• *Partnership*: Formal agreement not required, but strongly advised; if no formal agreement, Connecticut Uniform Partnership Act governs. • *LP*: Several formal requirements, including filing Certificate of Limited Partnership, which includes name, address, latest date to dissolve, general partner's name and address, and business description. • *LLP*: Several formal requirements, including filing Certificate of Limited Liability Partnership, which includes name and address, agent of record for the LLP, and business description.
Income taxes	• *All*: Business income reported on Form 1065; Form K-1 shows owner's share of income. Income passes through to owners and is reported on the owner's Form 1040. General partners income share is a form of salary and owner must pay self-employment tax in lieu of Social Security and Medicare taxes, on Form 1040, Schedule SE.
Deductibility of losses	• *All*: General partners may use business losses to offset their other income. There are limitations to the deductions limited partners are allowed and they should seek professional advice about deducting losses.
Choice of tax year	• *All*: Has same tax year as partners owning majority interest, usually calendar.
Sale of an interest	• *All*: An interest in a partnership is an asset in itself, so sale of a partnership interest generally results in a capital gain or loss to the owner.
Liquidation or dissolution	• *All*: Upon dissolution the owner and other partners get their interests back in cash or property; distribution is only taxed if cash plus property distributed exceeds adjusted basis of Partnership interest immediately before distribution.

Conclusion - partnerships, LPs, and LLPs

The three partnership forms of business offer a surprising range of tools for dealing with business management and legal liability. Each of them has its own characteristics and opportunities. Each also has challenges.

The general partnership form of business organization offers a great deal of freedom to two or more people starting a business together. Of course, that small step above the sole proprietorship form brings a big increase in complexity over the sole proprietorship because it involves agreements and extra paperwork. If an owner likes most of the attributes of a general partnership but is concerned about personal liability, or prefers not to share management rights with another partner, the partnership is not the right choice; a corporation or LLC is better.

Limited partnerships are useful in situations where a company has both participating and nonparticipating owners. LPs are also useful when parents wish to maintain control of a business while giving it away for estate tax purposes; they can make their children limited partners and the parents can become general partners in an LP.

LLPs are very useful for business owners who want the liability protection of a corporation and the tax flexibility of a general partnership.

LIMITED LIABILITY COMPANY

The limited liability company (LLC) form of business organization provides protection from personal liability for its owners, who are known as members. Unlike the limited liability partnership, which only has the tax attributes of a partnership, an LLC can choose to be taxed as a partnership or a corporation. LLCs are most often taxed as partnerships and this section of the chapter assumes partnership taxation has been elected.

The operations of an LLC are usually governed by a written operating agreement, or in absence of one, by the Connecticut Limited Liability Company Act. The LLC may be formed with one or more owners. The section of this chapter dealing with the single member limited liability company deals with one owner LLCs, this section of the chapter deals with LLCs with more than one member.

The following table summarizes the characteristics of an LLC.

Characteristics of Limited Liability Company (LLC)	
Personal liability	• Owner is not liable for debts and liabilities of LLC unless owner expressly guarantees them.
Separate legal entity	• Separate legal entity that may own property, sue, and be sued in LLC's name.
Management and control	• May be retained by the members or may be delegated through the articles of organization to Managers who are elected by members, but don't have to be members. Managers can be any type of entity.
Continuity of existence	• LLC has perpetual continuity of existence, like a corporation, unless specified termination date in articles of organization.
Transferability of interests	• Interest is considered personal property that can be sold or transferred, under the rules set up in original formation agreement.
Expense and formality of organization	• Several formal requirements, including filing of Articles of Organization of the LLC, which includes name and address, legal representative for the LLC, name of managers, and business description. Company must keep the articles at its office, along with list of past and present members, statement regarding contributions from each owner, and any other documents that are part of operating agreement.
Income taxes	• LLC is treated as a partnership for tax purposes (unless it elects otherwise), and reports its income on Form 1065, like a partnership. The income "passes through" to the owners and are reported on the owner's Form 1040. If the owner works for the business, the income of the entity is considered owner's "salary" and owner must pay self-employment tax in lieu of Social Security and Medicare taxes on Form 1040, Schedule SE. The income of a member who does not work for the LLC may not be subject to self-employment tax.
Deductibility of losses	• LLC members may use losses generated by the entity to offset owner's other income, but there are limitations to the deductions allowed and members should seek professional advice on this matter.
Choice of tax year	• Must adopt same tax year as partners owning majority interest, usually calendar year.
Sale of an interest	• An interest in an LLC is an asset in itself, so sale of an LLC interest generally results in a capital gain or loss to the owner.
Liquidation or dissolution	• Upon dissolution the owner and other partners get their interests back in cash or property; distribution is only taxed if cash distributed exceeds adjusted basis of LLC interest before distribution.

Conclusion – LLC

If the owner were currently operating the company as a sole proprietorship, corporation or partnership, the owner should evaluate the costs and potential benefits of conversion to an LLC. Generally, sole proprietorships, and partnerships may make the conversion without paying any taxes. Corporations, including "S" corporations, ordinarily incur tax costs that may outweigh the benefits of conversion. If the owner likes most of the attributes of the partnership and is concerned about personal liability, the LLC may be the way to go.

"C" CORPORATION

The "C" corporation form of business organization provides protection from personal liability for its owners, the shareholders. Corporations can give their employees such fringe benefits as stock options, pensions and group insurance more effectively than other types of business can. For that reason, the "C" corporation is the organization of choice for Connecticut's finance and industrial giants and nearly all publicly-traded companies. It is also the choice of successful smaller companies that wish to provide owners and employees the same benefits.

However, these advantages are paid for with a *double-tax* on corporate profits. When the "C" corporation makes a profit, it pays income tax on the profit. When the company distributes the profits - which have already been taxed - to stockholders as dividends, they pay personal taxes on the dividends.

> **NOTE** So, why would a small business choose the same business form used by United Technologies? One reason is that if the company pays most of its profits out as salaries to the owners, and pays them a very small dividend, there is no *double tax* problem. Another is that it gets superior tax writeoffs for fringe benefits. A third is that it doesn't have to have the same tax year as the owners, which can be a tax advantage!

Before choosing the corporate form of business for the company, the owner must carefully weigh the pros and cons. The "C" Corporation is one of two types of corporation. The legal characteristics of both types are identical; the tax characteristics are different.

The table on the following page summarizes the characteristics of a "C" Corporation.

Characteristics of "C" Corporation		
Personal liability	•	Owner is not liable for debts and liabilities of Corporation unless owner expressly guarantees them.
Separate legal entity	•	Separate legal entity that may own property, sue, and be sued in Corporation's name.
Management and control	• •	Management is centralized in Corporation's Board of Directors, who are elected by stockholders. In Connecticut, Board must have at least one member; the owner as sole Shareholder can also be the sole Director and President.
Continuity of existence	•	Corporation has perpetual continuity of existence, unless specified termination date in its Certificate of Incorporation.
Transferability of interests	•	Shares of a corporation are easier to transfer than any other entity; shareholders are free to sell any all of their shares. In a closely held corporation, usually a shareholder must first offer to sell their stock to other shareholders before selling to outsiders.
Expense and formality of organization	• • •	Several formal requirements, including filing of Certificate of Incorporation, which includes corporate name, purposes for which being formed, length of time for which being formed, maximum amount and type of capital stock to be authorized. Stock certificates must be issued to owners. Fee to the Secretary of State to officially register must be paid.
Income taxes	• • •	Separate legal entity that must pay its own income taxes. When dividend is paid to shareholders, it is taxed on shareholder's Form 1040, so there can be double taxation in that both the earnings and the dividends are taxed. To avoid double taxation, most corporations pay as much as possible to shareholders in deductible items such as salary, commissions, rent.
Deductibility of losses	•	Shareholder cannot deduct corporate losses against personal income. The Corporation retains the losses and can carry them back to get refunds of previous years' taxes paid or carry them forward to future tax years' taxable income.
Choice of tax year	•	Can choose any month as its fiscal year end; however Corporations that perform personal services may be required to use December 31 as a tax year end.
Sale of an interest	•	Stock in a "C" Corporation is an asset in itself, so sale of stock generally results in a capital gain or loss to the owner.
Liquidation or Dissolution	• •	Corporation has a taxable gain or loss on the property it sells or transfers in liquidation. Owner has taxable gain or loss on the difference between value of the property owner receives and the tax basis of the owner's stock.

Conclusion – "C" corporation

A "C" corporation is a form of business organization that offers many legal and tax advantages to its owners. It can also create some difficult tax problems for its owners. The "S" corporation, discussed in the next section of this chapter, eliminates some of those tax problems. Because the company is a small start-up business that could be converted to a "C" corporation in the future, "C" corporation status is probably not the way to go at first, but something to consider for the future.

"S" CORPORATION

An "S" corporation is identical to a "C" corporation for legal purposes. The main advantage of "S" corporation status is that it allows its shareholders most of the tax advantages of a partnership along with the legal advantages of a "C" corporation. The "S" corporation eliminates many of the problem of double taxation usually associated with the "C" corporation form of business organization, but keeps the corporation's advantages of limited liability.

NOTE — An "S" Corporation faces much more complicated tax rules than a partnership, LP or LLC, which makes it hard for a new small business to justify setting one up. Once widely selected as a small business form for its legal protection and tax breaks, the "S" corporation has lost its popularity, and the LLC is now a favorite.

The internal revenue service imposes several requirements on corporations that seek "S" corporation status. An "S" corporation must have these characteristics:

- United States corporation.
- No more than 75 shareholders.
- Shareholders must be individuals, estates, and some trusts.
- Nonresident aliens cannot be shareholders.
- No more than one class of stock.
- Cannot own or be owned by another corporation. However, recent federal legislation permits the creation of *Qualified Subchapter "S" Subsidiaries*, which can a help for companies with multiple locations or lines of business.

NOTE — You'll hear people refer to Subchapter "S" when talking about "S" corporations. That's a reference to the Internal Revenue Code of years ago. Nowadays, It's proper just to call them "S" corporations.

The table on the following page summarizes the characteristics of an "S" corporation.

Characteristics of "S" Corporation	
Personal liability	• Owner is not liable for debts and liabilities of Corporation unless owner expressly guarantees them.
Separate legal entity	• Separate legal entity that may own property, sue, and be sued in Corporation's name.
Management and control	• Management is centralized in corporation's board of directors, who are elected by stockholders. In Connecticut, board must have at least one member; the owner as sole shareholder can also be the sole director and president.
Continuity of existence	• Corporation has perpetual continuity of existence, unless specified termination date in its Certificate of Incorporation.
Transferability of interests	• Shares of a corporation are easier to transfer than any other entity; shareholders are free to sell any all of their shares. In a closely held corporation, usually a shareholder must first offer to sell their stock to other shareholders before selling to outsiders.
Expense and formality of organization	• Several formal requirements, including filing of Certificate of Incorporation, which includes corporate name, purposes for which being formed, length of time for which being formed, maximum amount and type of capital stock to be authorized. • Stock certificates must be issued to owners. • Fee to the Secretary of State to officially register must be paid. • Election must be filed with IRS on Form 2553 whereby the "S" corporation status is selected; must be filed within 2 ½ months of the start of any tax year.
Income taxes	• For Federal tax purposes, the income "passes through" to the owners and are reported on the owner's Form 1040. Connecticut has recently passed legislation that gradually recognizes "S" Corporation status. Until the phase in is complete, part of the earnings are taxed like a "C" Corporation, and the company pays income tax, and part of the earnings are taxed like a partnership and income tax is paid by the individual.
Deductibility of losses	• Shareholder can deduct corporate losses against personal income, however these loss deductions are limited to the owner's investment in the corporation. They may also be subject to limitations, so the owner should seek the advice of a professional.
Choice of tax year	• Generally required to have a December 31 fiscal year; if other than December 31 the company may have to pay advance tax payments to the IRS to simulate the cash flow of a calendar year.
Sale of an interest	• Stock in a "S" Corporation is an asset in itself, so sale of stock generally results in capital gain or loss to the owner.
Liquidation or dissolution	• Any gain or loss on liquidation flows through to the personal tax returns of the owners; owner has taxable gain or loss on the difference between market value of the property owner receives and the tax basis of stock.

Conclusion – "S" corporation

The "S" corporation form used to be the clear favorite for small companies that need the liability protection of a corporation. However, with the availability of the LLC and LLP, the complexity of "S" corporations has made them a much less desirable business form for small start-up businesses.

COMPLETING THE SETUP

After deciding on a business form for the company, the owner has several other important issues to consider and a number of steps to take before starting up. The Appendix has a checklist of start-up actions for each form of business organization discussed in this chapter. Other important issues to consider include:

- Accounting periods.
- Accounting methods.
- Ownership agreements.
- Fictitious names.
- Applying for tax numbers.
- Getting permission to do business.

Accounting periods

Every business must have an "accounting year." This is the annual accounting period the business uses for keeping records, figuring net income and paying income taxes.

There are two alternate accounting periods that the owner can use for the company:

- Calendar year. A year which ends on December 31.
- Fiscal year. A year which ends any other month.

The company adopts its tax year when it files its first federal income tax return. If it adopts a calendar year, the accounting year ends on December 31. A fiscal year is an accounting year ending on the last day of any month except December. The company continues to use the same accounting year unless it elects to change to a different one with the permission of the Internal Revenue Service. A business can use different periods for accounting and taxes. For example, the tax year could end December 31 and the accounting year could end June 30. But, most businesses find it convenient and less expensive to use the same period for both.

Generally, partnerships, limited partnerships, limited liability partnerships, limited liability companies and "S" corporations are required to use a calendar year as their tax year. Most corporations that provide professional services, such as a law firm, medical practice and dentists, must also use a calendar year even if they are "C" corporations. Most sole proprietorships and single member limited liability companies also use a calendar year because the owner files tax returns on a calendar year basis. As a result, generally, only businesses operating as "C" corporations can adopt fiscal years.

Accounting methods

A business figures its net income under one of two accounting methods:

- Cash method.
- Accrual method.

Cash Method
Under the cash method, income includes money that is received and expenses include money that is paid out. "Received," under the cash method, includes money that is available to the business.

Thus, a customer check sitting in the company's mailbox is "received," whether or not anyone takes it out.

Likewise, the cash method modifies the term "paid." It does not include expenses that are paid in advance. If the company owns merchandise or manufacturing inventory it cannot use the cash method of accounting; it has to use the accrual method. "C" corporations cannot use the cash method unless their average annual gross receipts are less than $5 million.

Accrual Method
Under the accrual method of accounting, income includes money that has been earned and expenses include those that are incurred. The goal of the accrual method is to match income earned and expenses incurred in the same time period.

Income is earned (and therefore taxable) when the business has a fixed right to receive the income and the amount of the income can be reasonably determined. Income can be earned in one year and received the following year.

Expenses are incurred by a business in the tax year that the business owes the expense and the amount of the expense can be reasonably determined. An expense can be incurred in one year and not actually paid until the following year.

If eligible, the owner should probably use the cash method for the company. The cash method is normally the one to use in order to reduce taxes. That is because income is usually lower under the cash method than it is under the accrual method.

Ownership agreements
If the company has more than one owner, the owners may have a disagreement and want to split apart or, one owner might die, become disabled or go bankrupt. Every business, regardless of business form, needs an agreement between the owners that avoids having the owners occupied in lawsuits trying to resolve the business' fate. A good business ownership agreement should deal with several possibilities:

- Death or disability of an owner.
- Sale of owner's interest.
- Retirement of an owner.
- Bankruptcy of the business.
- Bankruptcy of an owner.
- Policy disagreement between the owners.

Fictitious names
If a Sole Proprietorship or Partnership (entities that are not formed by a filing with the Secretary of State) does business using a name other than the owner's name, the name should be registered with the local town clerk. The name is registered by filing a Trade Name Certificate. Registration protects the company from another business stealing goodwill by using the same name. Trade or Servicemark registrations should also be considered by a business with long term growth potential. If the owner wants the company to become a name with statewide, regional or national recognition, the owner should seek the professional services of a Trademark and Servicemark, attorney as soon as possible.

Applying for tax numbers

The company probably needs at least three different identification numbers:

- A Federal identification number.
- A State unemployment identification number.
- A State tax identification number.

The company's CPA firm, payroll service or lawyer should have the forms to use for applying for these numbers. Companies can also get the forms from Community Accounting and Aid Services, the Connecticut Small Business Development Center, Internal Revenue Service, Connecticut Department of Revenue Services and the Connecticut Department of Labor. See the Appendix for addresses, phone numbers and web addresses for important government offices.

Federal Identification Numbers

Every business entity other than the Sole Proprietorship and Single Member Limited Liability Company must have a Federal employer identification number (EIN) to use as its taxpayer identification number. A Sole Proprietorship and Single Member Limited Liability Company can use the owner's social security number as its taxpayer identification number. However, a Sole Proprietorship or a Single Member Limited Liability Company must have an EIN if it:

- Pays wages.
- Files pension or excise tax returns.

The company can get an EIN by filing Internal Revenue Service Form SS-4, Application for Employer Identification Number. The EIN may also be applied for by phone, fax, or online.

Once the company registers for an EIN, the Internal Revenue Service automatically mails the necessary forms including tax deposits coupons, quarterly report forms, income tax forms and tax rate booklets. Register online at: http://www.irs.gov/businesses/small/

State Unemployment Identification Numbers

Any business that has employees must have a Connecticut unemployment identification number and pay state unemployment taxes. The company get this number by filing Form UC-1A, the application form for a Connecticut unemployment tax registration number. These are issued by the Connecticut Department of Labor, which issues the numbers by mail or phone. Register online at: www.ctdol.state.ct.us/.

State Tax Identification Numbers

A company has to register with the Connecticut Department of Revenue Services if it makes taxable sales, makes taxable purchases or has employees. The company can get this number by filing a Form REG-1, Application for a Tax Registration Number. The registration number costs a small filing fee for most applicants. Connecticut issues the number either by telephone or mail.

When it files Form REG-1, the company receives a sales tax permit. The permit lasts for two years and is renewed automatically. The permit must be displayed conspicuously at the place of businesses. A company in business without a permit is subject to a fine. The company also receives the necessary report forms and updates on tax regulations. Register online at: www.drs.state.ct.us/.

Getting permission to do business

The state and local governments regulate who can do business and where they can do it. There are two sources for these regulations: town zoning laws and regulations of the state agencies that issue professional licenses.

Zoning Laws

The local town zoning board decides what types of business can be operated from a residential area. The owner should check on regulations and visit the local zoning enforcement officer at Town Hall before starting to do business as a company at home. The owner should also visit the local zoning enforcement officer regarding a commercial business location. For example, some business zone areas that permit professional offices might prohibit retail sales establishments.

Professional licenses

Most skilled professionals, such as hairdressers and contractors, have to get special licenses before they can sell their services to the public. The state's Department of Consumer Protection regulates most of the licensed businesses. For licensing specifics, the starting place is the state's Web site: www.state.us.ct.

FORMING A BUSINESS ON THE WEB

A number of web based services allow business owners to expedite the registration process and reduce legal and processing fees traditionally charged such services. You may still need the services of an attorney to setup a business, particularly if the business has more than one owner. The following are some online services currently offered to business owners but exclude state filing fees:

www.companies-in-formation.com	$99
www.number1advantage.com	89
www.inc123.com	99
www.uslegalforms.com	49+
www.legalzoom.com	99

Every business entity other than the Sole Proprietorship (SP) and Single Member Limited Liability Company (SMLLC) is required to have a Federal employer identification number (EIN). SP and SMLLC can use the owner's social security number unless it pays wages or files pension or excise tax returns.

Business owners can contact the Internal Revenue Service directly on-line at www.irs.gov. All necessary tax deposit coupons, quarterly report forms, and other income tax forms will automatically be mailed to the registering business.

CONCLUSION

Business organization decisions can affect income taxes, legal protection and continuity of the company. A business owner should consult with accounting, legal, and insurance professionals before making a final decision. The decisions involves balancing tax advantages, administrative costs and legal protection. After making the decision, the owners should form the business and register with tax and regulatory authorities.

Appendix

Checklist for forming business organizations

All forms of business

_____ Apply for federal identification number with the Internal Revenue Service (if needed).

_____ Apply for state tax identification number with Department of Revenue Services (if needed).

_____ Apply for state unemployment ID with Connecticut Department of Labor (if needed).

Sole Proprietorship and Single Member Limited Liability Company

_____ File trade name certificate with the local town hall.

_____ File articles of organization with appointment of registered agent with CTSOS.

Partnership, LP or LLP

_____ File trade name certificate with local town hall.

_____ File certificate of limited partnership and designation of general partner with CTSOS. (LP)

_____ File cert. of limited liability partnership and appt of registered agent with CTSOS. (LLP)

_____ Consider preparation of a formal partnership agreement.

Limited Liability Company

_____ File articles of organization with appointment of registered agent with the CTSOS.

_____ Obtain an LLC kit with seal and membership certificates from a legal supply company.

_____ Adopt basic operating agreement, prepared by attorney or available in some LLC kits.

_____ Issue membership certificates to all members.

_____ Consider preparation of a more detailed operating agreement.

Corporation - "C" and "S"

_____ File certificate of incorporation with appointment of registered agent with the CTSOS.

_____ File first annual report with the CTSOS.

_____ Obtain corporate kit with seal and stock certificates from a legal supply company.

_____ Adopt corporate by-laws, prepared by attorney or available in most corporate kits.

_____ Issue stock certificates to all stockholders.

_____ File Form 2553 Election to be taxed as a small business corporation with IRS. ("S")

_____ Consider preparation of a stockholder agreement.

CTSOS= Connecticut Secretary of State. See address on following page.

Names, addresses and web-sites of important government offices

Internal Revenue Service
135 High Street
Hartford, Connecticut 06103
Telephone Number: 1-800-829-3676
Web-Site: www.irs.gov

Connecticut Department of Revenue Services
25 Sigourney Street
Hartford, Connecticut 06106
Telephone Number: 1-800-382-9463
Web-Site: www.drs.state.ct.us

Connecticut Department of Labor
200 Folly Brook Boulevard
Wethersfield, Connecticut 06019
Telephone Number: 1-860-263-6000
Web-Site: www.ctdol.state.ct.us/

Connecticut Secretary of State
30 Trinity Street
Hartford, Connecticut 06106
Telephone Number: 1-860-509-6000
Web-Site: www.sots.state.ct.us

Official State of Connecticut Web Site: www.state.ct.us/

All of these web-sites have official forms and instructions available in "PDF" Format. All you need to do is download the forms is a web-browser and a copy of Adobe Acrobat Reader. You can obtain a copy of Adobe Acrobat Reader for free at www.adobe.com.

INTRODUCTION

Insurance planning is an essential part of business management, because it helps the owners manage business risks, protect business assets and provide benefits to employees. This chapter is designed to help you make decisions about the types and amounts of insurance to carry and how to purchase the insurance. Like many topics covered in this book, insurance is a specialized field and owners can find many insurance professionals who can help them in their decision process.

Insurance planning is more than simply purchasing insurance products in the marketplace. It also involves making an assessment of the risks faced by the business and making a decision about how to deal with those risks. Sometimes, taking steps to reduce business risks is more economical than purchasing insurance.

We are grateful to the Insurance Information Institute for permission to reprint the descriptions of insurance policies found in this chapter.

ORGANIZATION OF CHAPTER

The chapter discusses the following topics:

- What is insurance and why have it?
- Insuring a home-based business.
- Liability insurance.
- Workers compensation insurance.
- Other types of insurance.
- Deciding on insurance coverage.
- Where to buy insurance, including pricing and reducing insurance costs.
- Managing risk.

This chapter discusses the risks that can impact your business and how insurance can help you deal with them. It also provides an overview of important insurance concepts. The chapter does not cover unemployment insurance, which is a form of payroll tax and is covered in the chapter on *Paying Employees*.

WHAT IS INSURANCE AND WHY HAVE IT?

If you own a business, eventually something will happen, such as an accident or theft, that is beyond your control or costs more to fix than you can afford. Without insurance, you'd have to set aside big cash reserves to pay for what might - but probably won't - go wrong.

Instead of having every business set up its own cash reserve fund, the insurance company sets up a single large cash reserve fund and charges its customers their fair share of that fund. The rate – or premium – charged depends on the type of insurance, the risk of loss, the company's type of business and other factors.

In addition, the insurance company provides a service to its customers of helping them control their risks, reducing both their losses and their insurance premiums. Finally, the insurance company helps its customers control legal costs, by providing a means for settling claims without having to resort to lawsuits.

Many small startup businesses skimp on insurance coverage in an effort to save money. They figure the risks covered by insurance seem unlikely so they try to stretch their homeowners and personal auto insurance or ignore insurance completely. The problem with their approach is that accidents *do* happen and mistake *are* made and they can result in severe property damage or in a costly lawsuit.

By purchasing insurance, the business owner:

- Makes better use of resources by not having to set aside reserves for losses.
- Protects assets by shifting the payment obligation to the insurance company.
- Gains peace of mind by knowing that the insurance company will cover claims.

In addition, in the case of employee benefits policies such as medical insurance, the company gains a recruiting advantage.

Insurance rates are based on the sharing of risks. Insurance companies evaluate their customers' exposure to business risks, arrange their customers into groups having similar risks, estimate the amount of losses and calculate a price - or premium - that covers the losses, administration and provides a profit. The estimated losses include the costs of defending against a lawsuit, such as lawyers, investigators, and professional witnesses, as well as the cost of a claim.

Types of insurance

Business insurance policies fall into three broad categories:

- **Protection of business assets.** Pays to repair, clean or replace facilities and equipment damaged, lost or stolen.

- **Assurance to other parties.** Reimburses other parties for their costs incurred.

- **Employee benefits.** Reimburses employees for their costs.

While it is management's business decision whether to purchase most insurance coverage, three are required by law:

- **Auto liability.** Required by state law.

- **Workers compensation.** Required for any company having employees, but optional for owners willing to waive their rights to coverage.

- **Occupational requirements.** The laws covering occupations sometimes either require liability insurance coverage or recommend it in such strong terms that should not be ignored.

> **NOTE** An excellent Web resource is www.iii.org the Insurance Information Institute website, which contains an overview of insurance and policies. You can also explore some of the links to other insurance sites that the Institute provides.

INSURING A HOME-BASED BUSINESS

Two problems arise in insuring a home-based business:

- **Inadequate coverage**. A homeowner's or renter's policy typically provides only $2,500 coverage for business equipment, which is usually not enough to cover the business property of a small business.

- **Risks not covered**. A business owner may need coverage for liability, professional liability lost income and other risks that aren't part of a homeowner's insurance package.

There are three main alternatives for insurance for a home business:

- **Homeowners policy endorsement**. This is group of inexpensive standard endorsements added to an existing homeowners policy to increase or extend the standard coverage. For a small additional premium, the standard $2,500 policy limit can be increased to $10,000 or more. Likewise, other coverages are possible:

  - **Incidental business occupancies**. Liability and property damage coverage for owners who occasionally do business from home.

  - **Business pursuits**. Coverage for salespeople, office employees and teachers who are not self-employed but perform some work from home.

- **In-home business policy**. This is a form of more comprehensive coverage for business equipment and liability than offered on a homeowners policy endorsement. These policies, which may also be called in-home business endorsements, vary significantly depending on the insurer. In addition to protection for business property, most policies reimburse for the loss of important papers and records, accounts receivable and off-site business property. Some pay for lost income due to business interruption in the event the home business premises is so badly damaged that it can't be used for a while. They also pay for the extra expense of operating out of a temporary location. Some in-home business policies allow a number of full-time employees, generally up to three.

  In-home business policies generally include broader liability insurance for higher amounts of coverage. They may offer protection against lawsuits for injuries caused by products or services, for example. In-home business policies are available from homeowners insurance companies and specialty insurers that sell stand-alone in-home business policies.

- **Business owners policy (BOP)**. This policy form was created specifically for small-to-mid-size businesses, and is an excellent solution if a home-based business operates in more than one location. A BOP, like the in-home business policy, covers business property and equipment, loss of income, extra expense and liability. However, these coverages are on a much broader scale than the in-home business policy. BOPs include:

- Property insurance for buildings and contents owned by the company

- Business interruption insurance, which covers the loss of income resulting from a fire or other catastrophe that disrupts the operation of the business. It can also include the extra expense of operating out of a temporary location.

- Liability protection, which covers the company's legal responsibility for the harm it may cause to others. This harm is a result of things that you and your employees do or fail to do in your business operations that may cause bodily injury or property damage due to defective products, faulty installations and errors in services provided.

BOP policies don't cover professional liability, auto insurance, worker's compensation or health and disability insurance.

Policy Forms

Homeowners and Business owners policies are sold with different levels of coverage usually referred to as *forms* – basic, broad or standard and special or all risk. The basic level is being eliminated and may not be offered in many states. Flood and earthquake may not be covered at all in a package policy and require specialized policies. The following table shows the differences among the forms.

Policy form	Coverage
Basic	Fire, lightning, explosion, windstorm, hail, smoke, damage caused by aircraft or vehicles, riot or civil commotion, vandalism, volcano eruption.
Broad or standard	All included in basic plus falling objects, weight of ice and snow, water damage (from a heating or cooling system, but not from flood or automatic sprinklers).
Special or all risk	What is not excluded in the policy is included. The common exclusions are: earth movement, government action, nuclear hazard, war and military action, flood.

Most insurance policies cover the *actual cash value* or ACV of property, which is the replacement value after deducting a depreciation allowance: the older the property, the larger the depreciation allowance. The idea of this practice is to reimburse for similar used property but the reimbursement is often too low to pay for reasonable replacement property in the open market. A more generous coverage, *replacement cost insurance* is available for an additional premium, and covers the cost of purchasing new replacement property.

LIABILITY INSURANCE

Liability insurance is the most important form of insurance for most businesses, because the claims can be the most devastating. For that reason, there are many different forms of liability insurance, including some there bundled with other insurance and those that are sold separately. The common forms are:

- General liability.

- Product liability

- Employment practices liability.

- Professional liability.

- Commercial umbrella.

- Directors and officers liability.

General liability

As defined by the online dictionary www.buyerzone.com, general liability insurance is: *a form of insurance designed to protect owners and operators of businesses from a wide variety of liability exposures. These exposures could include liability arising out of accidents resulting from the premises or the operations of an insured, products sold by the insured, operations completed by the insured, and contractual liability.*

General liability insurance is inexpensive for small businesses because most of them have no claims at all or very small claims, so it is common for small companies to find affordable liability insurance coverage in the hundreds of thousands or millions of dollars. For example, a small business might carry a policy for $1 or $2 million or more. The policy pays for defending a lawsuit as well as judgments and settlements.

The cost of a general liability policy varies greatly, depending on the nature the business, its past claims experience, type of entity (proprietorship, partnership, LLC) and the business location. In addition, it's important to read the policy carefully because many policies list things that they do not cover.

Product Liability

The purpose of product liability insurance is to cover damages caused by unsafe or malfunctioning products. This is a form of coverage that is customized for the type of business and it is often carried by insurance agencies that specialize in the businesses that they cover. Most insurance companies employ engineers and chemists who evaluate products for potential risks both to decide whether to insure the product and how to tailor the coverage if the risk is accepted.

Employment Practices Liability Insurance

Employment practices liability insurance (EPLI) covers businesses against claims by workers for violation of their civil rights or employment rights. The number of lawsuits filed by employees against their employers is rising and although most suits are filed against large corporations, no company is immune to them.

Recognizing that many smaller companies now need EPLI, some insurers provide this coverage as an endorsement to their Business owners Policy (BOP). Other companies offer EPLI as a stand-alone coverage. EPLI provides protection against most employee lawsuits, including claims of:

- Sexual harassment.
- Discrimination.
- Wrongful termination.
- Breach of employment contract.
- Negligent evaluation.
- Failure to employ or promote.
- Wrongful discipline.
- Deprivation of career opportunity.
- Wrongful infliction of emotional distress.
- Mismanagement of employee benefit plans.

The cost of EPLI coverage depends on the type of business, number of employees and risk factors such as whether the company has had past employment practices claims. The policy pays for defending a lawsuit as well as judgments and settlements. EPLI policies typically do not cover punitive damages, civil and criminal penalties or workers compensation claims.

Having a program to minimize the possibility of employee lawsuits is just as important as having EPLI insurance. Important elements of this program include educating managers and employees to avoid problems in the first place:

- Create effective hiring and screening programs to avoid discrimination in hiring.

- Post corporate policies throughout the workplace and place them in employee handbooks so policies are clear to everyone.

- Show employees what steps to take if they are the object of sexual harassment or discrimination by a supervisor. Make sure supervisors know where the company stands on what behaviors are not permissible.

- Document everything that occurs and the steps your company is taking to prevent and solve employee disputes.

Professional Liability

Professionals that operate their own businesses need professional liability insurance in addition to an in-home business or business owners policy. This protects them against financial losses from lawsuits filed against them by their clients.

Professionals are expected to have extensive technical knowledge or training in their areas of expertise. They are also expected to perform the services for which they were hired, according to the standards of conduct in their profession. If they fail to use the degree of skill expected of them, they can be held responsible in a court of law for any harm they cause to another person or business. When liability is limited to acts of negligence, professional liability insurance may be called "errors and omissions" liability.

Professional liability insurance is a specialty coverage. Professional liability coverage is not provided under homeowners endorsements, in-home business policies or Business owners policies (BOPs).

Commercial umbrella

This is a policy that allows a business owner to purchase a high limit of liability insurance that applies to a group of policies while allowing the limits of the individual policies to remain at reasonable levels. For example, if the company has a $1,000,000 automobile liability policy and a $1,000,000 general liability policy, it could purchase a $5,000,000 umbrella policy. This saves money by providing a $5,000,000 limit for each policy without the company having to purchase $5,000,000 for two policies. In addition, the umbrella policy usually provides extra coverage that may not be provided in any of the underlying policies.

Directors and officers

If the company is large enough to have outside shareholders, it may need directors and officers liability insurance. This insurance covers the legal expenses and settlements in situations where the officer or director is sued personally.

WORKERS COMPENSATION INSURANCE

Employers have a legal responsibility to their employees to provide a safe place to work and if the employee is injured on the job, to pay medical expenses and to continue paying wages while the employee recuperates. These costs are covered by workers compensation insurance, which is legally required insurance coverage in nearly every state. Depending on state procedures, the coverage is provided by private insurance companies or by a state-run insurance fund.

Workers compensation insurance covers workers injured on the job, whether they're hurt on the workplace premises or elsewhere, or in auto accidents while on business, regardless to who was at fault. It also covers the cost of work-related illnesses. Besides payments to injured workers, medical and rehabilitation services, it also provides death benefits to surviving spouses and dependents.

The amount and duration of lost income benefits, the procedures for medical and rehabilitation services and system administration are determined by the state workers compensation office. However, the insurance rates paid are determined by the insurance company and depend on three factors:

■ **Nature of work performed**. Jobs involving higher risk of injury naturally result in higher premiums.

■ **Company safety practices**. Employers that provide and enforce the use of safety equipment and provide safety training for employees can expect to pay lower premiums. A company that has a lot of accidents pays a higher premium even if the accidents aren't severe because the insurance company sees the number of accidents as a sign of poor safety practices.

■ **Insurance company procedures**. Companies that specialize in workers compensation insurance normally charge the lowest rates.

Workers compensation insurance must be bought as a separate policy. Although in-home business and business owners policies (BOPs) are sold as package policies, they don't include coverage for workers' injuries.

OTHER TYPES OF INSURANCE

The following sections discuss several common types of business insurance policy. It is impossible to cover every insurance coverage, because there are thousands, so we recommend consulting with a full-service insurance broker about the need for coverage.

Business interruption insurance

What happens if a business is shut down, wholly or partially, by events beyond the owner's control? Any number of things can cause this, including failure of air conditioning. power outage, fire, flood and even external events such as a fire in a supplier's business which interrupts material supply.

Business interruption (BI) insurance provides money to keep a business going until it can get back into operation. The money can be used to meet loan payments, pay key employees or pay ongoing expenses such as rent and property taxes. BI insurance can be as vital to business survival as fire insurance.

> **NOTE** Thousands of New York City businesses, their customers and suppliers learned about business interruption during the September 11, 2001 attacks. Most were closed for months and many never reopened because they ran out of money during the closures. BI insurance might have helped them to survive.

However BI insurance isn't the only solution. The best solution is to avoid an interruption by having a plan to prevent - or recover quickly from - an interruption. Known as a *disaster recovery plan*, it includes:

■ **Alternate workplaces.** Employee homes or offices in other areas.

■ **Backup communications.** These include beepers, cell phones, email and alternate Internet service providers.

■ **Alternate computer facilities.** Included are laptops and employee home computers.

■ **Spare parts.** For critical operating equipment, keep a backup unit or backups for vulnerable operating components.

Business interruption coverage is normally not sold separately, but is added to a property insurance policy or included in a package policy. BI covers the profits that would have earned, based on the company's financial records, had the disaster not occurred. It also covers operating expenses such as electricity, that continue even though business activities have come to a temporary halt. Generally, there is a 48-hour waiting period before business interruption coverage begins.

BI premium cost is related to the likelihood of an interruption. For example, the premium paid by a restaurant is likely to be higher than that paid by a real estate agency, because of the greater risk of fire. Also, a real estate agency can easily operate out of another location.

Extra expenses insurance

Extra expense insurance reimburses the company for the money it spends, over and above normal operating expenses, to avoid having to shut down during the restoration period. Usually extra expenses are paid if they help to decrease business interruption costs. In some instances, extra expense insurance alone may provide sufficient coverage, without the purchase of business interruption insurance.

Marine

If you import goods or have them manufactured for you overseas, you need Marine coverage, even it the goods are shipped by air. This insurance is usually arranged by the customs agent who is representing your business.

Inland marine

Originally an extension of Marine Insurance for when the goods are landed here, Inland Marine has grown to cover many things such as shipping goods, accounts receivable records, valuable papers, signs, plate glass, small tools and mobile equipment. Many of these coverages are included in the business owners policy. If the company owns special tools, unique inventory, special signs and similar property, there may not be adequate coverage in the standard business owners policy. In that case, the Inland Marine policy or endorsement may fill the gap.

Commercial auto insurance

Insurance coverages for a car used in a business are the same as for a car used for personal travel: liability, collision and comprehensive, medical payments (known as personal injury protection in some states) and coverage for uninsured motorists. However, when a vehicle is owned by a business, there are some additional requirements:

- The name of the business should appear on the policy as the principal insured rather than the name of the owner of the business. This avoids possible confusion if a claim has to be filed.

- Sometimes a standard personal auto policy provides enough coverage. However, the insurer can deny coverage if a car is used regularly in a business without being declared. Whether you need to buy a business auto insurance policy depends on the kind of driving you do. The insurance agent should be told about how vehicles are used in business, such as how much driving and where, who does the driving, whether employees are likely to be driving their own cars.

- The major coverages are the same, but a business auto policy differs from a personal auto policy in many technical respects. The insurance agent can explain the differences and options.

■   If you have a personal umbrella liability policy, there's generally an exclusion for business-related liability. In that case, be sure to have sufficient auto liability coverage.

Since auto claims can be very costly, Commercial Auto policies frequently include Loss Control services provided by the insurance company to train drivers and help prevent future claims.

Insurance for floods and earthquakes

Property insurance policies usually exclude coverage for flood or earthquake damage. If you operate in an area prone to floods or earthquakes, you'll need a special insurance policy or commercial property endorsement. The best way to find out if this coverage is needed is to contact government disaster-control offices, the company's commercial bank or an insurance broker. Fellow business owners are also a good source of information.

To purchase a flood insurance policy, contact an insurance agent or the National Flood Insurance program. For more information about this program call 1-888-FLOOD29 or look at its web site: www.fema.gov/nfip/. The federal government requires buildings in flood zones that don't conform to flood plain building codes to be torn down if damage exceeds 50 percent of the market value. Consider purchasing "ordinance or law" coverage to help pay for the extra costs of tearing down the structure and rebuilding it. If the policy contains a coinsurance clause, be sure the property is sufficiently insured to comply with the clause.

Earthquake policies have a different kind of deductible -- a percentage of coverage rather than a fixed dollar amount. Thus, if a building is insured for $100,000, with a 5% deductible, in the event of an earthquake, the owner is responsible for the first $5,000 in damage.

Business interruption insurance, which reimburses for lost income during a shutdown, applies only to causes of damage covered under the business property insurance policy. If the business premises are shut down due to earthquake damage, you'll need to have earthquake coverage to make a claim under a business interruption policy.

DECIDING ON INSURANCE COVERAGE

Making a decision about what - if any - insurance to purchase requires balancing the costs and benefits of insurance. The company that takes an overly cautious approach may spend far too much money. A practical approach is to analyze the company's situation and decide where to accept risk and where to insure against risk.

The analysis covers these areas:
■   Location.
■   People.
■   Vehicles.
■   Property and equipment.
■   Inventory.
■   Property of customers and others.
■   Products and services.

Location

Besides the cost of rebuilding a business premises, the value of the location itself and the form of occupancy are important. Having a prime location can justify extra coverage if the business can't return to it after a fire. For example, the right to operate a newsstand at a major bus terminal is worth much more than the right to operate one in a low-traffic area. Other factors include the terms of occupancy as shown in the table.

Leased space	The lease may list what coverages are required. Include improvements to the space. Consider liability for injury to the property of others.
Business condo	The condominium contract lists the insurance and coverages needed. These are usually minimums and may be inadequate for the business.
Owned building (owner's part)	The lender requires enough insurance to replace the building in case of total loss. Coverage should be for the full replacement value of the property with inflation protection. You may also want to include Ordinance or law coverage. Consider liability for injury to the property of others.
Owned building (tenant's part)	You need this coverage if you have tenants. Specify in your lease what insurance your tenants must carry and how they need to provide proof such as a certificate of insurance from their insurance carrier.
Owner's home	Provide coverage for business property and equipment. See the discussion of insuring a home business above.
Multiple sites	Insurance companies offer discounts and special packaging for a business with multiple sites

People

Adding employees means adding layers of risk, even in a small business.

Sole owner	Requires life and disability coverage.
Multiple owners	Company documents should define buyout terms and life insurance can be provided to fund them.
Family	Medical and dental insurance for families of owner and employees.
Employees	Workers Compensation Insurance is required. Health insurance benefits such as medical and dental to attract and keep employees. Errors and omissions coverage and life insurance on key employees.
Contractors	Contractors should carry their own liability, errors and omissions and disability insurance and provide a certificate of coverage for your files.

Vehicles

If vehicles are used other than for commuting to work, auto insurance policies must be reviewed for proper coverage.

Owner's personal vehicle	Notify insurance company of business usage of the vehicle and determine if the coverage is sufficient. If there are multiple vehicles, their business usage should also be covered.
Employee owned vehicles	If employees use their vehicles for business use, they should update their policies and provide proof of coverage. Provide additional coverage on company policies for employees' use of personal vehicles.
Rented vehicles	When renting a vehicle for business use, be sure rental agency knows the use and agrees to it. Be sure insurance covers business use.
Leased: registered in business name	Be sure leasing company and insurance company know and agree to business use. Normally you provide the insurance on a leased vehicle.
Owned: registered in business name	The business provides the insurance on an owned vehicle. Be sure the insurance company knows the kind and the extent of the business use.

Property and equipment

While a start up business may not have much property, the amount of property increases as the business grows. Property risks include fire, windstorm, flood, earthquake, theft and burglary.

It's important that the coverage is adequate. If the coverage is less than 80% of the property value, the business owner becomes a co-insurer with the insurance company. In that case, the insurance company is only obligated to pay its percentage of a loss.

Improvements	Improvements to leased space such as partitions, shelving, flooring and lighting are part of the business and should be included in insurance values. Consider higher cost of replacement if the building code demands higher quality.
Furnishings	These should normally be covered by replacement value insurance.
Liquid assets	Includes cash, checks, credit cards, securities and lottery tickets. The risk is employee theft and should be covered by a surety bond.
Tools and equipment	Consider special coverage for unique or self-constructed equipment.
Computer equipment	Provide for the theft, damage, accidental erasure or even malicious erasure of business records. Computer coverage should include the cost of replacing hardware and software and the rebuilding of information.
Fine arts	If the business premises is decorated with high-value artwork, the items should be reported to the insurance company and listed in a schedule to the policy.
Outside signs	Signs should be considered from both a property and a liability point of view.

Inventory

Inventory is a form of property that is treated differently because it turns over and loses value if it becomes stale or out of style.

All inventory	How hard is it to replace? Are employee theft and shoplifting covered?
Seasonal inventory	Do you have to store a large inventory to handle a peak season? Does insurance cover the peak values and storage location?
Perishables	Can the inventory be ruined by a power failure?

Property of customers and others

Customer goods stored	Will you be storing customer property? Examples are dry cleaners, auto repairer, tailor, consignment shop. Do you have a layaway service?
Customer goods held for repair	Do you store customer goods for repair? Consider the liability if the customer's property is stolen or given to the wrong person.

Products and services

Determine whether the company provides a service, or product that has a special risk. Some examples of the built-in risks are listed below.

■ **Manufacturing products.**

Product or service	Risk	Comments
Food or personal care products	Moderate to High	The major risk is product liability exposure: the product may injure someone.
Assembly only	Low	Generally this is the lowest risk.
Cutting or bending metal or other materials	Moderate	Greatest risk is injury to employees.
Smelting, melting metal or other materials	High	Highest risk of injury to employees and damage from fire and explosion.

■ **Selling or Merchandising.** Selling or merchandising generally has a lower risk overall, except for the sale of alcohol or medicines, which are unique areas of insurance and licensing and are handled by legal and insurance specialists.

■ **Services.** When selling a service, the company is responsible for the actions of individual workers. There are two insurance solutions to this risk, errors and omissions insurance and professional liability insurance. Both are specialized coverages but can be purchased from a conventional insurance broker.

WHERE TO BUY INSURANCE

Insurance purchasing is a little more complicated than that for other business products because of the vast number of choices to make. Although insurance is referred to as a product, it has an important service component which is the professional advice of the seller. This advice makes all the difference in arranging insurance coverage.

Whom to pick

The first step in getting the proper coverage for a business is to find the right insurance agent or broker, and the best source is a referral. These are some referral sources:

- Business friends and acquaintances.

- Agent or company that provides your personal insurance.

- Business trade associations. These may also sponsor insurance programs designed specifically for your business.

- Web sites.

If your business is very small, consider giving all of insurance to one agent or broker so there will be enough commission to pay for the time needed to do the job right. This practice helps to reduce overlaps - double coverage - and gaps - no coverage.

Insurance agents and brokers

Most commercial insurance is sold by licensed agents and brokers, while a growing amount of personal insurance is sold directly by insurance companies. The difference between them is important;

- **Both.** Licensed by the state insurance department. Paid a commission by the company whose policy you buy. Can sell any kind of coverage.

- **Broker.** Represents the business owner. Tend to handle larger accounts. Brokers gather your requirements and go to several insurance companies for bids. They may also create packages of coverage for a specialized industry and market directly to the industry.

- **Agent.** Represents the insurance company. Can represent multiple companies. Tend to handle small to medium sized customers. A small business is most likely to do business with a agent rather than a broker because an agent is used to dealing with owners of smaller businesses.

Company offices and Web sites

A growing number of companies sell directly to customers without going through agents. They do this through a local office or Web site. This is a safe, practical way to purchase insurance. However, as with any other direct sale situation, it's important to know the seller, including getting references and verifying the seller is licensed with the state insurance department.

Business insurance pricing

Business insurance prices depend on the risks involved and the nature of the coverage. The rates are applied either in advance or retroactively:

- **Advance pricing.** Fire insurance is an example of advance pricing. The building is assigned a rating based on the size of the building, its age, its condition, prior uses (which may have soaked the floors with oil), fire protection (such as sprinklers), the quality of local firefighting services. The rating is done by the insurance company or an independent inspection bureau. The premium is paid in advance and does not change until the policy is renewed.

- **Retroactive pricing.** Workers Compensation insurance is an example. The price depends on the kinds of jobs employees do and the number of employees in each job, which isn't known until one year after the policy takes effect. To deal with this uncertainty, the insurance company asks for a deposit premium at the beginning of the year which is based on an estimate of employment. When the year ends, the insurance company conducts a payroll audit to determine the actual employee counts in each classification and the business owner receives a charge or credit for the difference. This audit is conducted by mail or by an on-site audit, depending on the size of the payroll.

  The audit approach is also used for property insurance on inventory. If the inventory builds up for the annual peak season, gets sold off and then is reduced he rest of the year, the exposure varies. The inventory may also be located in leased or owned facilities beyond the basic business facilities. The business determines the inventory levels and locations each month and reports them to the insurance company. The insurance company sends an auditor in periodically to check the audit reports to the books.

The insurance company may want to use *composite rating* where a rate is developed based on all of the exposures and then related to a single factor such as sales. This method simplifies the audit process, since sales are the only value that needs to be reported and audited.

Shopping around

Prices vary from company to company, so it pays to shop around. In particular, companies or brokers that specialize in a type of insurance of industry can be very competitive because their larger specialized customer base gives them better buying power. The process of shopping around affords the opportunity to discuss different ideas and approaches to insurance protection.

Financial stability

It's very important to pick a company that is financially stable. The starting point is to be sure the insurance company is registered to do business in the state. If so, it means the company has the required minimum financial strength. It's also possible to check the financial health of insurance companies with rating companies such as A.M. Best (www.ambest.com) and Standard & Poor's (www2.standardandpoors.com/) and to consult consumer magazines.

MANAGING RISK

Since insurance pricing depends on risk, the best way to reduce insurance costs is by reducing risk. This is a process of analyzing business activities, identifying risky ones and developing a strategy to deal with them. Some practical strategies for small businesses are listed below.

■ **Deductibles and co-insurance.** Insurance policy premiums, can be reduced by increasing deductibles or decreasing coverage limits. These changes don't really reduce risks or insurance costs; instead, the business owner assumes more of the risk of financial loss. Deductibles represent the amount of money you pay before your insurance policy kicks in. The higher the deductible, the less you pay for the policy.

■ **Classify Employees correctly**. Workers Compensation premiums depend on the amount and classification of payroll. One strategy is to classify employees correctly to minimize the employees in the high risk jobs. Another is structure jobs to manage the amount of high-risk labor performed.

EXAMPLE

A group of workers process meat, part of which involves slicing, a high risk task. If all workers in the group perform slicing, all will receive the higher cost classification. However, if only one employee slices, that employee receives the high-risk classification and the rest receive a lower-risk classification. Beyond that, the company could eliminate slicing and purchase pre-sliced meats. The insurance company must be convinced that the classification change is legitimate.

■ **Outsourcing to contractors**. Functions and services that involve high insurance costs might better be subcontracted to other companies. Examples are metal plating, painting and package delivery.

■ **Supervision**. An investment in training for supervisors can pay off in reduced risk and insurance costs. These trained supervisors understand and enforce fire and other safety rules. They watch for litter, flammable materials, proper storage procedures and employee conduct. The training must be reinforced through annual retraining and periodic workshops.

■ **Modernize electrical systems**. That old Victorian building makes a cute restaurant, but the wiring that was installed by Thomas Edison himself may cause a fire that would burn it down on opening night. Having an experienced electrician evaluate the electrical system of a proposed location pays off in reduced premiums for fire and business interruption insurance.

■ **Reduce customer property**. Reduce the amount of customer property on hand by offering a reduced price for picking up property on time or prompt delivery.

■ **Fire resistant building**. A fire can destroy a business, even one with adequate insurance, because of the disruption of operations, smell of smoke and other factors. The things that you can do to avoid the fire will also reduce your insurance costs.

● **Fire walls**. Fire walls are fireproof (usually masonry) partitions that stop or slow the spread of a fire and also contain the water and smoke.

- **Fire Alarm**. Smoke, heat and fire detectors wired to a central alarm service get a faster response from the fire department and so there is less damage. Also the alarms need to be inspected and tested regularly.

- **Sprinklers**. Sprinklers will put out the fire. The problem is planning for and dealing with the water. Sprinklers decrease the cost of insurance on the structure, but impact the cost of insurance on contents such as inventory, furniture and fixtures that can be damaged by the water.

■ **Employee training**. Employees must be trained to provide good productivity and customer service. They should also be trained in good security and fire safety as well as safe work practices. Besides contributing to lowering of risks, this training also qualifies for insurance premium credits.

■ **Create good safety practices.** These include the following:

- Purchase fire extinguishers and train employees in their use.

- Handle fire sources and flammable materials correctly.

- Install fire alarms and provide 24 hour monitoring.

- Use good housekeeping.

- Learn good practices for lifting objects.

- Wear proper safety equipment.

INTRODUCTION
Small companies need money to start-up, operate and expand. Most of them get started with a small investment of the owners' savings, but, there are many other sources, and Connecticut has excellent sources and programs for business lending and investment. It still surpasses most other states in start-up capital investments. Recently, state and federal government agencies and banks have made millions of dollars available to small companies that want to expand and hire new employees.

This chapter discusses alternatives and procedures for raising money to start-up or expand a business. It reviews sources of money, the pros and cons of each source and how to get money from each source. It also reviews Federal and Connecticut government programs for small businesses and those owned by women and members of minority groups.

ORGANIZATION OF CHAPTER
This chapter discusses the following topics:

■　　Sources of capital … and risks.
■　　Determining start-up cash needs.
■　　Anticipating needs for more money.
■　　Debt versus equity financing.
■　　Debt financing.
■　　Equity financing.
■　　Sources of business capital.
■　　How lenders charge for loans.
■　　Preparing a proposal for financing.
■　　Getting outside help with the financing process.
■　　Small Business Administration programs.
■　　Financing and management assistance programs.
■　　Opportunities for minorities and women.

SOURCES OF CAPITAL...AND RISKS
Starting a business calls for having enough money to operate successfully through the company's formative years. Sources of start-up money include: individual investors, banks, federal, state and local government agencies, venture capitalists, customers and suppliers. The right source of money for a company depends on its situation; no two are exactly alike.

An entrepreneur, according to Webster's is "one who assumes the risks of business." Entrepreneurs must face one fact: lenders do not want to take on business risks. Therefore, they require collateral from the borrower to protect their loan. Banks, financial institutions and public agencies are required by law to protect their loans with collateral.

DETERMINING START-UP CASH NEEDS

It's a mistake to try to start a company on a shoestring, because it increases your chances of failure: the primary cause of business failure is cash shortages. If a company does not have enough cash to carry it through the start-up phase and keep it operating in periods of expansion, it can fail, even if its sales are expanding rapidly. During an expansion, a company needs money to buy inventory, finance accounts receivable, hire people and expand physical space. This requires more cash than when the company is growing slowly and can be financed from profits.

If the company starts out with too little cash and runs out of cash during the start-up phase, it might not be able to get cash to start over. So, the safest thing is raise more cash that you think you'll need so you'll have a fund available for emergencies and growth; we suggest a safety margin of about 10-20% above your estimated needs.

Of course, every company has different start-up cash needs, with service companies the lowest and manufacturing companies the highest. Even those that don't need expensive equipment have to pay operating expenses from the time of starting up until the company's revenues equal its expenses. Therefore, the starting point for figuring cash needs is the business plan, because it lists the equipment, furniture and personnel the company needs to get started.

The cash needs fall into the following categories:

- Equipment, furniture and fixtures.
- Security deposits for space rental, utilities, and similar charges.
- Office supplies and merchandise inventory.
- Franchise fees and organizational charges.
- Operating expenses for a start-up period of at least six months, if not longer.
- Personal living expenses for the start-up period. Because the company may not make a profit right away, it may not be able to pay the owner a salary.
- "Cushion," an emergency reserve, discussed in the next section.

The Developing a Business Plan chapter discusses the cash budget and some of its components, and the Appendix contains checklists of cash requirements and cash availability. This section shows how to develop a start-up budget and shows what a typical budget looks like.

 NOTE Most business advisors prefer to see entrepreneurs wait until they've accumulated enough money rather than start-up with inadequate funding.

The following is an example of a start-up budget.

Example - Business start-up budget

Start-up expense item	Amount
Equipment:	
Office furniture	$1,500
Fax machine	600
Telephone and installation	250
Deposits:	
Telephone	200
Electric	200
Rent	1,200
Insurance	800
Office supplies:	
Stationery with letterhead	500
Other supplies	300
Legal and accounting expenses to form corporation	1,500
Operating expenses for six months:	
Advertising	2,000
Auto and Truck	500
Insurance	800
Part-time secretary	4,000
Payroll taxes for secretary	600
Postage	600
Rent	3,600
Supplies	400
Taxes	250
Utilities and telephone	1,200
Personal living expenses for six months	10,000
(Details omitted to save space)	
Subtotal	$31,000
Reserve fund 10% of above	3,100
Total needed	$34,100

ANTICIPATING NEEDS FOR MORE MONEY

Once the company is in operation, despite thorough planning, many unexpected cash demands can happen. If the company fails to recognize, or plan for, these cash demands, it will have severe cash flow problems and may not even survive. Thus, most start-up companies need to set aside extra money for unexpected needs. One reason a company may need this "cushion" of extra money is to finance start-up losses for longer than originally planned.

Some other conditions to consider are listed below:

■ Expanding inventories to meet larger than expected customer requirements.

- Credit sales may result in a lag in cash inflows (outstanding accounts receivable) v. outflows (accounts payable), even if collections are timely.
- Sales growth or technology changes require investments in equipment and physical space.
- Changes by competitors or customers require changes in product lines
- Seasonal revenue fluctuations may require more money to purchase or build inventory before seasonal rushes, or to carry the company through the slow season.
- Loan repayment schedules may strain cash balances in slow operating periods.
- Economic conditions may cause a decrease in sales or a slowing of collections.

> **NOTE** The amount of this cushion depends on the type of business, size of the company, amount of risk, owner's experience, competitive market and many other factors. CPAs recommend a cushion of at least ten percent, and up to twenty percent, of the start-up cash budget.

DEBT VERSUS EQUITY FINANCING

A company can be financed either with *equity* or *debt* or a combination of both. Each source has different characteristics, purposes, control and risk factors. Each source has its place in financing a business start-up. First, one must understand the difference between the two.

- **Debt.** Money loaned to the company, or its owner, for use in the company. It has to be repaid, usually in regular installments and with interest.

- **Equity.** A permanent investment of cash or property in exchange for an ownership interest in the company. The money can come from the company owners' funds, outside investors or reinvested business profits. Equity capital never has to be repaid. Owners and other equity investors get their money back when they sell their investments in the company.

Debt financing

Debt financing can be any combination of secured or unsecured financing and long-term or short-term financing.

Secured loans v. unsecured loans

A secured loan is one for which the company has set aside assets to guarantee payment. The personal guarantee of the business owner is a common form of security if the business owner has an excellent credit rating or owns substantial assets to use as collateral. The owner guarantees payment on the loan in case the company cannot meet the payment schedule.

> **NOTE** Unsecured loans to small businesses are rare. Lenders know a small business can fail quickly and want to be assured they get paid back.

Short-term v. long-term loans

Short-term loans have to be repaid in less than one year. They are used to finance working capital such as accounts receivable and inventory. It is risky to use short-term borrowing to meet needs normally financed on a long-term basis. Using short-term funds for this purpose usually leads to business failure, because the company cannot meet the high payment demands.

There are four types of short-term debt for businesses. They all are designed to meet the working capital needs of a company. Practically every short-term loan to a small business is secured with a blanket lien, called a UCC-1, on the borrower's assets. This lien is recorded with the Secretary of State, and is part of the borrower's credit record until the loan is paid. The following table summarizes the types of short-term debt.

Available types of short-term debt	
Short-Term Notes	• Issued for periods of 30, 60 and 90 days. • Always repaid in full, with interest, on a fixed due date. • Interest is usually *discounted* or subtracted from the loan proceeds when the money is borrowed.
Lines of Credit	• Pre-approved loan for maximum amount for use when needed. • Interest rate varies with bank's base interest rate, called *prime rate*. • Bank's loan officer can advance any amount up to credit limit. • Usually borrowed in 30 day increments, and must be either repaid or renewed at the end of the 30 day period. • Line of credit to be paid in full at least once per year.
Revolving Credit Agreements	• Similar to line of credit except interest is paid separately, not discounted. • Money can be borrowed and repaid daily. • May be no requirement to pay in full once per year.
Letters of Credit	• Not a loan. Guarantee to third party to pay a specific sum when agreed upon circumstances or criteria are met. • Issuing bank charges commitment fee, usually 1% or 2% of loan. • Seldom intended to be used. Serves as payment guarantee, called a *standby letter of credit*.

Long-term loans are those whose repayment periods stretch beyond one year. Long-term loans should be used to finance tangible assets, such as equipment, vehicles, buildings, land, core working assets and even the purchase of a company. The reason long-term debt is used for these purchases is that their high cost makes it unlikely the company could repay the loans in less than one year.

There are two main types of long-term financing; the following table summarizes the differences between them.

Available types of long-term debt	
Term loans	• Maturity date exceeds one year, and not usually exceeding 10 years. • Paid in fixed periodic amounts, including interest; payments usually monthly, but can also be quarterly, semi-annually, or even annually. • Interest rates frequently float with the prime rate. • Secured by the general credit of the company, and the lender usually files a UCC-1 form to secure its position ahead of other creditors. • Small business owners usually have to personally guarantee the loan. • Loan agreement gives the lender priority interest in company assets, except assets that have been pledged as collateral for other loans.
Mortgages	• Used to buy real estate. • Usually have variable interest rates that fluctuate with the market. • Payment terms usually extend over 20 years. • May be written with long-term payment schedules, but required to be paid in full sooner, e.g, loan with 30 year terms with final payment in 10 years. Lender assumes borrower will refinance note or sell property before 10 years. Known as *balloon* loan.

Equity financing

The types of equity financing depend on the company's type of business organization. If a company needs outside investors to get started, the corporation or LLC company may be the best forms, because they shield investors from lawsuits and bankruptcies and allow easy transfer of ownership.

SOURCES OF BUSINESS CAPITAL

There are twelve main sources of capital for business start-up or expansion. Some sources work best for equity financing, and others are best for debt financing as shown in the following table.

Sources of business capital		
Source	**Equity**	**Debt**
Personal funds	Yes	Yes
Friends and relatives	Yes	Yes
Banks	No	Yes
Leasing	No	Yes
Suppliers	No	Yes
Asset based lenders	No	Yes
Joint ventures	Yes	Yes
Customers	No	Yes
Venture capital investors	Yes	Yes
Government backed loans	No	Yes
Government ventures	Yes	No

Personal Funds

The most common source of capital for new small businesses is the owners' savings. This source has three advantages: the interest cost is low; the money is fast and easy to get; and the money doesn't have to be repaid.

It would be a mistake for a company owner to drain the savings account for start-up money. There should be a cash reserve after business expenses are taken out. This includes cash for living expenses, children's education, personal emergencies, business problems and company expansion. Without these reserves, a company owner may have to tap the company for money; this may increase the risk of business failure. Personal financial planners recommend a reserve of six months' living expenses.

One way to conserve personal savings is to start the company as a part-time occupation, while the owner or spouse continues to work at another full-time job. In this case, earnings from the owner's other job can cover part of the company's operating expenses.

Another source of start-up capital is the owner's **retirement fund**. Often, the amount of money in a pension or retirement plan is significant. This is an excellent source of capital, but there are two risks in committing all or some of it to a start-up business. One is that a company owner who is near retirement should be careful about risking a main source of retirement income on a start-up. The other is that money taken out of pension funds is heavily taxed. Besides the tax on the withdrawal, there is a 10% penalty on *premature* withdrawals from pension plans. The owner should set aside money to cover income taxes to prevent severe financial problems at tax time. Borrowing from the retirement plan, if permitted, has the advantage of the interest expense being income to the plan as well as avoiding tax penalties on withdrawals.

Friends and Relatives

Friends and relatives can be a source of either equity or debt financing. The possible advantages of obtaining start-up capital from them include flexible repayment terms, lower interest rates and less outside control over the company. Friends and relatives are less likely to demand control over management methods, cash levels, inventory levels, payable levels or customer credit terms.

The disadvantages of borrowing from friends and relatives center on potential personal problems if the money is not repaid on time, or if the lender encounters emergency financial needs and wants to be repaid ahead of schedule.

Most friends and relatives lend or invest based on a personal relationship and not on the soundness of a business plan. Often, they do not understand the risks they are taking. Before accepting money from friends and relatives, company owners should ask them if they are willing and financially able to lose their entire investment. If they are not, the owner should think twice before accepting the money. Many personal relationships have been ruined over business loans and investments. The terms of loans should always be in writing, even those from friends and relatives. The Business Plan is the tool for developing the conditions surrounding personal loans, and for making sure such loans are based on economics rather than emotions.

Banks

Banks are seldom the direct source of either equity or debt for business start-ups, because they are reluctant to make loans to small businesses. However, they are an important indirect source. Many banks make personal loans or home equity loans to the owners of start-up ventures. Existing companies with profitable track records find banks a good source of financing. Some government fund sources (the Small Business Administration, for example) use banks to administer their programs. Thus, banks can be a starting point in the search for money.

A little basic research not only saves time, but also increases the likelihood the company's loan will be approved. A partial list of factors appears below.

Type of bank

A bank's charter limits the amount and kinds of money it can loan. Although savings banks are allowed to make business loans, commercial banks generally have more money available.

Risk considerations and personal guarantees

Regulations require banking institutions to protect against loan losses. As part of their protection policies, banks require business plans for two reasons: information about the borrower and proof that the borrower did a reasonable investigation. In addition, they request personal financial statements from the company's owners. If the borrower is a corporation, banks and other lending sources normally require the owners to guarantee the corporation's loan.

Risk analysis

Banks conduct their own investigation of the borrower's credit worthiness, evaluate the owner's business experience, study the business plan, compare the plan's financial projections to the performance records of similar companies and evaluate the personal characteristics of the potential borrower to determine the borrower's suitability. From these reviews, banks measure the risks present in the loan request.

Approval times

Depending upon the company's economic environment, the time required for an answer to the loan request can range from two to four weeks. Closing the transaction could add one to two weeks. If the borrower demands a quicker answer, the answer is usually "no."

Account relationships

It is helpful to request loans from a bank where the borrower is known as a customer (depositor, checking account, mortgage holder, etc.) If the company is to be located out of the bank's market area, the loan request should be directed to a bank in its proposed location. The owner should get an introduction before sending a loan request to a bank. A CPA, attorney or a business associate who is already a customer of the bank can make the introduction.

Investigating the bank

It is wise to investigate a bank before making a loan request, and to raise a few questions. Has the bank made loans to companies in the same business? Does the bank offer the services and have the resources to serve the business borrower? Does the bank cater to small or large companies? Is the bank in good financial condition? Who will the company be dealing with? What are the lending officer's loan approval limits? Who must approve the loan in question? Make the loan presentation to that person.

> **NOTE** — The bank investigates you, so why shouldn't you investigate the bank? Many small business owners are skittish about offending the bank by asking too many questions. Remember, they're in this for the money and the person you're dealing with is really a sales person who will be rewarded with a bonus or raise for bringing in more business. Ask away!

Leasing

Leasing is a popular and convenient way for small companies to obtain many types of physical assets, such as office equipment, vehicles and heavy machinery. Many manufacturers of industrial equipment offer lease purchase options as a way to increase sales. A traditional leasing arrangement requires the purchaser to make a down payment of the first and last months lease payment. Thus, the initial cash requirement is much less than if the purchaser uses a commercial bank to finance the purchase and is required to make a large down-payment.

Many leases of business property are really financing arrangements. The lessor charges a rental which covers the purchase price and interest on a loan to the purchaser/lessee. When the manufacturer is the lessor, it may charge higher lease rates than third party lessors or banks. This is because the manufacturer has to guarantee the purchaser's lease payment to its own lenders and writes leases to companies with lower credit quality. Third party lessors usually specialize in specific types of equipment, require more financial information from the purchaser prior to approving the lease, have more stringent lending requirements and offer lower interest rates than manufacturers/lessors.

Other options

Don't hesitate to seek creative sources of money, even if you've got plenty of capital behind you already. The more creative sources are cheaper and more flexible than banks and finance companies and are often easier to deal with. Some popular ones are summarized in the table on the next page.

Creative sources of money	
Suppliers	• Won't lend money but will allow extended payments of their bills. • Will develop custom products or contribute to promotional costs. • Usually don't charge interest on their money. • Beware not to become captive customer paying high product prices.
Asset based lenders	• Lenders that finance a percentage (usually under 75%) of liquid assets like inventory and accounts receivable. • Charge higher interest rates. • Require more detailed and more frequent financial reporting. • Offered by some banks through separate subsidiaries.
Joint ventures	• Common in high tech or service industries where small companies may have a product or service that compliments larger company's products. • Helps give small companies faster start-up and better market penetration. • Beware of being dependent on one customer or giving a large amount of control to the larger company.
Customers	• Will finance start-up companies to secure a source of supply, get access to a new or improved product, or get a more reliable source of supply. • Will provide outright investment, loan, joint venture, or an advance payment on purchases. • Usually don't charge interest on their money. • Be cautious the customer doesn't try to control company's marketing.
Venture capital	• Invest in start-ups, developing companies, and turn-around situations. • Can be individuals, groups of individuals, or fund managers. • Venture capitalist invests the money, and the founder puts up the idea or invention, sometimes known as *sweat equity*. • Sometimes require the founder to make a capital investment in the company as well to bind the founder during the difficult formative years • Monitor investments through board representation, regular financial reports and may insist on a voice in daily operations • Typical minimum investment is $500,000 to $1 million • Receive their profit when company sells or goes public. • Locate through CPAs, attorneys or Connecticut Venture Capital Network.
Government backed loans	• Federal programs include Small Business Administration and others. • State programs coordinated by Connecticut Department of Economic and Community Development (DECD).
Government ventures	• Fewer government equity programs than loan programs • Federal programs include SBA and Small Business Investment Company. • State programs coordinated through Connecticut DECD.

HOW LENDERS CHARGE FOR LOANS

Banks and other lenders earn money from the interest and fees they charge borrowers. They use the prime lending rate as a starting point. A safe loan is made at the prime rate. A more risky loan is made at a premium over the prime rate. A risky borrower also pays higher fee charges. A good place to start is with terminology:

Floating rate loans v. fixed rate loans

Floating rate loans have their rates tied to a base rate such as the bank's prime rate, the prime rate published in the *Wall Street Journal* or the United States Treasury Note rate. Interest rates are expressed in relation to the base rate, so a rate of *prime plus 2* means the bank adds 2 percentage points to the prime rate. Thus, if the prime rate is 8%, the customer pays 10%. This rate changes with the general interest market.

Fixed rate loans have interest rates that do not change over the life of the loan. To cover their risk, lenders boost the rate for fixed rate loans slightly over the current floating rate.

Simple interest v. discounted interest

Simple interest is a method of calculating interest by multiplying the yearly interest rate by current loan balance. Adjustments are made to the actual dollar amount of interest based upon the number of days the current loan balance is outstanding, using a 360 day year.

When interest is discounted, it is subtracted from the loan proceeds at the time the money is borrowed. *This standard practice increases the effective interest rate on the loan, because the loan proceeds are less than the amount borrowed.* The lending industry uses a standard practice of calculating loan interest based upon a 360 day year, which further increases the effective interest rate.

The example below illustrates how the amount of interest and the effective interest rate are calculated under the two different methods.

Comparison of simple and discounted interest		
	Simple	**Discounted**
Interest rate	10.0%	10.0%
Term of loan	1 year	1 year
Amount borrowed	10000	10000
Interest deducted	0	1000
Net amount received	10000	9000
Amount paid as interest	1000	1000
Total repaid to the bank, including interest	11000	10000
Rate of interest on money borrowed	10.0%	11.1%

Fees and Points

Fees and points are charged by lenders as a means of increasing the income on a loan without raising the stated interest rate.

Points are an advance fee designed to pay for the lender's cost of processing the loan paperwork. Points are expressed as a percentage of the loan amount, so a fee of two points on a $100,000 loan would cost the borrower $2,000.

A *commitment fee* is a charge to establish a lending arrangement that is available for future use. Commitment fees are common for letters of credit and revolving credit lines. When the borrower actually draws on a revolving credit line or letter of credit, it pays a usage fee in addition to the usual interest charge. This usage fee is typically less than 1% of the amount of the loan.

The actual interest rate, amount and types of fees charged by a lender varies, depending on the borrower's credit worthiness. They also depend on the amount of money a bank has available to lend, which is influenced by government regulations and the bank's financial condition.

PREPARING A PROPOSAL FOR FINANCING

Most lenders and investors require detailed information packages before they can consider advancing money. This package allows them to evaluate their chance of getting their money back and making a profit. More important, the package allows them to decide between competing uses for their money. A company that seeks funding must develop a proposal which persuades an investor or lender to advance money to it, rather than to other companies.

The typical complete financing package should contain the following information:

- **Business plan.** The business plan describes the company in detail, including the history, future plans, products or services, its industry, competitors, business strategy and key management. For a detailed discussion and example of a business plan see the *Developing a Business Plan* chapter.

- **Loan request.** The loan request describes the amount of money being requested, the proposed terms, use of proceeds, sources of repayment, available collateral and a repayment schedule.

- **Cash flow projections.** The cash flow projection shows future sources of cash from the company's normal operations, cash requirements to meet operating expenses and capital purchases, uses of money and projected payback schedule.

- **Financial statements.** For an existing company, financial statements for the past three years of the company, including balance sheet, statements of income and retained earnings, and a statement of cash flows. The owners' personal financial statements or copies of their income tax returns should be included, too.

- **Other Information.** any other information that may be of use in evaluating the loan request, such as owners' résumés, press releases, promotional materials, and product samples should be included.

The financing proposal should explain any unfavorable aspects of the company's past. These include bankruptcies, liens, loan defaults, slow payment history and lawsuits. If these are discovered during a credit check or financial review, they could kill the company's chances if they were not previously disclosed. By dealing with negative items early in the process, the company can present the favorable side of the story.

GETTING OUTSIDE HELP WITH FINANCING

Depending upon the size of the company, its prior loan experience and its financial sophistication, management may want to obtain outside experience in dealing with credit grantors or investors. Most financial institutions view the use of outside help favorably and not as a sign of weakness. Third parties can help in preparing the loan package, negotiating terms, and providing introductions to money sources. Among those qualified to help the company owner are CPAs, attorneys, the Service Core of Retired Executives, Community Accounting Aid and Services, Inc. and the Connecticut Small Business Development Center.

SMALL BUSINESS ADMINISTRATION PROGRAMS

The principal source of the Federal Government support for small business is the U.S. Small Business Administration founded in 1953. The SBA's objective is to generate and preserve jobs. The Department of Commerce and the Department of Agriculture have programs similar to those of the SBA. New or early-stage companies should work through the SBA, which can then direct them to other agencies if necessary. Starting with the SBA shortens the overall time in getting a helping hand.

SBA loans are not really loans at all but are guarantees of loans made by lending institutions, usually banks, and guaranteed to a maximum of 85% by the SBA. These guarantees reduce the lenders' risk and enables the lender to provide financing to small businesses who may otherwise be ineligible. The SBA can guarantee up to $2,000,000 of a private sector loan. The SBA does not make direct "grants" of money for starting a small business.

The SBA has a limited amount of money available for direct loans which are available only to applicants unable to secure an SBA guaranteed loan. This money is available only to certain types of borrowers such as businesses located in high-unemployment areas, or owned by low-income or handicapped people or Vietnam veterans.

SBA loan application procedures

The application process for an SBA loan is like that for a bank loan. The SBA deals with the private lender, not the applicant. The applicant submits a financing request to a participating lending institution. If the lender decides it requires additional support and can not merit the loan on its own, it submits the loan to the SBA under the guarantee program.

Businesses which expect to have their loan request referred to the SBA guaranty program should consider dealing with a lending institution which is designated as a certified lender with the SBA. The certified lenders program is designed to provide expeditious service on loan applications received from lenders whose policies procedures and forms are pre-approved by the SBA.

SBA loan guaranty programs

The 7(a) loan program is the largest of the SBA's financial assistance programs. There are a number of special loan guaranty programs under the 7(a) program. The following table summarizes a few of the more popular loans:

Types of loans available through the SBA 7(a) Program	
7(a)	• Maximum available - $2,000,000. • SBA guarantees up to 75% of the outstanding loan balance. • Business operating for a profit and falls within size standards. • SBA's primary loan program.
SBA Express	• Maximum available - $250,000. • SBA guarantees up to 50% of the outstanding loan balance. • Loans under $25,000 do not require collateral. • Revolving lines of credit allowed for maximum of seven years.
Low Doc	• Maximum available - $150,000. • Rapid turn-around (24-48 hours). • SBA guarantees up to 85% of the outstanding loan balance. • One-page SBA application form. • Eligible if purpose is to start or grow a business, annual sales are less than $5,000,000 and have 100 or fewer employees.

Other special loan programs offered by the SBA include:

- Export working capital program.
- CAP lines.
- CDC 504 program.
- Microloans.
- Delta.

You can get additional information about these programs on the SBA website at www.sba.gov.

Use of proceeds

SBA Loan proceeds may be used to establish a new company or to help in the operation, acquisition, or expansion of an existing company, including working capital; the purchase of inventory; machinery and equipment; and the construction, expansion and rehabilitation of business property.

Loan proceeds may not be used for: partial purchase of a company; funding lending institutions; real estate held for investment, speculation or rental; opinion molders such as magazines, newspapers, trade journals, radio or television; live entertainment; schools; religious organizations and their affiliates; refinance existing debt; repay delinquent state or federal withholding taxes.

Eligibility

To be eligible for SBA loan help, a company must qualify under SBA size criteria. For business loans, eligibility depends on the average number of employees or on sales volume, product type or industry, as shown in the following table.

General SBA eligibility standards by industry	
Manufacturing	Maximum number of employees range from 500 to 1500
Wholesaling	Maximum number of employees may not exceed 100
Services	Annual receipts may not exceed $4 to $29 million
Retailing	Annual receipts may not exceed $6 to $24.5 million
Construction	Annual receipts may not exceed $6 to $28.5 million
Special Trade Construction	Annual receipts may not exceed $7 million
Agriculture	Annual receipts may not exceed $500,000 to $10.5 million

Documentation requirements

Documentation requirements will vary by lending institution and size of loan. The following is a common list of information requested:

- Business plan.
- Financial statements for three years (existing businesses.)
- Personal income tax returns for two years.
- Business income tax returns for three years (existing businesses.)
- Personal financial statements.

Collateral

It requires sufficient assets be pledged to adequately secure the loan to the extent they are available. Personal guarantees are required of all principal owners of a business. Liens on personal assets of the principals also may be required, where business assets are considered insufficient to secure the loan.

Maturity

Loan maturity varies with the economic life of the assets being financed and the applicant's ability to repay, subject to the following maximums:

Use	Maximum maturity
Working capital	up to 5-7 years
Machinery and equipment	up to 10-15 years
Building construction or purchase	up to 15-25 years

When loan proceeds are used for a combination of purposes, the maximum maturity can be a weighted average of the maturities or a sum of equal monthly installments for all the maturities. The weighted average produces a level payment for the life of the loan. The sum of the maturities produces unequal installment payments.

Interest rate

The interest rate for guaranteed loans reflects prevailing market rates. It can be a fixed or variable rate. Interest rates are competitive with the rates offered through traditional bank loans. The rate is usually based on the prime rate published in the *Wall Street Journal* plus a spread. Direct loans are made at a fixed rate which is set quarterly by the SBA.

Prepayment penalty

Prepayment penalties can be added to loans with maturities of 15 years or longer. The penalty fee is assessed when there are substantial voluntary prepayments made during the first three years after the date of the first disbursement. The fee is calculated as a percentage of the prepayment amount. The percentages can range from 1% to 5%.

FINANCING AND MANAGEMENT ASSISTANCE PROGRAMS

The following table summarizes several other special loan, financing, and management assistance programs that are offered by the SBA, federal government agencies, and state government agencies.

Loan financing and management assistance programs	
Certified Development Company (CDC)	▪ Provides fixed-rate financing for construction or rehabilitation of owner-occupied or leased premises. ▪ Net worth must be under $6 million, profits under $2 million. ▪ Funds may be used for construction or acquisition, equipment and soft costs such as appraisals and surveys. ▪ SBA portion cannot exceed $750,000 or 40% of project, whichever is less; maturity can be 10 or 20 years. Owner must put 10% down.
Small Business Investment Company (SBIC)	▪ Provides long term loans and/or venture capital to small companies. ▪ Privately owned investment companies licensed and regulated by SBA. ▪ SBIC's success is linked to profitability of companies it finances, so some SBICs focus on companies with significant growth potential. ▪ May provide management help to protect their investment. ▪ Net worth must be under $6 million, profits under $2 million. ▪ Terms of investment are negotiable, but usually at least 5 years. ▪ Also: Minority Enterprise SBIC (MESBIC); specialize in small companies owned by socially/economically disadvantaged persons.
Minority Business Development Agency	▪ Agency of the U.S. Department of Commerce designed to serve minority business interests with over 100 Minority Business Development Centers around the country which provide management, marketing, and technical assistance to minority business owners.
U.S. Department of Education	▪ Opportunities to small businesses performing management consulting, program evaluation, computer-based projects, student testing materials, audio-visual materials, and other professional services.

Loan financing and management assistance programs	
U.S. General Services Administration	■ Handles purchases by Federal government and runs procurement efforts aimed at minority and women-owned businesses to encourage them to bid on proposals.
Bureau of Indian Affairs	■ Run by U.S. Department of the Interior, provides information on Tribal Resources Development Program and financing information for Native-American business owners.
Women's Bureau of Department of Labor	■ Seeks to expand business opportunities for women-owned companies. ■ Promotes the welfare of women workers.
Minority Business Development Agency	■ Helps minority entrepreneurs who need assistance in starting a company by putting them in contact with other government programs and providing catalogs, publications and other information on minority businesses.
Small Business Administration (SBA)	■ Office of Minority Small Business and Capital Ownership Development serves as an advocate for minority businesses and assists in supplying resources and obtaining other agency assistance for minority owned businesses. ■ Office of Women's Business Ownership seeks opportunities for women-owned businesses in government and private business programs.
Connecticut Department of Economic Development	■ Administers Business Outreach Centers, Office of Small Business Services, Connecticut Development Authority loans, other programs. ■ Programs always changing and being added, so check with CAAS and local business advisors for possible state assistance programs.

OPPORTUNITIES FOR MINORITIES AND WOMEN

All levels of government are working to assist minority-owned and women-owned businesses, and many agencies are set up to offer them special help. There are also many sources for funding, management help, education and consulting. This chapter has listed a few, but it is impossible to list them all. Many local sources may prove to be the bridge in locating state and federal help.

■ **Chambers of commerce.** Local chambers of commerce, especially those in cities, provide start-up help and information, including access to resources and self-help networks.

■ **Hartford Economic Development Corporation.** HEDCO is a nonprofit organization serving Greater Hartford. Its purpose is to help minority and women-owned businesses to get financing. It also serves as a source of information for all businesses.

■ **Libraries.** Public libraries and university and college libraries offer many business publications, books, and reference materials for minority and women owned businesses.

CONCLUSION

The financing for a small company is a critical aspect of starting up. Without enough money to start, *and keep going through the start-up period*, the company can't survive. This aspect of start-up demands plenty of planning and work.

There is plenty of money out there for qualified, hard-working business owners. They must take the time to find the money in the many government programs and departments and they must understand that these programs are not handouts. They are loan programs, and the lenders expect to get their money back to lend to other small business start-ups.

Chapter 8
Keeping Good Business Records

INTRODUCTION

There are many factors that determine the success of a company: management, employees, service, product, financing, competition, marketing and the economy. However, the main measure of success of a company is found in the financial numbers it produces: sales, profits, assets and capital. This measurement system is the way the owners see if they are on track to achieve the business plan, it is the way lenders see if the business is worthy of loans and it is the way tax authorities assess business taxes. The company's business records are the *only* source of this financial information.

Good records allow business managers to analyze their successes and plan for the future. They allow banks and investors to understand business results. Basically, good records are essential for complete and accurate business tax returns.

Poor records, on the other hand, seriously undermine business managers' credibility with banks, investors and tax collectors. Poor records can lead to lost tax write-offs and higher tax penalties and assessments. Basically, poor records prevent managers from controlling the company.

ORGANIZATION OF CHAPTER

This chapter discusses the following topics:

- Components of a good records system.
- Practical forms of business records.
- Computer systems.
- Managing and summarizing information.
- Using accounting data to manage.
- How to improve the company's records.

The chapter contains many examples of business records, most of them prepared with the popular computer accounting program, QuickBooks. We recommend you use a computer system because it is the cheapest way for you to keep good records. However, there are several good systems and we leave the choice of system to you. Later in the chapter, there is a discussion of the available systems and features you should expect to find in these programs.

COMPONENTS OF A GOOD RECORDS SYSTEM

There is no universally correct records system. The system's structure must be tailored to fit the needs of the company. There is only one universal objective: to keep the system as simple as possible. A well-designed system will pay for itself by reducing bookkeeping time and accounting fees and by providing essential information for effective business management. There are many sources of help in designing a business records system, including the company's CPA firm, one-write system vendors, business consultants from Community Accounting Aid Services and the Connecticut Small Business Development Center and computer consultants.

There are six basic business records. Most companies should use them all, although the form will vary considerably between companies. Accountants refer to these records as the *books of original entry* because they are the source of all other business documents, including tax returns and financial statements. The source of data for a journal is a *transaction* or business activity and the journal serves as a summary of a group - day, week, month or year - of transactions.

The table below shows the six basic records and the transactions that make them up.

Summary record	Transaction source
Sales register	Invoices to customers
Cash receipts register	Customer payments
Purchases register	Supplier invoices
Cash disbursements register	Checks or cash payments
General register	Special adjustments
Payroll register	Employee paychecks

In a larger company, these records might be subdivided into many components. For example, a manufacturer might have a different sales record for each type of product line or each type of customer. In a small company, it is possible to combine some records, such as payrolls and cash disbursements and some, such as the sales journal, may not even be needed in a small company.

This section discusses the purpose, and shows an example of a simple version, of each type of business record. Accountants use the terms *journals* and *ledgers* to refer to these records. The term *books*, used interchangeably in this chapter, means the same thing.

Sales journal

This journal records each sale of goods or services. Its purpose is to keep track of sales, amounts due from customers and the Connecticut sales tax collected from customers. It is a record of the individual invoices or sales slips from customers. If the company sells on credit, the sales record allows it to keep track of the customer name and amount owed for each sale. In QuickBooks, the way this is maintained depends on whether the company sells on credit or requires payment in full at the time of sale:

- In a *credit sale,* you create an invoice, which lists the items or services sold, print it and mail or hand it to the customer. The accounting system saves the sales transaction, which can be printed in the form of a sales journal or any other format. The system also adds the invoice to the amount due from the customer.

- In a *cash sale,* the transaction is added to total sales but because it is already collected, it isn't added to the customer account. You might still prepare an invoice for the customer's records.

An example of a sales journal is shown below. It shows both cash and credit sales.

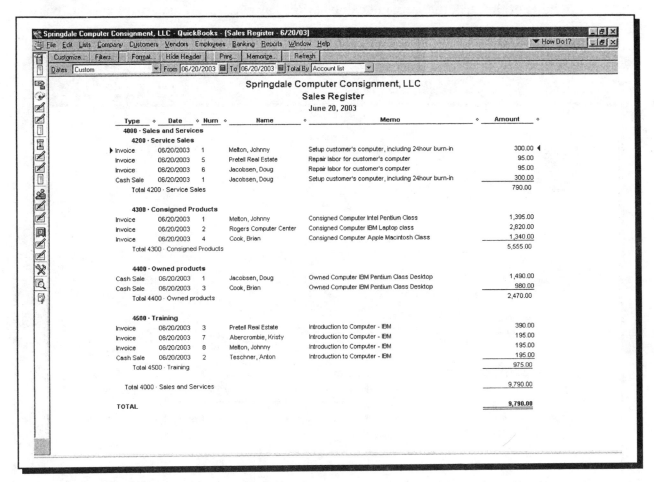

One important purpose of the sales journal is to record transactions on which sales taxes must be collected. The Connecticut sales tax report form requires companies to start with their total sales and to show - and explain - deductions for transactions that are not taxable. Your system should be capable of producing a report that classifies sales by tax category. If you keep a manual record of sales, it should contain columns into which the different tax categories can be entered. In its simplest form, the manual sales record should have these columns:

Date	Invoice	Customer	Taxable	Nontaxable	Tax collected	Total
6/20/03	1	Melton	1,395.00	300.00	83.70	1,778.70

Companies that have many different types of exempt sales may need to have several *nontaxable* columns. Likewise, if the company sells several types of services or products, it may need to expand the number of columns to accommodate the main types.

A related record is the *accounts receivable record*, which keeps track of amounts due from customers. This is an important feature for following up with slow-paying customers:

- In a computer accounting system, transactions are identified with the customer's name and the details of the customer account can be printed as needed. A statement appears below.

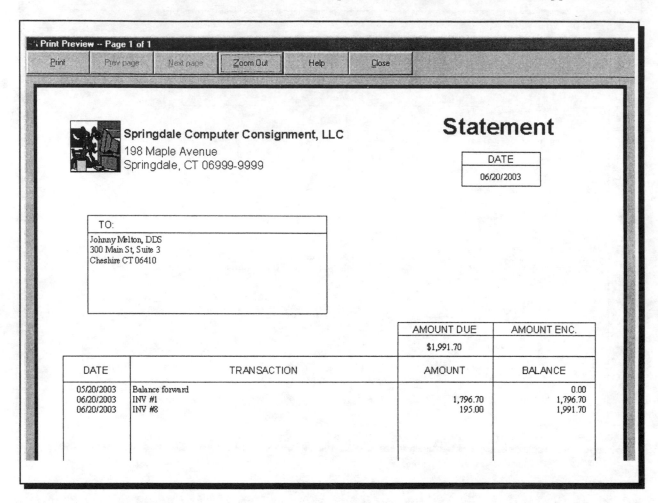

- In a manual system, one record is kept for each customer, either on a 5" x 8" card or on 8½" x 11" paper. When a sale is made to a customer, it is posted to the customer's record, adding to the customer's balance. When a payment is received, it is deducted from the balance. The card is copied and mailed to customers as a reminder notice.

For *cash sale* businesses such as grocery stores, retail shops and restaurants, the sales journal and accounts receivable record are not necessary, because the cash receipts journal contains all the necessary information. When the cash journal is used as the main sales record, it must be modified to capture the necessary sales tax information.

Cash receipts journal

Every company has to have a cash receipts journal to record the money it receives. Like the sales journal, the cash receipts journal records every deposit of money in a useful format for tax and business analysis. The source of the receipt is important information. Cash receipts sources normally fall into three groups: (1) cash from credit customers in payment of their accounts, (2) cash from cash sales, and (3) cash from miscellaneous sources. Sales receipts must be identified separately from bank loan proceeds, transfers from other cash accounts, money invested in the company, insurance claims, vendor refunds and similar non-business receipts. Poor records could result in sales taxes or income taxes being paid on money that should not be taxable.

An example of a simple cash receipts journal and sample entries is shown below.

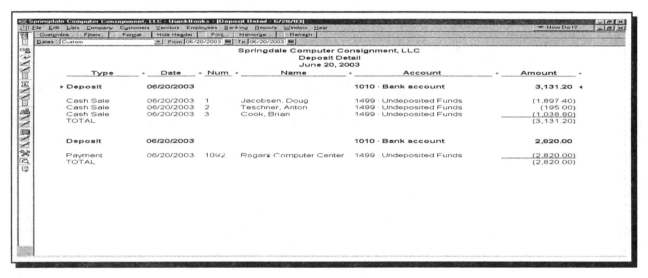

This report shows the amounts deposited and the details of each deposit, which makes it possible to verify the deposit amount on the bank statement. If the company uses a cash register, the "log-out" total tape is posted to the cash receipts journal and the daily tapes are stored for future reference.

The sales journal and the cash receipts journal measure the same thing: income to the company. However, there are two important differences between them:

■ The sales journal contains only sales to customers, while the cash receipts journal includes non-business cash received such as from loans or refunds.

■ The sales journal is a record of sales *at the time they are earned* while the cash receipts journal does not record the sales *until the cash is received*. For companies on the accrual basis of accounting, accountants enter a sale in the income statement when it is earned and not necessarily when the cash is received.

Purchase journal

The purchase journal is used to record goods and services used in the business. The journal shows the date, source, cost and description for every purchase.

A purchase journal has two purposes:

- If the company purchases on credit (that is, when it receives goods or services but has not yet paid for them), the purchase journal allows the recording of expenses when they occur, rather than when they are paid.

- The purchase journal is the source of information to keep track of accounts payable - amounts owed to suppliers.

An example of a purchase journal is shown below.

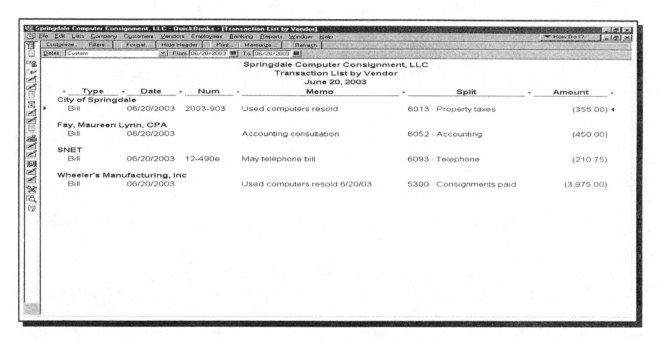

The format of a typical manual purchase journal varies considerably among companies, depending on the type and size of the company and how the company manages its payments. The usual format contains columns for each expense category like the one below.

Date	Supplier	Amount	Resale	Taxes	Accounting	Telephone
06/20/03	City of Springdale	355.00		355.00		

A real-life purchase journal might have 20 or 30 columns: one each for the company's different expense categories. For many small businesses, this journal may not be necessary. That is because a small company may not have a large enough volume of credit purchases to justify the cost of the extra record-keeping. A small company will find that an accounts payable record does the job well enough. The company's CPA or business advisor can help with this decision.

The *accounts payable* record that links to the purchase journal resembles the customer accounts receivable record and works the same way. One record is kept for each supplier. Purchases are posted to the supplier's record, adding to the balance. When an invoice is paid, the payment is deducted from the supplier's balance. A vendor ledger is very similar to the customer ledger discussed earlier in this chapter.

Cash disbursements journal

Like the cash receipts journal, this journal must be maintained for every company. It records all the money the company pays out, regardless of the purpose. The journal records the date paid, who it was paid to, the check number, the amount and what it was for. The term *cash* does not refer to payments made with currency or dollar bills. Currency payments are normally recorded in the cash receipts journal because they are typically made out of the day's receipts. As with cash receipts, accuracy in this journal is critical.

The format of the cash disbursements journal is similar to that of the purchases journal. Both records must be able to identify the details of each transaction. This categorization is known as the *chart of accounts*, described later in this chapter.

General journal

A general journal is used to record a few transactions that cannot be recorded in the normal transaction journals. This journal is normally maintained by the company's CPA or bookkeeper, who uses it to record adjusting, closing and correcting entries on the company's books. The following important accounting events are recorded on the books by means of the general journal:

- Depreciation of fixed assets. The adjustment that reflects the gradual decline in value of the company's office furniture, equipment, buildings and vehicles.

- Bad debts. The reserve fund set aside to cover the possibility of loss when a customer's ability to pay is in doubt.

- Future payments. The amount of a current year's expense that will have to be paid in a future year but for which the company has not yet received an invoice.

Payroll journal

This journal gives essential details about payroll paid to employees. In addition to containing all the information to prepare W-2 forms for employees, it has vital information on insurance coverage and shows the amount of taxes withheld from employees' paychecks, which must be paid over to the Federal and state governments. The following page has an example of a payroll journal.

For more information about payroll, refer to the Payroll and Payroll Taxes chapter for a complete discussion.

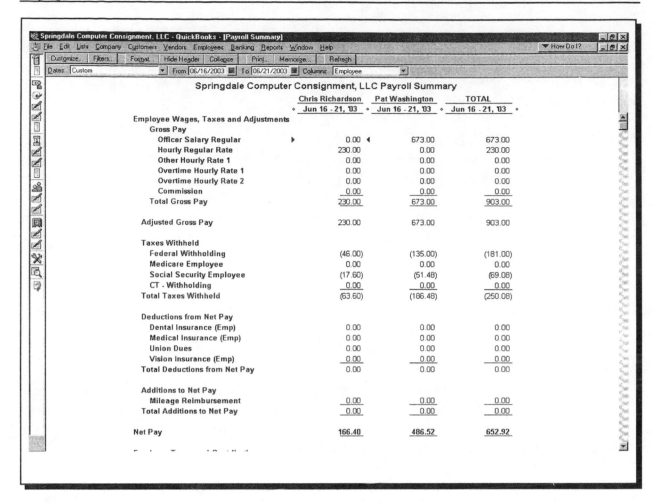

PRACTICAL FORMS OF BUSINESS RECORDS

Printed versions of all of the above journals are sold by most office supplies stores and business forms vendors. These companies sell standard records systems that can be customized for most companies. There are many publishers of these records, so it is only possible to mention the main categories.

Weekly or monthly accounting records

These systems are designed for very small businesses and are widely sold in stationery stores. The best known are published under the "Dome" name. They allow a small company to keep track of cash receipts and disbursements transactions. They are also portable; they are easily carried in a truck, car or briefcase, making it convenient to keep business records up-to-date. However, they are not practical for a company that sells on credit, because they don't provide a way to keep track of amounts owed by customers. There are some versions for specific businesses, such as in-home childcare.

One write systems

A *one-write* system uses carbon strips or carbonless paper to record journal information at the same time that business documents are prepared. By writing the information once, company personnel save time and reduce errors in posting journals.

A one-write sales system is an example. When an invoice is prepared for a customer, the sales information is being posted to the sales journal and to the customer accounts receivable card at the same time. When payment is received, the data is posted to the bank deposit ticket, cash receipts journal and customer's account card - all at the same time.

The cash disbursements one-write system is the most popular. When a check is prepared, it updates a disbursements journal and vendor record at the same time, through a carbon stripe on the back of the check. Other systems are available for purchase journals, payroll, inventory records and other applications.

Like the Weekly Accounting Records discussed above, the one-write system is convenient to carry around.

COMPUTER SYSTEMS

A computer accounting system is a practical way to keep the records for most small businesses. Of course, the cost of a computer is much higher than that of any other record-keeping system. However, the long-range cost is comparable, or even cheaper, for three reasons:

- The computer records system saves on outside bookkeeping and accounting costs.

- The computer system gives owners faster access to company information such as sales, customer receivables and supplier payables.

- The computer system saves the owner's time, improving productivity.

- The computer system allows easy access to historical records and budget information, making it easier to use information to manage the business.

- The business is likely to need a computer anyway, for correspondence, advertising, mailing lists and other non-accounting tasks. Adding the accounting system is a small added cost.

The key to an effective computer installation is the software. It must process the company's information, be easy to use, and be able to grow with the company without being so full-featured that employees are unable to learn to use it.

Most of the computer hardware on the market today will be more than adequate for small business accounting, so resist the urge to overbuy, which results in purchasing hardware that is obsolete before its power can be used. Remember that when implementing a computer system, training is the most expensive ingredient. It is very important to choose your software carefully so that your company experiences as little down time as possible. However, for a company to survive today it must take advantage of technology and with the dropping prices of computers these days it's the right time to get connected.

Pros and cons of computer accounting

Pros:

- Computers can significantly decrease time needed to gather and organize information.

- Better information allows owners and managers to make better decisions.

- Computerization saves money on accounting fees.

- Owners and managers receive business financial information much faster.

- Computerization combines many operations into one.

- Computerization may provide for increased profits and improved morale.

- Computerization may increase customer satisfaction.

Cons:

- Purchasing hardware and software requires forethought and planning.

- The initial purchase of software and hardware could be costly.

- Personnel must be trained on the new software.

- Some employees are not comfortable with computers.

Hardware selection

Once the decision to computerize has been made, the first thing to do is get a computer system. For small-company business systems, there are two elements:

- **Computer unit.** Earlier in this chapter, we reported that business records systems aren't demanding applications and even the least powerful computer on the market has adequate computing power for a small start-up business.

  A network card, modem, and Internet access (either through a dial-up connection or through a high speed service like cable or DSL) are essential because software must be updated regularly to fix bugs; updates are delivered via the Internet.

  Computers running Microsoft Windows versions are the most popular and have a vast amount of software available. Apple computers have a niche following among graphics professionals, but owners will find a limited business software market.

- **Printer.** A laser printer is essential because it allows business owners to produce crisp invoices, checks and reports quickly on plain paper. Color laser printers are coming down in price and soon will be a viable option for small businesses. Ink jet printers are cheaper and provide color capability, but may not provide the hands-off trouble-free performance needed at higher volumes of transactions in a small business.

Software options

The first step is to research the software programs available. The market consists of hundreds of different systems. Three ways to narrow the field are to shop around, ask other small business owners what they are using and ask accountants what software they would recommend.

Most small startup companies can fill their needs with very inexpensive, yet full-featured systems. The five most popular programs are listed below.

Product	Developer	Phone/Web site	Price
QuickBooks Pro	Intuit P.O. Box 7850 Mountain View, CA	(800) 4-INTUIT www.quickbooks.com	$299
MYOB Plus	MYOB US, Inc. 300 Roundhill Drive Rockaway, NJ 07866	(973) 586-2200 www.myob.com	$249
One-Write Plus	Peachtree Software 1505 Pavilion Place Norcross, GA 30093	(800) 228-0068 www.onewrite.com	$99
Peachtree Complete Accounting	Peachtree Software 1505 Pavilion Place Norcross, GA 30093	(800) 228-0068 www.peachtree.com	$299
Simply Accounting Pro	Simply Accounting 13700 International Place- Suite 300 Richmond, BC V6V 2X8	(800) 773-5445 www.simplyaccounting.com	$99

These systems all contain the basic records systems needed for small businesses:

■ General ledger, budgeting and financial statements.

■ Customer invoices and accounts receivable.

■ Vendor invoices and accounts payable.

■ Payroll and employee records.

Besides these features, there are other features available that small business owners may find useful. They are usually low cost add-ons. If these features are important, they should be included on the company's software shopping list.

■ **Multiple currency accounting.** Sending invoices to foreign customers in their home currency.

■ **Professional time billing.** Keeping track of accounting and billing for professionals who charge by the hour.

■ **e-mailing of forms and reports.** Sending invoices and other documents via the Internet.

- **Multiple price levels.** Maintaining different selling prices for different customers.

- **Vacation and sick pay accruals.** Keeping track of employee vacation and sick time.

- **Printing of W-2s and 941 forms.** Creating the forms directly on a laser printer so as not to have to purchase preprinted forms.

- **Password protection.** Allowing different users to have different levels of access to the system.

- **Network-ready multiple users.** Allowing several different users to use the system simultaneously over a network.

- **Job cost tracking.** Summarizing the cost and profit on contracts such as construction jobs.

- **Fixed assets management.** Keeping track of major investments in equipment.

- **Inventory tracking.** Maintaining records of in-stock levels as well as reorder quantities, inventory cost calculations, product assemblies, and multiple price levels.

- **Electronic payments.** Making direct deposits to the bank accounts of vendors and employees. Making collections directly from the bank accounts of customers.

- **Point of sale.** Managing cash register information, including direct connection to an electronic cash register. Usually includes point of sale hardware such as cash drawers, bar code scanners and receipt printers.

- **Job estimating.** Preparing the selling price calculation for a large complex contract.

Support plans
Once a software package has been purchased, the user is given the option of purchasing any updates at a reduced price as soon as they are available to the public. These updates are the new software package on the market, with complete documentation. In some cases the annual updates are included in the original purchase price.

In addition, each software package includes phone numbers for technical support, help when installing, questions on the basics as well as advanced questions.

Making the decision
Choosing a software package should not be a casual decision. Before shopping around, list the functions which are necessary for the company and locate those software packages which fulfill your needs. Then, compare any special offers that might be included, cost of the original package, cost of updates, demands and limitations on the computer hardware and compatibility with other software. Once this is done the rest is easy. All that is left to do is read the manual and work with the program to learn its features, strengths and shortcomings.

Backing up computer data
The small computer environment is inherently unstable, and many things, including electric power irregularity, human error and software bugs can cause computer crashes. If a crash occurs, the company may lose valuable business data. The purpose of computer data back-up is to provide a way to recover from computer crashes and give a solid starting place from which to recreate files in case of emergency. The easiest way to do this is to date your transaction batches and back-up tapes

or disks. The back-up should be done daily. Back-ups should be stored off the premises in a fireproof container as a precaution if there is any loss of data on the computer.

 We can't say enough about the need for frequent data backup. The data may be worth more than the computer it resides on!

MANAGING AND SUMMARIZING INFORMATION

The system for keeping track of any business records consists of accounts. An account is the basic storage unit for accounting data. There is a separate account for each asset, liability, component of owner's equity, revenue and expense. The book which contains all the accounts is called the ledger. In order to be able to find an account in the ledger easily, the accounts are numbered. The account number tells both the location of the account and its financial statement classification. The list of numbers and the corresponding account names is called the *chart of accounts*.

The use of a chart of accounts facilitates analysis of business records and preparation of reports such as the balance sheet and income statement. Accountants use account numbers because they process the data by computer. Also, it makes it easier to put the information in order. For example, the balance sheet is the first report in the financial statements, followed by the income statement. The balance sheet always lists assets first then liabilities and owner's equity. The income statement shows revenues first then expenses.

A simple chart of accounts for a small company might use a four digit number for each account where the 1000s are used for assets, the 2000s for liabilities, the 3000s for owner's equity, the 4000s for revenues and the 6000s for expenses. The Appendix shows an example of a chart of accounts.

USING ACCOUNTING DATA TO MANAGE

The purpose of this section is to explain what the accounting professional does with the company records to turn them into financial statements. It is a basic explanation of two important financial statements. It also discusses how small company owners can use accounting data to estimate the company's income. Finally, it explains the significance of the accounting information. This discussion is not a substitute for a meeting with the company's accountant or financial advisor to learn to understand the statements and how to use the information to run the company and make business decisions.

The information from the registers is summarized and the totals are used to prepare financial statements and tax returns. Many company owners will prefer to turn the summarized records over to a CPA or other accounting professional to be processed into financial statements. Besides getting the job done, this allows the business manager to use the services of a professional to interpret the information while the owner concentrates on running the company.

Using either a computer system or paper-based techniques, the accountant accumulates the company data into another record called a *general ledger*. From the general ledger, all reports are prepared, including company financial statements, sales tax reports and income tax returns. The general ledger is the starting point for tax examiners and auditors when they look at the company's books.

The following flow chart shows a simplified flow of data from basic documents to the end product.

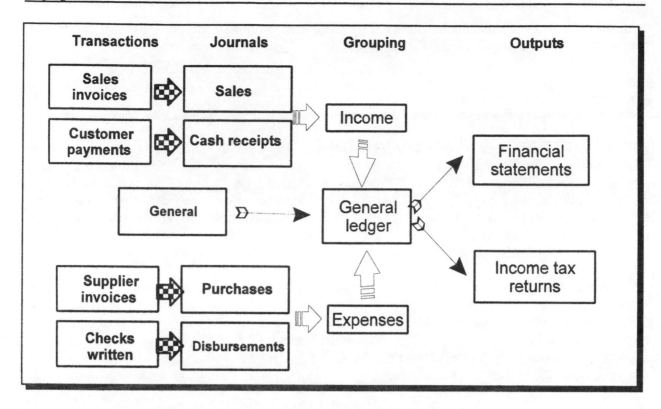

There are two main financial statements: the income statement and the balance sheet.

Income statement

This statement shows the components of profit or loss for a company. It can cover any period of time, from a month to a year, but never more than a year. Typical small businesses have an income statement prepared either quarterly, semi-annually or annually. Larger ones do so every month, because larger businesses find it harder, and riskier, to rely on personal observation to evaluate the company's financial success.

The following page shows the annual income statement for Springdale Computer Consignment, LLC. In most cases, it is possible to get a *rough approximation* of the company's income by entering data from company accounting records. The Appendix contains a worksheet that can be used for this purpose. This worksheet will produce an estimated income statement, not a substitute for a professionally prepared income statement.

Of course, the most important item on the income statement is the net income after taxes. Beyond that, however, the format of the income statement allows a fast analysis of company performance. Each main component of the statement has a meaning.

Springdale Computer Consignment, LLC
Income Statement
January through December 2003 and 2002

		2003	**2002**
Income:			
4000	Sales and Services	$229,790	$200,000
Cost of Goods Sold:			
5000	Cost of Goods Sold	137,575	120,100
Gross Profit		92,215	79,900
Expenses:			
6000	Payroll Expenses	49,429	41,210
6010	Rent and occupancy	6,355	6,000
6020	Insurance	1,200	1,200
6030	Advertising	4,200	4,200
6040	Supplies	1,000	1,000
6050	Professional Fees	2,450	2,000
6060	Credit card fees	4,000	3,080
6070	Depreciation and Amortization	6,000	6,000
6080	Interest Expense	8,400	9,100
6090	Communications	2,211	2,000
6240	Miscellaneous	1,000	1,000
6350	Travel & Entertainment	1,000	1,000
	Total Expenses	87,244	77,790
Net Income		$ 4,971	$ 2,110

Comparison to prior periods or to a budget
To be truly useful, the income statement should have comparative figures to the previous year or to the company's budget. Few small businesses have formal budgets. Those that do, and use the budgets as goals, find it helps them to improve profitability. The simplest budget for any company expresses management's goals for sales and net profits. This two-factor target allows managers to make action plans to achieve the goals. If the goals are not met, corrective actions can be taken.

Cost of sales
Cost of sales is a term used to define the cost to produce, buy or modify the item being sold. Anything that is part of the product or touches the product directly is a part of the cost of sales. Any material used is the first and most obvious cost of sales, but also included are costs of production or service such as the wages of anyone involved in producing a product or providing a service. All expenses included in cost of sales vary directly with sales. That is, the more widgets that are sold or the more services performed, the greater the cost of sales.

Gross profit
Gross profit is the profit after cost of sales is subtracted from sales and before any other expenses are deducted. This figure is an important measure of profitability. To be successful, a company must sell its goods or services for enough above cost to pay operating expenses and make a profit.

Operating expenses
Operating expenses are costs, other than cost of sales, incurred in running a business. Whether one widget is sold or one hundred, these costs remain relatively the same. Some common examples are utilities, rent and office expense. Obviously, as sales increase, there comes a point when operating costs will increase but the relationship is not a direct one.

Net income before taxes
This amount - revenues minus costs minus operating expenses - is significant for two reasons:

■ It is the main measure of the company's financial progress and success. Lenders use it to determine if the company is credit-worthy.

■ It determines how much tax a company pays.

Federal and state income tax
These are an expense of doing business and making a profit and are included as expenses in a company's financial statements.

Net income after taxes
This is the net increase in owner's equity resulting from a company's operations. Net income equals revenue less cost of goods less operating expenses less income taxes.

Balance sheet

A balance sheet normally accompanies any professionally prepared income statement. It is also required for all financial statements requested by banks. The balance sheet is a report of the company's *assets* and *liabilities*. It also shows the amount of the owners' interest or *equity* in the company. The equity is the amount by which the assets exceed the liabilities.

The balance sheet is a snapshot at a specific moment in time of the assets the company owns, the amount it owes to others, and the amount of the owners' stake in the company. It shows the resources available to run the company, how much of those resources are already committed, how liquid the assets are and whether the liquid assets are adequate to pay the company's bills.

The following page shows a balance sheet for Springdale Computer Consignment, LLC. As with the income statement, it is possible to estimate the company's balance sheet from readily available information. The Appendix contains a worksheet that can be used for this purpose. Of course, this worksheet is not a substitute for a professionally prepared balance sheet.

Springdale Computer Consignment, LLC
Balance Sheet
As of December 31, 2003 and 2002

	2003	2002
ASSETS		
Current Assets:		
1000 Cash	$62,603	$59,655
1200 Accounts Receivable	4,199	0
1300 Inventory	45,000	40,000
Total Current Assets	111,802	99,655
Fixed Assets:		
1510 Furniture and equipment	20,000	20,000
1520 Accumulated depreciation	-12,000	-8,000
Total Fixed Assets	8,000	12,000
Other Assets:		
1700 Organization costs	4,000	6,000
1900 Security deposits	3,000	3,000
Total Other Assets	7,000	9,000
TOTAL ASSETS	126,802	120,655
LIABILITIES & EQUITY		
Current Liabilities:		
2000 Accounts Payable	12,991	6,500
2101 Payroll Liabilities	326	0
2200 Sales Tax Payable	360	0
Total Current Liabilities	13,676	6,500
Long Term Liabilities:		
2250 SBA Note Payable	82,000	88,000
Total Long Term Liabilities	82,000	88,000
Total Liabilities	95,676	94,500
Equity:		
3000 Member's Equity	25,000	25,000
3900 Retained Earnings	1,155	-955
Net Income	4,971	2,110
Total Equity	31,126	26,155
TOTAL LIABILITIES & EQUITY	$126,802	$120,655

Limitations of financial statements

When preparing or reading financial statements, there are two things to remember:

- **Historical asset valuations.** The assets on the balance sheet are valued at what they originally cost, not what they are really worth. This difference is most apparent for real estate and other assets that fluctuate in value. In times of rising real estate values, real estate holdings may be worth more than they are valued on the company balance sheet.

  However, traditional financial statements do not increase the values to the higher market values. If the difference is critical, the company should hire an appraiser to prepare a separate valuation of the company. This is usually only necessary when the company wants to borrow money.

- **Net income is influenced by the company's selection of accounting practices.** Depreciation, discussed in the Developing a Business Plan chapter, is the operating expense that expresses the gradual wearing out of the company's equipment and furnishings. This expense depends on the choice of service lives for these assets. When you choose a short life, depreciation is higher and profits are lower than when you choose a long life.

> **NOTE** — When looking at the financial statements of a company, it's important to learn the company's accounting practices, especially if you are thinking about buying the company. Owners like to show low profits to the tax collectors and high profits to lenders, investors and buyers; they can do so with their choice of accounting practices. When CPAs prepare financial statements, they're required either to list the practices or to warn the reader that they've been omitted. If they're omitted, be sure to ask what they are!

HOW TO IMPROVE THE COMPANY'S RECORDS

Accountants know there can be a strong correlation between good records and good profits. Companies that keep good records seem to be more profitable than those that don't. Good records allow managers to: resolve customer billing questions; avoid double-paying bills; analyze selling prices and costs; withstand tax audits. This section offers a few suggestions.

Spend time on setup

Good records reduce accounting fees, so the money spent to set up good records returns as future cost savings. This is really a two step process. The first is to design the records system and put it into operation for one or two months. The second is to review the results of the trial operation and fine-tune record keeping formats and procedures.

Use a qualified trained bookkeeper

Whoever keeps company records, the owner, a spouse, employee or outside bookkeeper, should be properly trained and understand the importance of maintaining good records. Sources of this training include community college, bookkeeping seminars, the company's accountants and many others. Truly good bookkeepers are valuable; they make life easier for business owners and protect them from tax problems. Bookkeeping requires skills and discipline. A poorly trained bookkeeper or one who does not have the required skills could be very costly.

Keep records up to date

Financial information is useful only if it is timely. Each month should be treated as a separate business cycle and records should be up to date at the end of every month. Month end procedures should include totaling receipts and disbursements journals and balancing cash, accounts receivable, accounts payable and bank loans. A good tool is the month-end *closing checklist*, a list of the things to do to complete the company's record-keeping at the end of the month. Your CPA can customize one for you. *Then, after monthly procedures, print and review the income and expense reports that come from the accounting system.*

Organize records

The company's records consist of journals and the original documents that support them, including cash register tapes, customer invoices, bank statements, paid bills and canceled checks. They should be filed so they can be retrieved quickly. The law requires these documents to be kept for at least three years. The Appendix contains a checklist of how long to keep records.

Keep business and personal finances separated

Many business owners feel they can do whatever they please with their company funds and records. This is not necessarily true. In the eyes of the IRS, the bank and the courts, the company is a separate entity and the owners are required to keep an arms-length distance from it. The best way is for owners to treat their companies as if they were unrelated. Besides separate records, the money should be separate. Unless an expenditure is directly related to the company, it should be paid directly from the owners' personal checking accounts. If an expenditure is partly personal and partly business, the personal part should be paid from personal funds and the business portion paid from the company account. This separation reduces the potential for error, reduces bookkeeping time, saves on accounting fees and reduces audit problems with the IRS.

Understand and use available financial information

A regular review of company financial performance helps keep the company on track and avoid future problems. The two basic financial statements, income statement and balance sheet, were discussed in the previous section. They are the starting point for financial reviews. The form the two basic statements take and how often they're needed depend on the company size and other factors. The form can range from an approximation to CPA-prepared statements.

Then, read them carefully, ask questions and *don't ignore financial danger signals*. It's hard for the owners and founders of small businesses to look objectively at their creations. Good financial information allows that objective look. Too often, business owners ignore financial information when it shows mistakes in judgement. This carelessness can be costly. If the financial statements show a decision is wrong, recognize the error and correct it. The real measure of success is the long term prosperity and growth of the company. Mistakes along the way are learning tools and can contribute to the long term success of the company.

CONCLUSION

Good record keeping is essential to every company no matter what the size. Even the smallest company must prepare tax returns and be able to explain the numbers used if audited by the Internal Revenue Service. As a company grows, financial results must be known in order to manage the company successfully and to make business decisions based on reliable information.

Appendix

Chart of accounts

Springdale Computer Consignment, LLC
Account Listing - June 20, 2003

1000	Cash		5400	Purchases for Resale
1010	Bank Account		5500	Outside Instructors
1020	Cash Register Drawer		6000	Payroll Expenses
1200	Accounts Receivable		6001	Owner Salary
1120	Inventory Asset		6002	Employee Salary
1300	Inventory		6003	Payroll Taxes
1500	Furniture and Equipment		6010	Rent and Occupancy
1501	Cost (Furniture and Equipment)		6011	Rent
1502	Depreciation (Furniture and Equipment)		6012	Repairs
1700	Organization Costs		6013	Property Taxes
1701	Cost (Organization Costs)		6020	Casualty Insurance
1702	Amortization (Organization Costs)		6021	Liability Insurance
1900	Security Deposits		6022	Disability Insurance
2000	Accounts Payable		6030	Advertising
2101	Payroll Liabilities		6040	Supplies
2111	Direct Deposit Liabilities		6041	Marketing
2200	Sales Tax Payable		6042	Office
2250	SBA Note Payable		6050	Professional Fees
2300	Truck Loan		6051	Legal Fees
3000	Member's Equity		6052	Accounting Fees
3100	Member's Contribution		6060	Credit Card Fees
3200	Member's Draw		6070	Depreciation and Amortization
3300	Retained Earnings		6080	Interest Expense
3001	Opening Bal Equity		6081	Finance Charges
3900	Retained Earnings		6082	Loan Interest
4000	Sales and Services		6090	Communications
4200	Service Sales		6091	Postage and Delivery
4300	Consigned Products Sales		6092	Printing and Reproduction
4400	Owned Products Sales		6093	Telephone
4500	Training Sales		6100	Bank Service Charges
4600	Finance Charge		6240	Miscellaneous
5000	Cost of Goods Sold		6350	Travel & Entertainment
5200	Service Labor and Supplies		6310	Automobile
5300	Consignments Paid		6360	Entertainment

Income statement worksheet

_____
Company name

_____
Date

Sales $_____

Cost of goods sold
    Materials   _____
    Subcontract   _____
    Direct labor   _____

                                                      _____

Gross profit   _____

Operating expenses
    Salaries   _____
    Rent and utilities   _____
    Administrative   _____
    Marketing   _____
    _____   _____

       Total operating expenses   _____

Net income before taxes   _____

Federal income tax   _____
State income tax   _____

Total income tax   _____

Net income after taxes $_____

Balance sheet worksheet

_____
Company name

_____
Date

Assets

Current assets
    Cash   \$ _____
    Accounts receivable   _____
    Inventory   _____
        Total current assets   _____

Property & equipment
    Equipment   _____
    Vehicles   _____
    Furniture   _____
    Total property and equipment   _____

    Less accumulated depreciation   _____
        Net property and equipment   _____

Total assets   \$ _____

Liabilities and Shareholders' Equity

Current liabilities
    Accounts payable   \$ _____
    Notes payable, due in one year or less   _____
    Accrued expenses & taxes   _____
        Total current liabilities   _____

Other liabilities
    Notes payable, due after one year   _____

Shareholders equity
    Common stock   _____
    Retained earnings   _____
        Total shareholders' equity   _____

Total liabilities & shareholders' equity   \$ _____

Records retention guide

One year
- Cash reports
- Department forecasts
- Inventory tags and tickets
- Packing slips
- Production orders, reports
- Requisitions
- Returned goods notices

Two years
- Audit reports-internal
- Departmental reports
- Express receipts
- Import-export documents
- Parcel post receipts
- Payroll receipts
- Purchase price records
- Purchase quotations
- Sales orders
- Shipping orders
- Standards, efficiency records
- Stores records

Three years
- Bills of lading
- General correspondence

Four years
- Time cards

Six years
- Accounts payable records
- Accounts receivable records
- Bank statements
- Canceled checks, stubs
- Cash slips
- Claims, claims correspondence
- Customer orders
- Deposit slips
- Diversion notices
- Draft registers
- Employee earnings ledger
- Inventory records
- Medical records
- Payroll data
- Purchase orders
- Receiving slips
- Shop work orders-capital accounts
- Termination of employee records
- Vendor's debits and credits
- Vendor's invoices
- Withholding statements

Permanent
- Accounts payable ledgers
- Accounts receivable ledgers
- Appropriations-capital accounts
- Audits, external
- Blueprints, product records
- Capital stock books
- Cash books, cash register tapes
- Corporation meeting minute books
- Cost, inventory
- Employee record cards
- Financial statements
- General ledger, journal
- Government reports
- Group insurance records
- Notes payable, receivable registers
- Production summaries
- Property records
- Tax returns-corporate
- Voucher registers

One-write bookkeeping services in Connecticut

Accu-rite Inc./Accounting Systems Specialists
12 Chapel Street
Wallingford, CT
(203) 265-5686

Data Management, Inc.
537 New Britain Avenue
Farmington, CT 06034
(800) 243-1969

Accounting Forms Company
3460 Main Street
Hartford, CT   06120
(860) 247-2086

Other bookkeeping systems:

Dome Publishing, sold in most stationery stores.

INTRODUCTION

Having to hire employees is good news; it means the company has grown to the point where the owners can't keep up with the workload by themselves. It's the first step toward creating a self-perpetuating enterprise. It's also not so good news; it adds a large amount of administration. Even if a company employs only a single worker, it has to follow the same federal and state payroll regulations as employers that have large payrolls. This chapter and the following chapter cover the two aspects of being an employer: paying a payroll and handling employees' legal rights.

Every Connecticut employer must withhold three taxes from all employees' pay: federal income taxes, state income taxes and Social Security taxes. The employer must deposit these withheld taxes with Federal and State collectors promptly. These withheld funds become the personal responsibility of the employer's owners and managers. If they are not deposited, the government can seek payment directly from the owners and managers. Besides taxes withheld from employees' pay, the employer must also pay, from its own funds, Social Security taxes, federal unemployment taxes and state unemployment taxes.

ORGANIZATION OF CHAPTER

This chapter discusses the following topics:

- Payroll record keeping.
- Payroll preparation alternatives.
- Federal payroll taxes.
- Federal payroll tax deposits.
- Connecticut payroll taxes.
- Connecticut payroll tax deposits.
- Forms required from employees.
- Registration forms required for employers.
- Recurring payroll reports.

PAYROLL RECORD KEEPING

Payroll preparation is one of the company's most challenging responsibilities, because the rules covering payroll change every single year and because the records have to be very good to comply with the law. These records include details of hours worked, taxes withheld and payments made. The company must report summary information to tax collectors every quarter and submit detailed information once each year. Many small companies find it tempting to ignore these numerous, costly and complex procedures. By doing so, they face even more costly penalties.

There are two types of payroll records: basic employee information and earnings information. Basic employee information includes the following:

- Name.
- Address.
- Sex.
- Date of birth.
- Social security number.
- Withholding exemptions.
- Occupation.
- Period employed.
- State employed in.
- Pay rate and history of raises.

The personal information is normally kept in file folders for each employee, which should also contain the employee's application, performance evaluations, reprimands, health insurance data, and similar information.

> **NOTE** Many employers make the mistake of asking for this information on an application form. Discrimination laws make it illegal for employers to ask for any information that would disclose an applicant's ethnic, racial or religious background, marital status, or number of dependents. This information is best gathered *after* the employee is hired.

Earnings information includes all the data needed for payment calculations and to prepare government reports. The company must keep a record, for each payroll period, of the following information about each employee's earnings:

- Gross wages paid.
- Federal income tax withheld.
- State income tax withheld.
- Social Security and Medicare taxes withheld.
- Fringe benefits withheld, or paid.
- Net wages paid.

If the employee is paid by the hour, the employer must also keep a record of:

- Hours worked.
- Overtime hours worked.

Earnings information must be summarized each quarter and at the end of the year for government reports of wages, taxes and withholding. Records of employment taxes must be retained for at least four years and be available for Internal Revenue Service review. These should include all copies of returns filed along with dates and amounts of tax deposits made. The detailed records of hours, payments and withholdings should be kept for three years. Connecticut only requires employers to keep records for three years. The Appendix in the Keeping Good Business Records chapter contains the contact information for the IRS, Connecticut's Department of Revenue Services, and Connecticut's Department of Labor.

PAYROLL PREPARATION ALTERNATIVES

There are several ways to pay employees and maintain employee earnings information, and the company is free to use whatever means it wants, as long as the records are accurate and complete. There are two main alternatives: prepare the payroll internally or hire an outside service to do it.

Internally prepared payroll

When payroll is prepared within the company, two things are required: a system for preparation and someone to stay informed about changes in payroll regulations. The information about payroll regulations comes from three sources:

■   IRS payroll booklet, Circular E, which is issued annually in December. This covers income tax and Social Security tax regulations.

■   Connecticut payroll booklet, Circular CT, which is issued whenever Connecticut payroll regulations changes take place, normally every two years.

■   Notifications as needed from the Department of Labor on changes in the unemployment insurance rate.

The advantage of a self-prepared payroll is flexibility; the payroll can be prepared and checks handed out in a single step. The disadvantage is that someone in the company has to invest the time both to prepare the payroll and to learn the rules. For that reason, it's not a good idea to prepare your own payroll, but if you want to, there are three alternatives:

■   **Individual record card.** This is a paper record, usually 5" x 8" or 8½" x 11," that records every paycheck paid to the employee during the year. It is subtotaled at the end of each calendar quarter and totaled at the end of the year. These subtotals and totals allow the company to prepare quarterly reports of taxes and unemployment insurance. Payroll record cards can be purchased from stationery and office supply stores and one-write vendors. If the company uses a one-write system, the payroll record card is filled out at the same time as the paycheck is written.

■   **Payroll book.** These books are sold in stationery and office supply stores and allow the company to summarize both employee information and company payroll figures. A popular brand is the DOME payroll book.

■   **Computer.** In-house computer preparation is a realistic payroll alternative, because of the available computer programs which are both full-featured and inexpensive. All the systems listed in the Record Keeping chapter contain excellent payroll modules and can handle the needs of most small companies. With a laser or inkjet printer, they produce professional-looking results, including paychecks and government payroll report forms. Through third-party providers, they also provide many of the features, including direct deposit of payroll, that are available through outside payroll services. Because requirements change almost every year, the company needs to purchase an annual update and should consider an annual subscription for telephone support.

Payroll preparation services

Many small businesses have decided the most economical and efficient way to handle payroll is to turn it over to a payroll service. The advantage of this alternative is that the company doesn't have to pay for - or spend time with - forms, software, tax tables or regulations. The disadvantage is that the company is tied to a production cycle with data reported to the payroll service three to four days before payday.

 If you place a value on company employees' time to process payroll, the real cost of a payroll service for a small company is less than doing it yourself.

Outside payroll preparation is a simple five-step process:

- At a scheduled time, the company reports its payroll information through a call-in, fax or computer communications procedure. This takes place one to three days before payday.

- The service then prepares the checks and delivers the package to the company. If there are multiple locations, checks can be delivered to each one.

- The service makes direct deposit of pay to the bank accounts of those employees who authorize it and issues checks for the rest.

- The service then electronically pays all federal and state taxes. Most services are fully liable for the accuracy and timeliness of the deposits so the company is no longer responsible and cannot incur penalties.

- Quarterly and at the end of the year, the service prepares the government payroll reports.

Payroll processing is a competitive business, and the service companies strive to offer low prices and good service. The Appendix lists the major payroll services operating in Connecticut. They offer similar, but not identical, services.

Some of the offerings of payroll services are listed in the table below.

Payroll service offerings	
New business kit	A free kit containing all federal and state new business applications and all new hire paperwork.
Direct deposit	The employee's net pay is electronically deposited to one or more bank accounts on payday.
Check signing and Insertion	The owner's signature is laser printed on the check, which is sealed in an envelope for security and confidentiality.
Lump sum bank transfer	The entire net pay is electronically moved to a separate bank account set-up by the payroll service on which the payroll checks are cashed. The business owner no longer has to reconcile the payroll account.
Section 125 plans	A way to reduce employee and employer payroll taxes through a pre-tax health care contribution.
Human resource management	Professionally finished employee handbooks, assistance with safety compliance and COBRA administration to name just a few services. Replaces an HR department for a small company.
State unemployment Insurance services	The payroll service becomes the address of record with the Department of Labor, replies to all claims, appeals, determinations and requests for separation of documentation.
Workers' compensation pay-as-you-go service	Workers' compensation premiums are electronically collected and remitted to the insurance carrier every pay period. Collections are based on actual, not estimated payroll dollars. This service eliminates the down payment and additional premiums due with the final audit.
Internet reporting Service	This service adds convenience and flexibility by allowing businesses to receive their payroll on the Internet.

A new competitor in the payroll service arena is the Web-based service offered by many of the standard payroll services and a growing number of Web-only payroll processors. These are included in the payroll processing services list in the Appendix.

FEDERAL PAYROLL TAXES

Federal payroll taxes fall into three categories:

■   Federal income tax withholding taxes paid by the employee.

■   Social Security and Medicare taxes (FICA - Federal Insurance Contributions Act) paid by the employee with matching contributions by the employer.

■   Federal Unemployment taxes (FUTA - Federal Unemployment Tax Act) paid by the employer.

Details on all three types of taxes are found in the Internal Revenue Service Employer's Tax Guide, known as Circular E. This publication is automatically sent to all companies that have employees. It may also be obtained by mail or phone from the IRS. See the Appendix for current addresses and toll-free numbers.

Federal income tax withholding is calculated on individual employee data (wages, marital status, exemptions, and frequency of payroll). Commonly used tax tables are listed in Circular E.

Employee wages subject to federal income tax withholding include all pay rendered for services performed. This can be in the form of salaries, vacation pay, sick pay, bonuses, and commissions. Employee wages may be in the form of cash or other sources. There is no limit to the amount of wages subject to withholding taxes.

Employees may also be compensated in the form of fringe benefits. A fringe benefit is anything of value given to employees in addition to their salary or wages. There are taxable fringe benefits, the value of which must be added to the employee's gross earnings to be taxed for federal, FICA, and unemployment taxes. Some examples of this are employer-provided cars, prizes, memberships in country clubs, airfare, vacations, and tickets to entertainment or sporting events. Circular E contains a complete list of the items that are taxable.

There are also non-taxable fringe benefits which can be given to employees and are not included in their earnings.   Some examples are: qualified employee discounts on company products, working condition fringes, employer provided meals and on-site athletic facilities.

Federal Insurance Contributions Act withholdings, or FICA, consists of two component parts - Social Security and Medicare, using different wage bases for each component. The rates and wage bases change every year, usually increasing by a small amount. These are published by the IRS in Circular E and by Connecticut in Circular CT. The changes take place on January 1 each year, and are published in Circular E. Medicare, on the other hand, has no wage base limit. Employees must contribute a percentage of their gross payroll dollars to Medicare tax, regardless of how much they earn during a calendar year. Managers should be sure to check the Circular E each year for changes in tax withholdings and wage base limits.

While employees must contribute 6.2% of their gross earnings to Social Security and 1.45% to Medicare, the employer is responsible for matching contributions. The following table shows how the tax would be figured for an employee earning $90,000.

Payments for an employee earning $90,000			
Wage base	**Rate**	**Employer Share**	**Employee Share**
Up to $87,000	7.65%	6,655.50	6,655.50
over $87,000	1.45%	43.50	43.50
Total		6,699.00	6,699.00
Note: Check IRS publications for current rates.			
Components of FICA rate:			
Social Security Tax	6.20%		
Medicare Tax	1.45%		
Total	7.65%		

FUTA

Like Social Security, Federal Unemployment Tax also has a wage base limit. Unlike Social Security, FUTA is an employer tax and is not withheld from an employee's paycheck. Employers are responsible for paying FUTA on the first $7,000 in wages paid to each employee. The tax rate for FUTA is 6.2%, but the IRS allows each employer to deduct a maximum credit of 5.4% for state unemployment taxes paid, resulting in a net federal unemployment tax rate of .8%. All wages up to the first $7,000 paid to each employee are taxed at .8% for a maximum of $56 per employee per year.

FEDERAL PAYROLL TAX DEPOSITS

There are two recurring federal tax payments:

- Federal income tax withholding and FICA taxes, which are combined into a single payment known as a Federal 941 deposit.

- FUTA payment, known as a Federal 940 deposit.

Federal 941 Deposits

Federal payroll taxes must be deposited according to the frequency assigned each company by the IRS. Each November the IRS advises businesses what their deposit status is for the following year. New businesses generally start out with a monthly tax depositing frequency for their first year of business. The five components of a 941 deposit (federal withholding, employee social security, employee medicare, employer social security and employer medicare) must be paid by the 15th of the following month for monthly tax depositors. For example, all tax liabilities incurred for checks dated in January are due by the 15th of February. If the 15th is not a banking day, the deposit is due the following banking day. After the first year of business, deposit frequency is determined by the IRS with reference to a prior period's liability. The prior period is called the lookback period.

The table below shows the requirements for making 941 tax deposits.

Deposit requirements for payroll taxes	
Deposit Rule	**Deposit Due**
Quarterly rule. If at the end of the quarter your total tax liability is less than $500.	You may pay the taxes to the IRS with your Form 941 quarterly return, or you may deposit them by the due date of the return.
Monthly rule. If your total tax liability during the look-back period was $50,000 or less.	You must deposit the taxes accumulated in any month by the 15th of the following month, so long as your total tax obligation is at least $500 but not more than $100,000 (see one-day rule below).
Semi-weekly rule. If your total tax liability during the "lookback" period was more than $50,000.	Taxes accumulated for pay dates of Wednesday through Friday must be deposited by the following Wednesday. Taxes accumulated for pay dates of Saturday through Tuesday must be deposited by the following Friday.
$100,000 one-day rule. If your accumulated tax reaches $100,000 or more on any day in a deposit period:	Taxes must be deposited by the next banking day whether an employer is a monthly or semiweekly depositor. If a monthly depositor accumulates $100,000 on any day it then becomes a semi-weekly depositor for the remainder of the calendar year and for the following calendar year.

FUTA deposits

The FUTA tax for each quarter must be paid on or before the last day of the calendar month following each quarter. There is an exception - if the tax liability is less than $100, it is not necessary to make a deposit. That liability can be carried over to the next quarter.

To calculate its FUTA due for each quarter, the company multiplies its total gross wages subject to FUTA times .008. For example, if the total wages subject to FUTA were $21,000, the deposit amount would be $168.

Electronic payment

The IRS requires most companies to make their payroll tax deposits through the Electronic Federal Tax Payment System (EFTPS). There are three ways to make an EFTPS deposit:

- **Debit Method.** A TFA (Treasury Financial Agent) electronically debits the business bank account and transfers the money to the IRS.

- **Credit Method.** A local bank is notified by the business of the amount to be paid. The financial institution debits the business bank account and transfers the money to the IRS.

 NOTE Either of these two methods require that the business owner file Form 9779 enrolling with the IRS. You can also do either method online at www.fms.treas.gov/eftps/.

- **Bulk Filing Method.** Most payroll service companies will enroll the client and electronically deposit to the IRS on behalf of the client.

Deposit coupons

The Form 8109 deposit coupon is a deposit procedure for both 940 and 941 taxes when EFTPS isn't available or isn't required. Situations in which the Form 8109 deposit would be used include new taxpayers not yet set up for EFTPS, small companies not ready to use EFTPS, or when the company switches payroll services and there is a break in deposit service. The deposit is made at most commercial banks.

NOTE The bank provides a receipt for tax deposits. This is an important record to keep to prove the date and the amount of the deposit. The IRS takes up to three years to audit tax deposits, so tax receipts and canceled checks should be kept at least that long.

Federal deposit penalties

Tax deposits are a serious matter. Employers should give tax deposits priority above all other payments because:

- Besides penalties, the IRS charges interest at 1/2% per month from the date of the return to the date the tax is paid. The maximum interest payable is 25% of the tax deposit.
- The deposits are the personal responsibility of business owners and managers.
- Penalties and interest can cost an additional 40% of the original tax due.

CONNECTICUT PAYROLL TAXES

There are two forms of Connecticut state payroll taxes:

- State income taxes paid by employees.
- State unemployment taxes paid by employers.

Employers must withhold *state income tax* from all employees who are working in Connecticut. Like the federal income tax, the amount of state income tax to be withheld from an employee is determined by four factors: filing status, number of allowances, rate of pay and frequency of pay. The information needed to correctly withhold from an employee can be found in the CT W-4. The withholding rates and amounts can be found in the Connecticut Circular CT. To order a Connecticut Circular CT, contact the Department of Revenue Services.

State unemployment tax is paid by the employer. Like FUTA, state unemployment tax also has a wage base limit that changes every year. The state unemployment tax is calculated using the contribution rate that the Department of Labor assigns to each business. The rate that is assigned is determined by the employer's "experience rating". This rate moves up or down each year depending on the number of unemployment claims filed against the company - the more claims the higher the rate. In March, the Department of Labor sends a notice to all Connecticut employers informing them of their rate for the year. New businesses are all assigned a standard rate until their experience rate is determined.

CONNECTICUT PAYROLL TAX DEPOSITS

The two different state tax payroll payments go to two different state agencies on two different forms, one for income tax and the other for unemployment insurance tax.

Income taxes

These deposits are made with a coupon similar to that for the Federal withholding taxes: Connecticut Form CT-WH. Employers must deposit state taxes with the same frequency as for payments to the Internal Revenue Service. Whenever the company reaches the point at which a Federal payment is required, it must make a state payment, regardless of the amount that has been withheld. To obtain a state withholding number and coupon book, new business owners must file a Reg-1, the application for a tax registration number. This is filed with the Department of Revenue Services. After a tax ID number is assigned, the Department of Revenue Services will mail the employer a coupon book. The Department of Revenue Services will notify payers who are required to pay by electronic funds transfer.

Unemployment taxes

The state unemployment tax due is reported and paid quarterly with Form UC-2 within one month after the end of each calendar quarter. The tax is calculated and remitted with the form. This tax is deposited with the Connecticut Department of Labor. To obtain a state unemployment number, new business owners must file a UC 1-A with the Department of Labor. The quarterly unemployment tax and the UC-2 are mailed to the Department of Labor.

FORMS REQUIRED FROM EMPLOYEES

The employer must obtain three forms from every employee:

- IRS form W-4.
- Connecticut Form CT-W4.
- Immigration and Naturalization Form I-9.

The *Employee's Withholding Allowance Certificate (Form W-4)* may be obtained from the local Internal Revenue Service office, by calling the IRS toll free number, downloaded from the IRS website, from the company's CPA, or from the company's payroll service. This form must be retained in each employee's personnel file. The W-4 provides the basic information required for payroll calculations: employee name, address, social security number, marital status and tax exemptions. If the employee chooses no withholding, the employer must send a copy of the W-4 form to the IRS.

The *Connecticut Employee Withholding Allowance Certificate Form (CT-W4)* is similar to that for the IRS. If the employee chooses no withholding, the employer doesn't have to withhold and doesn't have to send the form to the Department of Revenue Services. However, all Form CT-W4 for all newly hired or newly re-hired employees must be sent to the Department of Labor within twenty (20) days.

The *Employment Eligibility Verification Form (Form I-9)* applies to every employee hired after November 6, 1986. Failure to comply may result in civil fines of from $100 to over $1,000. The I-9 and a booklet explaining how to use it may be obtained by calling the Immigration and Naturalization Service toll free number, 1-800-375-5283, or from the IRS website. This form must be filed in the employee records.

REGISTRATION FORMS REQUIRED FOR EMPLOYERS

In order to make payroll payments, every employer must register for identification numbers with several government agencies. These are required for all employers, regardless of the form of business organization. The chapter on Choosing the Right Legal Organization contains a full description of the forms.

Three identification numbers are necessary for payroll payment:
- Federal Employer Number - IRS Form SS-4.
- Connecticut Identification number - Connecticut Form REG-1.
- State Unemployment Tax Registration Number - Form UC-1A.

After the company has received its Federal, State and Unemployment Identification numbers, it will automatically receive the necessary quarterly and annual forms and information booklets that it needs to administer payroll. It must then file regular reports, as discussed in the next section.

RECURRING PAYROLL REPORTS

Having a payroll means having to make regular reports to the IRS and Connecticut, regardless of the number of employees on the payroll. These reports fall into two cycles, quarterly and annual, and are produced automatically by all payroll service bureaus and by most payroll software.

Quarterly reports

For reporting purposes, the year is divided into four quarters:

First quarter	January 1 through March 31
Second quarter	April 1 through June 30
Third quarter	July 1 through September 30
Fourth quarter	October 1 through December 31

At the end of every quarter, three payroll reports are required. All are due on or before the last day of the month following the calendar quarter as shown in following table.

Quarterly payroll reports	
IRS Form 941	Reconciliation of federal income tax withholding, FICA withholding and federal deposits.
Connecticut Form CT-941	Quarterly reconciliation form similar to IRS Form 941.
Connecticut Forms UC-2 and UC5A (combined form)	Unemployment taxes and wages paid to each employee, listing employee name, social security number and gross wages for the quarter. Companies with 250 or more employees must report via magnetic tape or disk.

Annual reports

Every January and February are active months for employers. Besides the normal quarterly reports, they must furnish employees, the IRS, Social Security Administration, and the State with detailed information statements. There are four annual reports as shown in the following table.

Annual payroll tax reports		
Form	Title	Due
Form 940	Federal unemployment report	January 31 to IRS
Form W-2	Wage and tax statement	January 31 to employee Feb 28 to SSA with W-3
Form W-3	Transmittal of income and tax statements	Feb 28 with copies of all W-2s to Social Security Administration
CT-W3	Wages paid and taxes withheld	Feb 28 to CT Department of Revenue Services

If an employer issues 250 or more W-2s in a year, they have to be filed via tape or disk. There is a penalty of $50.00 per individual form for failing to file electronically.

 Good records make the recurring tax deposits and reports a simple transfer of data, insuring timely deposits and saving penalties.

CONCLUSION

While the process of doing payroll and calculating tax deposits is a non-profitable aspect of running a business, it is very important that it is done correctly. Too many small business owners fall into the trap of trying to manage too many administrative details instead of focusing on growing the business. Using a payroll service is a way to insure that the processing, tax deposits and reports will be done on time and accurately, eliminating the chance of penalties. A new business owner who opts to do payroll should follow a few basic rules:

- Stay abreast of all federal and state tax law changes.
- Keep accurate records of all payments made to employees.
- Keep accurate records of all deposits made to the IRS, Connecticut Department of Revenue Services and Department of Labor.
- Don't fail to make deposits of payroll taxes. They are the owner's personal responsibility. As an owner, if you can't make the deposit, don't take a paycheck.

Appendix

Sources of taxpayer assistance

State taxes	Department of Revenue Services 25 Sigourney Street Hartford, CT 06106 (860) 297-5962 or (800) 382-9463 www.drs.state.ct.us
	Connecticut Department of Labor 200 Folly Brook Boulevard Wethersfield, CT 06109-1114 (860) 263-6550 www.ctdol.state.ct.us
Federal taxes	Internal Revenue Service 135 High Street Hartford, CT 06103 (860) 240-3349 (800) 829-1040 www.irs.gov
Immigration	Immigration and Naturalization Service Ribicoff Federal Building 450 Main Street Hartford, CT 06103 (860) 240-3171

Payroll processing services

Automatic Data Processing 100 Corporate Drive Windsor, CT 06095 (860) 687-7900	Paychex Payroll Services 100 Great Meadow Rd, Suite 202 Wethersfield CT 06109 (860) 257-0677
Data Management, Inc. 537 New Britain Avenue PO Box 789 Farmington, CT 06034 (800) 243-1969	Payroll 1 160 West Street, Building 1 Cromwell, CT 06416 (800) 385-6844
Virtual Payroll (Web payroll provider) Margate FL (888) 531-5300	Paycom Online (Web payroll provider) Oklahoma City, OK (405) 841-6900

INTRODUCTION

Employers must be aware of a variety of restrictions that federal and state laws have placed on the employment relationship, including hiring and screening techniques. For example, the Americans with Disabilities Act contains limitations on interviewing, and hiring. Title VII of the Civil Rights Act of 1964, the Age Discrimination in Employment Act, and the Connecticut Fair Employment Practices Act also provide significant protections to employees. Besides the penalties allowed in statutes and regulations, employers can pay hefty damages to employees - or even employment applicants - who are successful in court.

ORGANIZATION OF CHAPTER

This chapter discusses the following topics:
- Employment advertising.
- Applications.
- Interviewing.
- Employee record keeping.
- Payroll decisions.
- Paying overtime.
- Exempt employee.
- Employee v. independent contractor.
- Employing minors.

SUCCESSFUL RECRUITMENT

Getting the right employee - and avoiding discrimination claims - depends on doing several things right, from advertising to position descriptions to interviewing, evaluating the applicant and making an offer. At each step there are risks and opportunities to make things happen right.

Employment advertising

Successful recruiting can be a significant and costly challenge to any employer. Employment ads should list the basic position requirements, such as minimum education, experience, or specialized training so potential applicants can determine if they meet the desired qualifications. However, employers must be careful to avoid including any language that expresses a hiring preference or discrimination, such as race, gender or nationality under federal and state discrimination laws.

 Web-based recruiting has grown strongly as a practical tool. Expect to pay much less for this means of advertising and to receive more applications. We recommend www.careerbuilder.com.

Job descriptions

A job description is a written outline of the responsibilities of a job or position and a listing of the duties involved in carrying out those responsibilities. Job descriptions may be used as a basis for job evaluations and job rankings and for determining rates of pay for new or changed jobs; they are also used in the interview stage of the hiring process to explain responsibilities of a job or position to an applicant. Job descriptions are a valuable means by which an employer can communicate its expectations about job functions and duties. They also tell employees what duties and responsibilities they are expected to perform. A job description should be up to date, and the essential functions of the job should be clearly emphasized. It may be helpful to have the current employees' input about the job description.

Job descriptions and the Americans with Disabilities Act

Although there is no federal law requiring employers to prepare them, job descriptions play an important role in complying with the Americans with Disabilities Act (ADA). The ADA prohibits discrimination against a "qualified individual with a disability who, with or without reasonable accommodation, can perform the essential functions of the job." The ADA does not define what constitutes the *essential functions* of a job but permits employers to define what the employer believes are the essential functions. A written job description is considered evidence of the employer's judgment about which functions of a job are essential.

> **NOTE** — An *essential function* is a life function, such as seeing, lifting, walking, sitting, standing or hearing that an employee must be able to use in carrying out a job. Including a list of these functions in a position description provides fair warning about a job's physical challenges, reducing the risk of ADA claims.

Application forms

When recruiting, it is important to ask all applicants to fill out written applications, even if they furnish résumés. The company can create its own application form, purchase it from many business forms stores or find it in a great many business textbooks. A standard application insures that the same information is obtained about every applicant and that no information is gathered that might suggest the company used discrimination in employment decisions.

There can - and should - be different application forms for different positions, such as clerical, sales, manufacturing, professional and managerial. The following table contains a list of things that belong in a good application form.

Items for an employment application	
At-will	Employment may be terminated by either party at any time, for any reason, with or without notice. No employee has authority to make any representations to the contrary.
Certification	Include statement certifying that applicant was truthful in completing the application, no information affecting application was withheld, and employee can be fired if application was untruthful or withheld material information.
Discretion of employer	Applicant's hours and/or shift may change at employer's sole discretion.
Employer's policies	Applicant agrees to obey employer's rules and policies and acknowledges that rules may change. Employee may be fired for disobeying.
Medical exam	Disclose whether employer requires passing a medical examination or separate drug testing. Exam must be given *after* making an offer, not before.
Release	Applicants must sign a release permitting previous employers to release information about the applicant's employment. Release should be on a separate page and sent along with any request for information from previous employers.
Affirmative action	If employer is a government contractor/subcontractor who must complete an annual affirmative action plan, information on race, gender and other statistics should be entered on a form that can be separated from the rest of the application. That information should not be part of the application that goes to supervisors and should be maintained separately.

Criminal records check

The portion of the job application that contains information about the arrest record of a job applicant must be withheld from anyone interviewing the applicant, other than those in the personnel department or in charge of employment. If an employer rejects an applicant because of a conviction, the employer must advise the applicant, by registered mail, of the evidence relied upon and reasons for the rejection. Conviction information is available to the public for any purpose.

Credit checks

The Fair Credit Reporting Act (FCRA) allows the use of consumer credit reports for employment purposes, including hiring and promotion decisions, where the consumer has given written permission. A consumer credit report can be oral, written or any other communication of information by a consumer reporting agency on a consumer's credit worthiness, credit standing, reputation or character, used to establish a consumer's eligibility for credit insurance or employment.

Employers must certify that the consumer credit report is being obtained for a permissible purpose and that it will not be used for any other purpose. Under the FCRA for "employment purposes" means for the purpose of evaluating someone for employment, promotion, reassignment or retention as an employee. Employers who use consumer credit reports must notify the potential employee when an adverse decision is made based on a consumer credit report. The notice must include the following:

- Name, address, and telephone number of the agency that provided the report.
- That the agency did not make the decision and cannot explain why it was made.
- The right to obtain a free copy of the report if requested within 60 days.
- The right to dispute the accuracy or completeness of information with the agency.

The employer must also make a clear and conspicuous written disclosure to the applicant before the report is obtained, in a document that consists solely of the disclosure, that a consumer credit report may be obtained. Employers must obtain prior written authorization from the prospective employee and certify to the consumer reporting agency that the above steps have been followed, that the information being obtained will not be used in violation of any federal or state equal opportunity law or regulation, and that, if any adverse action is taken based on the applicant report, a copy of the consumer credit report and a summary of the applicant's rights will be provided to the consumer. Before taking an adverse action, the employer must provide a copy of the consumer credit report as well as the summary of the consumer's rights. Connecticut law and the FCRA both require a credit bureau to correct any misinformation in its files when presented with proof of the error.

Interviewing

An important step in the interview process is the preparation step, because it can save time in the interview and improve the interview's focus. Before an applicant is interviewed, ask the following questions:

- Is the job description current and free of obvious inaccuracies?

- Does the applicant seem to meet the minimum lawful requirements established for the position? (e.g., if a high school diploma is required, did the applicant graduate?) If the information given by the applicant does not meet the requirements, the employer need not interview the applicant.

- Are there any large gaps in the applicant's work record?

- Has the applicant worked for you before?

- If so, can anyone provide further information on this applicant?

Prohibited interview questions

An employer may not ask questions that are likely to elicit information about a disability or any other protected class status. Therefore, questions about the existence, nature, or severity of a disability, such as whether the applicant has heart disease, whether the applicant has ever filed for workers' compensation, what prescription drugs the applicant is currently taking, or the amount of alcohol the applicant consumes each week, are not permitted. Likewise, questions about an applicant's status as a member of protected class are also not allowed. In addition to disability protected classes include age, sex, race, color, marital status, religion, pregnancy, national origin, sexual orientation, or ancestry. The following are some prohibited questions:

- Do you need reasonable accommodation to do this job?
- How many days were you sick last year?
- Do you have trouble performing activities like standing, lifting, walking, etc.?
- Have you ever filed a workers' compensation claim?
- What medications are you currently taking?
- How much alcohol do you drink?
- How old are you, when were you born?
- Are you currently married, do you plan to get married?
- Are you pregnant, do you plan on having children?
- What religion do you observe?
- Do you celebrate any special religious holidays?
- Do you attend church? Which one?

Employers may make a job conditional on results of a post-offer medical exam or inquiry. However, employers must individually evaluate the employee's ability to do the job. Applicants may be asked to describe or demonstrate how they will perform a job, only if this question is asked of all applicants for a position, regardless of whether they have a disability. The focus must be on the applicant's ability to perform the job, not on the disability. Employers can ask about the applicant's ability to perform all tasks, not just essential functions.

Allowable interview questions

An employer may ask about the applicant's ability to perform specific job-related functions, e.g. describe how applicant would perform a function, can applicant meet the position's attendance requirements. Examples of questions employers may ask:

- Can you move 50 pounds from point A to point B?
- Do you have a valid driver's license? (If the job is as a driver.)
- Can you sit for two hours at a time?

- Can you read a video display terminal?
- Can you reach the top of a six-foot-high filing cabinet?
- Are you capable of standing for three hours at a time?
- Would you be able to arrive to work by 8:00 a.m. every day?

Where an employer reasonably believes that a worker needs a reasonable accommodation (either because the applicant voluntarily disclosed a disability or because the applicant has an obvious disability), the employer may ask whether and what type of accommodation will be necessary.

Interviewers may not ask applicants whether they will request leave for medical treatment or for other reasons related to a disability. However, they *may* tell applicants about the employer's work hours, leave and attendance policies, and any other special attendance needs of the job, and then ask them if they can meet those requirements. If an employer asks questions about attendance at previous jobs, the questions should not refer to illness or disability.

Effective Interviews

The employment interview is an opportunity - to learn about an applicant's motivation, likes, dislikes, experiences and skills - and a risk - to dig into topics that border on illegal discrimination. In today's environment, applicants prepare for interviews and try to show themselves in the best possible light. The most effective technique in interviewing is to get the applicant talking - as much as possible - by asking open-ended questions that invite more than just yes/no answers. When that happens, the caution that normally is found in a job interview disappears and the applicant reveals much more than was ever intended. The interviewer's best tool is to introduce the unexpected into interviews.

> **NOTE** Many applicants prepare themselves to answer hypothetical questions, so it is better to ask about real work place situations and how the applicant would handle them. For example, you may have a position that requires the applicant to handle several tasks at the same time under pressure. You might want to ask if the applicant had ever held a job that required more than one task at a time to be done. If so, ask, "How did you handle the situation?" The answer may reveal a great deal about the applicant.

The ADA and anti-discrimination laws have severely limited many of the topics that can be discussed in an employment interview. The safest and most effective technique is to ask only job related questions. The main concern in an interview is whether the applicant can perform the job. Ask questions that will help you make that determination. Job related questions such as those in the following table are appropriate.

Examples of allowable interview questions	
Previous Job	How big was your last company?
	What job did you last perform?
	How did you like it?
	Was it routine?
	Was it exciting?
	What did you like best about it? What did you like least about it?
	Why did you leave your former employer?
	What kind of references would you receive from your former employer?
	Would you be rehired?
Prior Wages	What were your wages at your prior job?
	Were you satisfied with your level of wages? If not, why?
	How frequently were increases given?
	What were they based upon -- merit, productivity or something else?
	How many increases did you receive, if based upon merit?
	How do you think employees should be compensated?
Fringe Benefits	What benefits did you receive at your prior job?
	What did you think of the fringe benefits provided at your previous employer?
	Did you pay any part of your insurance coverage?
	How were you advised by the prior employers as to your benefits -- insurance booklets, employee memo, bulletin board notices, handbook?
	How frequently were benefits changed?
	Did you feel that you were provided sufficient information about benefits?
Promotions	Were you ever promoted in your prior jobs?
	On what basis were you promoted -- length of service, merit?
	How do you think employees should be compensated?
Prior Supervisors	What did you think of your supervisors?
	Did you get along with them?
	What kind of person was your prior supervisor? A strict disciplinarian? Easygoing?
	What kind of supervisor do you like to work for?
	What do you expect from a supervisor?
Other questions	Describe your past employment history.
	How does your schooling and training prepare you for the job we're discussing?
	If hired, are you able to furnish proof of your eligibility to work in this country?
	Are you applying for full-time or part-time work?
	What hours and days are you available for work?
	Are you able to meet our attendance requirements and get to work on time?
	What kind of job duties are you interested in?
	Why do you believe you are qualified for this job?
	What do you think would be important for the job for which you are applying?
	We will make a reference check. What will your previous supervisor will say about you?
	Are you currently using drugs illegally?

The interviewer should review the questions asked on the employment application with the applicant to ensure accuracy and to answer any questions the applicant may have about the job.

After the interview: some simple steps

The period after an interview is important for forming a conclusion about the applicant's fitness for the job. These few steps will improve things:

■ **Document thoughts and comments immediately after the interview.** Don't let any time pass and take a few minutes to write down impressions of the applicant, particularly in areas deemed important to filling the position.

> **NOTE** — Write these notes on a separate piece of paper, not on the application and do not include references to age, race, gender, disability or similar factors. Even if the company doesn't discriminate, having these references in the file is damaging.

■ **Check references given by the applicant.** Remember that applicants normally provide only the names of favorable references, so use the reference-checking process to go beyond the applicant's list. You might, for example, ask a listed reference for the name of someone else who worked closely with the applicant.

RECORD KEEPING REQUIREMENTS

In addition to payroll records, employers must also maintain separate and confidential files for various types of employee information. There really are three separate files, and employees have differing rights to the three.

■ **Medical records.** This consists of all papers, documents and reports prepared by a physician, psychiatrist or psychologist that are in the possession of an employer and are work-related or upon which such employer relies to make any employment-related decision. Connecticut law requires that medical records be kept for at least one year after an employee leaves.

■ **Security Files.** These files include memoranda, documents or collections of information relating to the investigation of losses, misconduct, or suspected crimes, and investigative information maintained under government requirements, provided such memoranda, documents or information are maintained separately and not used to determine an employee's eligibility for employment, promotion, additional compensation, transfer, termination, disciplinary, or other adverse personnel action.

■ **Personnel Files.** Under the Connecticut Personnel File Act, a "personnel file" includes papers, documents, and reports pertaining to an employee that are used or have been used by an employer to determine such employee's eligibility for employment, promotion, additional compensation, transfer, termination, disciplinary or other adverse personnel action including employee evaluations or reports relating to such employee's character, credit and work habits.

A "personnel file" does not mean stock option or management bonus plan records, medical records, letters of reference or recommendations from third parties including former employers, materials used by the employer to plan for future operations, information contained in separately maintained security files, test information (the disclosure of which would invalidate the test), or documents that are being developed or prepared for use in civil, criminal or grievance procedures.

The distinction is important, because of legal requirements. Federal and state law both require that medical records be kept in confidential files, separate and apart from a personnel file. State law requires that medical records be kept for at least one year after termination of employment. In addition, Connecticut law gives employees the right to access to their personnel files, but not to the other two files.

Employee access to personnel files

Anyone currently or formerly employed, including people in managerial positions, must be permitted to inspect their personnel file within a reasonable time after making a written request to the employer. The inspection must be during regular business hours at a location at or reasonably near the employee's place of employment.

 The employer must keep the personnel file for at least one year after the end of the employee's employment.

Retaining files on premises

The employer may require that inspection of personnel files or medical records take place on the company's premises in the presence of a company official.

Removal or correction of information

If an employee disagrees with any of the information contained in a file or record, removal or correction may be agreed upon by the employer and the employee. If the employer and employee cannot agree, the employee may submit a written position statement, that the employer must keep permanently in the file.

Disclosure to third parties

Individually identifiable information contained in the personnel file or medical records of employees cannot be disclosed by the employer to anyone not employed by or affiliated with the employer without the written authorization of the employee except:

- Dates of employment.
- Employee's title or position.
- Wage or salary.

Disclosure may also be made:

- To a third party that maintains or prepares employment records or performs other employment related services for the employer.
- To a lawfully issued administrative summons or judicial order, including a subpoena.
- To a request by a law enforcement agency for an employee's home address and dates of attendance at work.
- For a medical emergency or to advise an employee's physician of a medical condition of which the employee may not be aware.

- To comply with federal, state, or local laws and regulations.
- Under the terms of a collective bargaining agreement.

PAYROLL DECISIONS AND POLICIES

When setting up the payroll system, make it work for you by incorporating as many elements into the process as possible. Some questions you might ask are: should you pay weekly or get DOL permission for bi-weekly, semi-monthly or monthly; will it be best to process the payroll in house or use an outside service; would you and your employees benefit by using electronic funds transfer thereby reducing costs and errors?

Policies about hours - regular and overtime - and salaried versus non-salaried employees depend on whether an employee is considered *exempt* or *non-exempt* from the Federal Fair Labor Standards Act and Connecticut Wage laws. These laws determine minimum and overtime wages based on employees' duties and responsibilities. *As we go to press, Congress is planning a major change to this law which may become effective soon.*

Determining exempt status

To determine whether an employee is exempt from overtime provisions, employers should carefully examine the job duties of each employee whom it believes is exempt. An experienced, highly-paid employee may appear to be a supervisor, but might lack the authority to exercise independent judgment and discretion in decisions about hiring, firing, evaluations, imposition of discipline, etc.

> **NOTE** — The titles we use and the importance we place on employees' job roles can help us walk into a trap. Take group leaders. They're valuable employees, who may attend management meetings. However, these employees often do not truly supervise two or more full-time employees or fit within any of the exemptions and thus may fail to meet the requirements to be considered exempt from overtime.

There are four groups of employees who are exempt from wage and hour laws:
- Executive employees.
- Professional employees.
- Administrative employees.
- Outside salespeople.

Anybody else is non-exempt and must be paid overtime and receive the other benefits of the wage and hour laws.

Executive exemption

An executive employee must be paid a salary of at least $155 per week and meet the following criteria:
- Primary duty to manage a company, branch, division or department.
- Regularly directs the work of two or more full-time employees, or equivalent.
- Has authority to hire or fire or recommend hiring, firing, promotion, or similar actions.
- Regularly exercises independent judgment and discretion.
- Devotes over 80% of time to above functions. Can be 60% in service or retail companies.

If the employee earns $250.00 or more per week, only the first two requirements apply.

Professional exemption

A professional employee is one who earns $170 a week and:

- Performs work requiring advanced knowledge or does original and creative artistic work or teaches in an educational institution.
- Regularly exercises independent judgment and discretion.
- Does work that is intellectual and varied and where the output rate can't be standardized.
- Devotes over 80% of time to above functions.

If the employee earns $250.00 or more per week, only the first two requirements apply. The salary level doesn't apply at all to lawyers, doctors, medical interns or teachers.

Computer systems professionals fall into a gray exemption area. Those who work as highly skilled jobs with computer software are normally exempt, while those who work operating or repairing hardware are normally not exempt. A computer professional who earns at least $27.63 per hour is normally exempt.

Administrative exemption

An administrative employee is one who is paid a salary of at least $155 per week and:

- Does office or non-manual work to implement management policies or the company's general business operations.
- Regularly exercises discretion and independent judgment.
- Is either an executive or administrative assistant to a top executive or a staff employee with specialized skills who does specialized work under only general supervision.
- Devotes over 80% of time to above functions.

If the employee earns $250.00 or more per week, only the first two requirements apply.

 NOTE Job titles can be misleading. Some secretaries who do mainly secretarial work are called *administrative assistants*, but they aren't exempt employees unless they meet the exemption requirements.

Outside salespersons exemption

An outside salesperson is one who regularly works away from the employer's office:

- Making sales.
- Obtaining orders or contracts.
- Devotes over 80% of time to above functions.

Salary payments

Each of the exemption categories requires the employee be paid a salary. This means they must receive their regular salary even though they sometimes work less than 40 hours in a work week. Deductions are permitted under federal law only if the employee:

- Is absent for a day or more due to personal reasons other than illness.
- Is absent due to illness and receives sick pay instead of salary.
- Takes Family and Medical Leave Act leave.

WAGE PAYMENT LAWS

These statutes are separate from the minimum wage and overtime laws and apply to all employees, regardless of position or exemption status. All nonexempt employees must be paid at least minimum wage.

Minimum wage

The Connecticut minimum wage is set at least at ½% higher than the federal rate:

January 1, 2003	$6.90
January 1, 2004	$7.10
January 1, 2005 and later	www.ctdol.state.ct.us

Payday

Payday must be every week no more than eight days after the end of the pay period. Employers may have other paydays, such as biweekly, but they must have permission from the Department of Regulation of Wages. There are three other rules for payday:

- If the payday falls on a holiday, employee must be paid preceding work day.
- All money due on pay day must be paid; no hold back is allowed.
- Payment must be cash or check, or, if employee requests, direct deposit.

 Direct payroll deposit is an inexpensive, convenient employee benefit. Just make it automatic for each employee at hiring time. The payroll service provides the form.

Payment upon termination

An employee who quits or is laid off must be paid in full on the next regularly scheduled pay day, but an employee who is fired must be paid in full before the next business day.

Disputed wages

If there is a question over the amount of wages due, the employer must pay all wages conceded to be due. Paying this amount doesn't affect the employee's rights to further payments, and the employer can't ask the employee to sign a waiver of further wages.

Allowable deductions

The employer may make deductions from employee paychecks only in two situations:

- Those required or authorized by law, such as child support, income tax and FICA.
- Those the employee has consented to, such as medical insurance and savings.

Employment information notification

The employer must notify the employee, at the time of hire, the pay rate, payday, working hours, sick day policy, vacation policy, and fringe benefits policy.

- The employer must also notify employees in writing of changes in this information.

■   An employer's failure to document this information leaves the employer vulnerable to the interpretation of the Courts or the Department of Labor.

Fringe benefits upon termination of employment

The only legally required fringe benefit is the continuation of medical insurance by IRS COBRA regulations. Others, such as severance pay or unused fringe benefits, aren't required but if the employer has a practice of making these payments, it must do so according to the policy.

 It's best to be consistent about payments to former employees, because past practices become company policy that has to be followed in the future.

Pay stubs

The pay stub must list the hours worked, straight time wage, overtime wage, itemized deductions, and net earnings. For exempt employees, hours worked, straight and overtime wages may be omitted.

Tips

The restaurant and hotel industries must follow special rules covering tips and the minimum wage. The payroll service handles the computations automatically and is the best source for timely information on rules and procedures.

Paying overtime to non-exempt employees

Non-exempt employees must receive overtime pay for all hours worked beyond 40 hours in any work week, regardless of whether the employee received approval to work overtime.

■   **Work week.** A work week is any seven consecutive day period, which doesn't have to match the calendar week. Once an employer determines the work week, it may not be changed in order to minimize the payment of overtime.

■   **Overtime pay.** Overtime is paid at 1½ times the employee's regular rate of pay. The regular rate of pay is determined by calculating all compensation paid to the employee in the work week, then dividing that amount by the actual number of hours worked.

The regular rate does not include expense reimbursements, sick pay, holiday pay, vacation pay, fringe benefits, shift differentials and similar non-work payments. It does include production bonuses.

■   **Daily overtime.** Daily overtime is not required. If an employee works two hours overtime one day and two hours less another day within the work week, no overtime is due.

■   **Averaging work weeks.** An employer *cannot* average two work weeks in determining whether an employee is due overtime pay. For example, an employee who works 35 hours one week and 45 hours the next week must be paid overtime for the second week.

■   **Compensatory time off:** Comp time, where an employee receives time off in exchange for overtime, is forbidden unless it is given during the work week.

EMPLOYEE VERSUS INDEPENDENT CONTRACTOR

One important aspect of managing a payroll is determining whether a worker is classified as an employee or an independent contractor. Making the determination of whether an individual is an employee or an independent contractor is a question of fact that rests primarily on the amount of direction and control that an employer has the right to exercise over a worker. This distinction affects an employer's tax payments:

■ If an employer-employee relationship exists, the employer must withhold federal and state income, and FICA tax, pay federal and state unemployment taxes and meet federal and state requirements on wages and hours.

■ If the worker is an independent contractor, the employer is relieved of all tax responsibilities. The worker is responsible for all taxes. In addition, the company does not have to pay workers' compensation and other employee benefits costs.

By definition, an employee is one who is paid to work under the control and direction of the company. The right of a company to exercise direction and control is sufficient to establish an employee/employer relationship. Direction and control means the employer's right to determine what work is done as well as how it is done. An independent contractor is someone typically hired to do a specific job and the one doing the hiring has no right to control the manner in which the job is done. The independent contractor is generally paid a lump sum after the job is completed.

The employer should make a careful analysis to ensure the correct classification of all workers. It might be tempting to classify employees as independent contractors to save on taxes. But, if they are later found to be employees, the employer faces severe penalties and interest and may have to use company funds to pay taxes that could have been withheld from employees' wages. Further, if a worker is not included with those covered by workers' compensation, the employer risks a costly lawsuit.

If an employer unintentionally disregards the withholding requirements for an employee, the penalty rate is 20% of the original tax due and the original tax must be paid as well. If the withholding rules are intentionally disregarded, the penalty rates are doubled. In addition, state and federal unemployment taxes would also be collected along with the penalties and interest assessed on those amounts.

The Internal Revenue Service has established "common-law" guidelines to be used in determining the status of workers. Below are the factors the IRS takes into consideration in determining the relationship of a worker to the company. The factors are somewhat subjective, but if several of them apply, the worker could be considered to be an employee and not an independent contractor.

The IRS has a procedure for determining, in advance, whether a worker is an employee or independent contractor. The company can get this determination by filing Form SS-8, which asks for the details of the worker's relationship to the company.

IRS guidelines to determine employee or contractor status

1.   The worker must comply with instructions on when, where and/or how a job must be done.
2.   The worker is subject to periodic training.
3.   The services of the worker are adapted to the continuing operation of the business.
4.   Services are rendered personally by the worker, and thus do not permit substitute labor.
5.   If the worker has the capacity to hire, supervise and pay others at the employer's direction the employee is considered to be acting as a representative of the company.
6.   The worker enjoys a continuing relationship with the employer indicating a permanent relationship.
7.   The worker has set hours to perform a job thus limiting freedom to come and go.
8.   The worker is full time.
9.   The worker performs the job on the employer's premises.
10.   Services are performed according to a sequence set by the employer.
11.   The worker is expected to submit periodic oral or written reports.
12.   Payment is made by the hour, week or month rather than by a lump sum for a job.
13.   The worker is reimbursed for travel and business expenses.
14.   Tools and materials necessary to complete the job are furnished by the employer.
15.   The worker does not maintain a substantial investment in the employer's premises.
16.   The worker does not realize a personal profit or loss from the performance of the job.
17.   The worker does not work for more than one firm at a time.
18.   The worker's services are not available to the general public or other employers.
19.   The employer has the right to fire the worker.
20.   The employer does not have the right to terminate the relationship without incurring a liability.

Connecticut also uses an *ABC test* to determine if there is an employment relationship for unemployment compensation Under the ABC test, *any* service provided by a worker is considered employment, unless the following apply:

A.   The employer does not provide control or direction to the worker.

B.   The work performed is not an integral part of the employer's business or is not performed at the employer's place of business. For example, in a machine shop, roof repair could be done by an independent contractor, but machining could not. However, machining done off-location could be independent contractor work.

C.   The worker normally provides the service as a self-employed person.

EMPLOYING MINORS

Persons under eighteen years old are permitted to work, but with restrictions on maximum hours, and excluding some industries. Generally, a minor may not work:

- More than 6 hours during a regularly scheduled school day, unless the day is followed by a non-school day.
- More than 8 hours on non-school days.
- More than 32 hours per calendar week when school is in session.
- More than 48 hours when school is not in session.

However, there are different restrictions for several industries. In addition, every employer who employs someone under 18 years old must obtain a certificate of age and keep it on file at the place of employment. The age certificate is provided by the employee's school administration under Connecticut Department of Education rules.

The Fair Labor Standards Act permits parents to employ their own children, regardless of age, directly and exclusively. The Act does not apply to family owned businesses or to any other relative and allows employment in any occupation except ones involving manufacturing, mining or the use of power equipment or machinery. In addition, a child so employed is exempt from Social Security and other employment taxes.

NOTE — So as a sole proprietor, you could employ a son or daughter and pay the child up to the standard deduction amount. The money would be a tax deduction for the business but totally tax-free income for the child! You could even pay up to $2,000 more than the standard deduction and make an IRA contribution on the child's behalf. Of course, you should provide your child with either a 1099 or a W-2 and the child has to file an income tax return even though there is no liability for taxes.

CONCLUSION

Although this chapter discusses various laws about employment issues in Connecticut, employers must be aware that laws can, and often do change. Therefore, before implementing or changing any policy, it is important to be sure that policy changes comply with all current federal, state and local laws. The information provided here is intended as an educational tool and should only be used as a stepping off point, from which employers must make their own policy decisions and seek appropriate advice.

Appendix

Time and hour restrictions for minor children

The following summary of Department of Labor rules is intended only for general guidance. The full rules are available on the DOL's Web site www.ctdol.state.ct.us./wgwkstnd/wgminors.htm or in the law, which is available from the address listed in the Web site.

16 & 17 year-old students during school weeks

- General rule for Monday to Thursday: May work between the hours of 6AM and 10PM, 6 hours per day, 32 hours per week.
- General rule for Friday to Sunday: May work between the hours of 6AM and 10PM, 8 hours per day.
- Exceptions: may work until a later time in the restaurant, recreational, amusement, theater retail, mercantile industries, and may work later during school vacations.

16 & 17 year-old students during non-school weeks

- May work 8 hours per day, 48 hours per week, 6 days per week.

16 and 17 year old non-students

- May work 9 hours per day, 48 hours per week, 6 days per week.

14 and 15 year-olds' working hours

- Work day throughout the year: may work between the hours of 7AM and 7PM.
- Work day from July 1 to Labor Day: may work between the hours of 7AM and 9PM.
- Work hours on school days: 3 hours
- Work hours on non-school days: 8 hours
- Work week in school weeks: 18 hours
- Work week in non-school weeks: 40 hours

14 & 15 yr. old's Permitted employment*	14 & 15 yr. old's Prohibited employment
Agriculture	Restaurant/food service
Street trades, e.g., news delivery, baby-sitting	Recreational establishments
Hospitals**	Manufacturing industries
Convalescent homes**	Mechanical/service industries
Hotels and motels**	Mercantile/solicitation
Banks	Theatrical industry
Insurance companies	Barber shops
Professional offices, e.g., lawyers, CPAs	Businesses not listed as permitted employment
Municipalities, e.g. library, recreation.	
Golf caddies.	
Acting.	
Household chores for private homeowners	

*15 year-olds only may be employed in retail/mercantile establishments, as baggers, cashiers, or stock clerks during non-school weeks only. Working papers are required.

** No food service or laundry work allowed

INTRODUCTION

Tax planning is an important part of every company's business planning. There are two goals we are trying to achieve when doing tax planning: pay the lowest possible legal amount of taxes and make sure the tax plan we decide on doesn't change our overall business plans and goals. The first step in tax planning is to select the best form of business organization from the many options currently available. The next step is to understand applicable tax laws and regulations, and to consider the tax results of business decisions. The third step is to keep good business records.

This chapter covers the second step: tax laws and regulations, and tax results. The tax consequences of many business actions depend on the form of business organization: Sole Proprietorship, Partnership, Limited Liability Company or Partnership, Single-Member Limited Liability Company, "S" Corporation or "C" Corporation. Therefore, the chapter was designed to be read selectively. This way, readers can review all of the materials pertaining to their form of business organization in one place and do not have to read through the discussion of other types of organization.

ORGANIZATION OF CHAPTER

This chapter discusses the following topics:

- Taxation procedures and implications for each of the major business types: sole proprietorships, single-member limited liability companies, partnerships, limited liability partnerships, limited liability companies, "C" corporations and "S" corporations.
- Calculating net income.
- Tax computation, credits and other taxes.
- Estimated taxes.
- Tax traps for business owners.

The chapter discusses the way in which the different business entities are structured. So, before reading the chapter, you may find it helpful to review the material in the chapter entitled *Choosing the Right Legal Organization*. In that chapter, we discuss the legal differences and in this chapter, we discuss the differences in how profits are taxed, how money can be taken out of the business by the owners and provide some pointers to keep in mind.

The last part of the chapter contains two important sections. One describes important tax writeoffs and how to take advantage of them. The other lists tax traps: things that can trip up owners of small companies.

SOLE PROPRIETORSHIPS AND SMLLCs

Net income taxed at individual level
The *net income* of a sole proprietorship or an SMLLC is directly included in the individual federal income tax return of its owner. The gross income and allowable deductions are shown on Schedule C (Form 1040), Profit or Loss from Business. Once the net income has been computed on Schedule C, it is included with the owner's other tax information (i.e., wages, interest, etc.) to determine the owner's tax liability.

Assets of a sole proprietorship
A sole proprietorship has no legal existence apart from its owner. As a result, each asset or liability of a sole proprietorship is treated as a separate business asset or liability of the individual owner.

Withdrawals from a sole proprietorship
If a business operates as a sole proprietorship, the owner doesn't receive a salary, so no federal income tax is withheld when the owner takes money out of the business. Instead, the owner takes a *draw*. The company sets up a *drawing account* on its books to keep track of the money the owner takes out. This account should identify money withdrawn for personal use or used to pay personal expenses, to separate it from money paid for business expenses.

> **NOTE** There is no tax affect when the owner transfers money into, or out of, a sole proprietorship because the draw is not considered a deductible expense in calculating the net income. Whether the owner withdraws the money or leaves it in the business, tax is based on the business' income.

Because there is no tax withholding from draws, the owner must be sure to make quarterly estimated tax payments to both the Internal Revenue Service and the Connecticut Department of Revenue Services. These are discussed below under *Estimated Taxes*.

Federal self-employment taxes
A sole proprietor whose income from self-employment totals $400 or more must pay *self-employment tax* in addition to regular income tax. Proprietors do not have to pay social security tax, so the self-employment tax is the proprietor's version of Social Security. Thus, the rate is linked to the Social Security tax rate. The tax is figured on Schedule SE (Form 1040), Self-Employment Tax. Sole proprietors can deduct half of this self-employment tax on their personal income tax return - Form 1040, page 1.

State income taxes

A sole proprietor's taxable business income for State of Connecticut tax purposes is generally the same as the federal income. This amount is reported on Form CT-1040, Connecticut Individual Income Tax Return, and is included with the proprietor's other income, such as wages, interest and dividends, just like the federal Form 1040. If the proprietor loses money for the year, that loss can be offset against the proprietor's other income. Connecticut does not have a separate self-employment tax, but, like the IRS, it requires proprietors to make estimated tax payments, discussed later in the chapter.

The following summarizes the proprietor's income tax obligations. In addition, the sole proprietor must collect and pay the same payroll, excise and sales taxes as any other business owner.

Income tax checklist for a sole proprietorship		
Type of tax	**Form required**	**Due date**
Federal taxes:		
Income Tax	Schedule C (Form 1040)	Same as Form 1040 (April 15th for calendar year individuals).
Self-Employment Tax	Schedule SE (Form 1040)	Same as Form 1040.
Estimated Tax	1040-ES	15th day of 4th, 6th and 9th months of tax years and 15th day of 1st month after the end of tax year.
State taxes:		
Income Tax	CT-1040	Same as federal.
Self-Employment Tax	Not applicable	Not applicable.
Estimated Tax	CT-1040ES	Same as federal.
Business Entity Tax	OP-424	SMLLC's only

PARTNERSHIPS, LPs, LLPs AND LLCs
Not a taxable entity - net income taxed at partner level

A partnership is not a taxable entity. A separate U.S. Partnership Return of Income (Form 1065) is filed, but no tax is paid. The information from this return is used by the partners to prepare their personal tax returns. Thus, each partner's share of partnership net income (or loss) is taxed at the individual level. The following table summarizes the partnership's tax obligations.

Income tax checklist for a partnership, LP, LLP or LLC		
Type of tax	**Form required**	**Due date**
Federal taxes:		
Income Tax	Partner reports share of partnership income on Form 1040.	Same as Form 1040. (April 15th for calendar year individuals)
Self-Employment Tax	Partner reports share of partnership income subject to self employment tax on Schedule SE (Form 1040).	Same as Form 1040.
Estimated Tax	Partner includes partnership income in calculating estimated tax payment requirement on 1040-ES.	15th day of 4th, 6th, and 9th months of tax year, and 15th day of 1st month after the end of tax year. (April 15, June 15, September 15 and January 15 for calendar year partnerships.)
Annual Return of Income	Partnership files Form 1065.	15th day of the 4th month after end of tax year. (April 15 for calendar year partnerships.)
Tax Information to Partners	Schedule K-1	Same as Form 1065.
State taxes:		
Income Tax	Partner reports share of partnership income on Form CT-1040.	Same as federal.
Self Employment Tax	Not applicable.	Not applicable.
Estimated Tax	Partner includes partnership income in calculating estimated tax payment requirement on CT-1040ES.	Same as federal.
Annual Return of Income	Partnership files Form CT-1065.	Same as federal.
Business Entity Tax	OP-424	Same as federal

Allocation of net income to partners

In determining their individual income tax liability for a year, partners must include their share of partnership income, whether or not it is actually paid out to them. This income is reported to the partners on Schedule K-1.

A partner's distributive share of partnership income is normally computed as described in the partnership agreement. The tax rules for this allocation of partnership income are extremely complex but for most small business partnerships, the income is divided by predefined shares. If there is an ownership change during a tax year, the income has to be apportioned accordingly.

Self-employment tax

A partner's share of partnership income is generally considered self-employment income. As a result, most partners pay self-employment taxes on their share of partnership income if their total net earnings from self-employment is $400 or more. Partners do not pay social security tax; the self-employment tax is the partner's version of Social Security. Thus, the rate is linked to the Social Security tax rate. The tax is figured on Schedule SE (Form 1040), Self-Employment Tax. Partners can deduct half of this self-employment tax on their personal income tax return-Form 1040, page1.

Assets of a partnership

Generally, neither the partners nor the partnership recognize gain or loss when assets are contributed to a partnership. This general rule applies whether the partnership is just being formed or is already operating. Once assets have been contributed to a partnership, they are considered partnership assets for federal income tax purposes, as well as for most other purposes.

Partner's basis in a partnership

Partners must keep track of their *basis* in a partnership for several reasons. One reason is that the *basis* represents the limit of partnership losses that partners may deduct on a personal tax returns. Another is that a partner must pay capital gains tax on any distribution of property that exceeds the partner's *basis*.

> **NOTE** — The Basis is the amount, for tax purposes, that something costs. Generally, if a partner contributes property other than cash to a partnership, the partnership's basis in that property is the same as the partner's basis in the property. The partnership then uses this basis in its accounting records for figuring depreciation and capital gains.

A partner's original basis in a partnership equals the money and the basis of property the partner contributes to the partnership. The partner's basis is then increased by any partnership liabilities the partner assumes and decreased by any of the partner's personal liabilities assumed by the partnership. After the partnership begins operating, the partner's basis is continually adjusted.

The original basis is increased by:

- Additional contributions to the partnership.
- The partner's share of partnership income and gains (whether taxable or not).
- An increase in the partner's share of partnership liabilities.

The original basis is decreased (but not below zero) by:

- Money and property distributed to the partner.
- The partner's share of partnership losses and deductions (whether deductible or not).
- A decrease in the partner's share of partnership liabilities.

Once a partner's basis has been reduced to zero, any remaining or additional partnership losses are postponed until such time as the partner has enough basis to absorb them.

Withdrawals from a partnership

When a partner withdraws cash from a partnership, there is no taxable gain unless the withdrawal exceeds the partner's basis in the partnership. Partners withdrawals of their original investments normally aren't taxable. Neither is withdrawal of the current year's income, even if the withdrawal takes place earlier in the year than the income is actually earned.

> **NOTE** — If a partnership distributes property other than cash (or securities) to a partner, there is generally no gain or loss to either the partner or the partnership. Instead, the partner takes the property with the same basis that the partnership had in the property, but not exceeding the partner's basis in the partnership.

State income taxes

Connecticut also taxes a partner's share of partnership net income at the partner level. The amount taxable is usually the same amount as reported on the partner's federal return. This amount is reported on Form CT-1040, Connecticut Individual Income Tax Return. Individual partners must make estimated tax payments throughout the year on Form CT-1040ES.

Connecticut, like the IRS, requires a partnership information form. This Form, CT-1065, reports financial and partner information but requires no tax payment, because the partners include the income on their personal returns.

LLPs and LLCs

We include these two types of business in the partnership category because they are treated the same as a partnership. LLCs and LLPs can be the ideal form of business for many family, startup and entrepreneurial businesses. Either of these should afford the same degree of legal protection as a corporation. If they have at least two owners, these entities are taxed as partnerships; using the same forms (Federal Form 1065 and Connecticut Form CT-1065) and taxed at the individual level only, not the entity level.

Although LLCs appear favorable on the surface there is a trap for the unwary. You should be aware that an LLC or LLP can elect to be taxed as a corporation. The election is a simple one, made on the tax form. When that happens, some of the undesirable things about a corporation, such as double taxation, kick in.

 An LLC or LLP, if not properly set up, could end up being taxed as a corporation, so it is a good idea to seek professional advice before making any final decision.

Also, as with a conventional partnership, the LLC or LLP can face termination (for tax purposes) if it finds itself with only one owner.

"C" CORPORATIONS

Net income taxed at corporate level

The net income of a "C" corporation is taxed at the corporate level. This is because a corporation is considered a separate entity for federal income tax purposes. A Corporation files a federal income tax return annually on either Form 1120, U.S. Corporation Income Tax Return, or Form 1120-A, U.S. Corporation Short Form Income Tax Return.

Like a sole proprietorship or partnership, a corporation's net income equals its gross income less allowable deductions. However, "C" corporations are entitled to special deductions that other forms of business do not receive. These include a deduction for dividends received from other corporations and deductions for the owners' medical insurance and pension contribution.

The following table is a summary of the "C" corporation's tax obligations.

Income tax checklist for a "C" corporation		
Type of tax	**Form required**	**Due date**
Federal taxes:		
Income Tax	Form 1120 or 1120A	15th day of 3rd month after end of tax year.
Estimated Tax	(Deposits made with commercial bank or electronically)	15th day of 4th, 6th, 9th and 12th months of tax year.
State taxes:		
Income Tax	Form CT-1120	1st day of the 4th month after end of tax year.
Estimated Tax	Forms CT-1120 ESA, ESB, ESC, ESD.	15th day of 3rd, 6th, 9th and 12th months of tax year.

Assets of a corporation

If a shareholder contributes assets to a corporation, the transaction usually doesn't create a tax gain or loss to the shareholder or the corporation. Once assets have been contributed to a corporation they are considered corporate assets for federal income tax and all other purposes.

If a shareholder contributes property other than cash to a corporation, the corporation values the property at the shareholder's basis, regardless of the property's market value. The corporation then uses that basis for figuring depreciation and gain or loss on the sale of that asset.

Withdrawals from corporations - double tax

If a corporation distributes either cash or property to the shareholders, this is usually considered a dividend, and the shareholder pays tax on the current value of this dividend. However, the dividend is not tax deductible for the corporation. *The corporation and the shareholder both pay tax on the same income.*

Not all distributions from corporations are taxable dividends. A corporation can make a *return of capital* distribution to shareholders. This occurs when the corporation has distributed all of its accumulated earnings and then makes another distribution. That distribution is considered a return of the shareholders' original capital in the corporation. A return of capital is not taxable unless it exceeds the shareholder's current basis in this stock.

 Distributions of property, returns of capital and complete liquidation of a corporation can pose federal income tax problems. In these complex situations the advice of a tax professional is needed.

Status as shareholder/employee

Because a corporation is a separate legal and taxable entity, a shareholder who works in the corporation is an employee, and cannot take *draws* as a proprietor or partner would. Therefore, payments to a shareholder for services are considered wages, and the company must withhold and pay all normal employment taxes from these wages.

State income taxes

Unlike sole proprietorships or partnerships, corporations are treated - and taxed - by Connecticut as separate entities. This tax is normally figured on net income, but there are three possible taxes: income tax, capital tax or minimum tax. A Connecticut corporation figures its tax all three ways and pays the highest of the three.

Tax on net income

The starting point for determining the Connecticut income tax is federal taxable income. Specific adjustments are then made to either increase or decrease this amount. Once federal taxable income has been determined, the following adjustments are made to arrive at state taxable income:

- Additions include:
  - Interest income exempt from federal tax.
  - State income taxes.
  - Federal operating loss carry over.
  -
- Deductions include:
  - Dividends received from other corporations.
  - Capital loss carry over.
  - State operating loss carry over.

The state tax on this net income is figured at a flat rate. There are two adjustments to this tax. One applies to corporations that do business in other states. These corporations adjust their tax for profits that are taxed by other states. See *Doing Business in More Than One State* for more information. Another adjustment is for state tax credits, such as those for job development. See *State Tax Incentives* for more information.

Tax on capital

The tax on capital is a tax on the average equity of the corporation. The tax is computed by multiplying the average amount of this stockholders' equity by a flat tax rate. The tax rate is quite low, so the tax applies mainly to large corporations.

Minimum tax

Connecticut charges a minimum tax of $300 even if the corporation has no taxable income.

"S" CORPORATIONS

Requirements of an "S" corporation

An "S" corporation is a regular corporation that elects to be taxed in a manner similar to a partnership. This means the corporation will generally not pay any federal income tax, the income is taxed to the individual shareholders. An "S" Corporation is formed the same way as a regular "C" corporation, and has the same legal protection and legal requirements. A corporation qualifies to be an "S" corporation by meeting several requirements. It must:

- Be a corporation organized in the United States.
- Have only one class of stock (although some can be voting and some non-voting).

- Have no more than 75 shareholders, and all must consent to "S" Corporation status.
- Have only individuals, estates, allowable trusts and tax exempt entities as shareholders.
- Have shareholders who are citizens or residents of the US.
- File a timely election with Form 2553 to be taxed as an "S" Corporation.

Net income taxed at shareholder level

As mentioned above, an "S" corporation is generally not a taxable entity. It files a separate U.S. Income Tax Return for an "S" corporation (Form 1120SI), but in most cases it pays no tax to the IRS. Instead, the shareholders pay personal income tax on their pro-rata share of "S" corporation taxable income. Each shareholder receives a Schedule K-1 which lists their share of "S" corporation taxable income. This income is taxable even if the shareholder doesn't receive it. A shareholder's share of "S" corporation income is figured on ownership percentage. If there is an ownership change, the percentage is adjusted.

The following table is a summary of income tax requirements for an "S" corporation.

Income tax checklist for an "S" corporation		
Type of tax	**Form required**	**Due date**
Federal taxes:		
Income Tax	Form 1120S	15th day of 3rd month after end of tax year.
Estimated Tax	Shareholder includes "S" corporation income in calculating estimated tax payment requirements on 1040-ES	15th day of 4th, 6th, and 9th months of tax year, and 15th day of 1st month after the end of tax year.
Tax Information to Shaareholders	Schedule K-1	Same as for 1120S
State income taxes		
Income Tax	Form CT-1120SI	First day of 4th month after end of tax year.
Business Entity Tax	OP-424	Same as CT-1120S

Assets of an "S" corporation

If a shareholder contributes assets to an "S" corporation, the transaction usually doesn't create a tax gain or loss to either the shareholder or the corporation. Once assets have been contributed to a corporation they are considered corporate assets for federal income tax and all other purposes.

If a shareholder contributes property other than cash to an "S" corporation, the corporation values the property at the shareholder's basis, regardless of the property's current fair market value. The corporation then uses that basis for figuring depreciation and gain of loss on the sale of that asset.

Shareholder's basis in an "S" Corporation

Basis rules, similar to those for partnerships, apply to "S" corporations. These rules play a significant role in determining whether a shareholder can deduct "S" corporation losses. They are also instrumental in determining whether distributions from an "S" corporation are taxable as either dividend income or capital gain, or constitute a tax-free return of capital. Rules similar to the rules for calculating a partner's basis are generally applicable to "S" corporations. However, only amounts loaned to the "S" corporation directly by the shareholder, rather than that person's share of the "S" corporations liabilities, will increase the shareholder's basis.

Withdrawals from "S" Corporations

A principal benefit of electing to be an "S" corporation, is the avoidance of the "double tax" that applies to regular corporations. "S" corporation shareholders are taxed on their shares of income earned by the "S" corporation, whether or not distributions are made. If the "S" corporation makes a distribution to its shareholders, the distribution is generally tax free.

State income taxes

Connecticut "S" Corporations receive the same special treatment allowed under federal tax law. The exceptions are those items separately stated for federal purposes such as dividends, rental income, capital gains and charitable contributions; these are passed directly to the "S" corporation shareholders, who report them on their personal income tax returns. Connecticut tax laws were recently changed, so that eventually Connecticut will treat "S" Corporations in the same manner as federal tax laws.

NOTE — We are currently in the midst of a "phase-out" of the previous Connecticut "S" Corporation tax structure. A portion of Connecticut "S" Corporation income is subject to taxation, which is calculated at the same rate as Connecticut "C" Corporations, and the balance passes through to the individual.

Finally, Connecticut "S" Corporations are entitled to many of the same state tax credits as Connecticut "C" Corporations, on the portion of their taxable income that is subject to Connecticut taxation. See the discussion of State tax credits for further details.

An "S" corporation uses Form CT-1120SI to report the tax liability of its owners. Otherwise, the same adjustments, tax rates, compliance procedures and other rules for "C" corporations apply to "S" corporations. A full explanation can be found in the "C" Corporation section.

CALCULATING TAXABLE INCOME

The first step in calculating a company's net income is to compute gross income. Gross income includes any income received in the operation of a trade or business, such as income from the sale of products or services. It also includes interest, dividends or rents that the company receives. Gross income can be received in cash, property, or services.

Bartering has become increasingly popular in recent years. Bartering is the trading of one company's products or services for the property or services of another company. Income from Bartering is included in the calculation of the gross income.

Allowable deductions

The company deducts the expenses that are allowed under the tax laws from the gross income. This does not include *all* the company's expenses, because some are disallowed, and some are only partly deductible.

General rules of deductibility

To be deductible, a business expense must be **ordinary** in the business and **necessary** for its operation.

- An ordinary expense is one that is common and accepted in the line of business.
- A necessary expense is one that is helpful and appropriate for the business.

All business expenses must first meet this test in order to be deductible. If an expense is partly for business and partly personal, the personal part must be separated from the business part, and only the business part is deductible. If a corporation tries to deduct the personal expenses of its owners, the payment can be characterized as a taxable dividends.

Meal and entertainment expenses

Generally, in order to deduct meals and entertainment expenses, the company must be able to show that these expenses are directly related to the business. Meal and entertainment expenses falling into one of the two categories discussed above are generally only 50 percent deductible provided they meet these tests

- Traveling away from home (whether eating alone or with others) on business.
- Entertaining business customers.
- Attending a business convention, reception, meeting or luncheon.

In order to deduct most travel, meal and entertainment expenses incurred, regardless of the nature of the expense, you must have proof of the expense such as a diary, an explanation of the business purpose and if the amount is over $75, a receipt.

Automobile expenses

The IRS rules for deducting expenses for business use of a car are very strict. Only business travel (not commuting to work) is allowed, and a car must be used more than 50% for business in order for expenses other than mileage to be deductible.

> **NOTE** *If* the car is used more than 50% for business, the owner is entitled to deduct reasonable operating costs, such as gas, garage rent, repairs, oil, licenses, tolls, lease fees, insurance, tires, parking fees, depreciation, car washes, and property taxes.

If a car is used for both business and personal purposes, the expenses are split between business and personal use. This may be done by keeping a log of business and personal mileage, and figuring a percentage split.

> **NOTE** Let's take an example. Say a machine repairer drives a car 30,000 miles during the year, 20,000 miles for business and 10,000 miles for personal use. The repairer can claim only 67% (20,000 ÷ 30,000) of the car's operating cost as a business expense.

An alternative to figuring actual expenses is the standard mileage rate, published by the IRS which can be found on the IRS website or from the IRS toll-free number. To use the standard mileage rate, the taxpayer must:

- Own the car;
- Not use the car for hire (i.e., as a taxi); or
- Not operate a fleet of cars using two or more at the same time.

The standard mileage rate may only be chosen the first year the car is used for business. If the standard rate isn't chosen in that first year, it can never be used for that car in any other year. As with other personal expenses, personal use of a company-owned car may constitute taxable income (either compensation as a taxable fringe benefit or dividend if a corporate shareholder) and may *still not be a deductible expense to the business.*

Interest expense

Interest expense for business is generally fully deductible, but the company must be able to prove that the money from the loan was used for a business purpose. If a business purpose can't be proved, the interest expense is classified as personal interest and isn't deductible.

> **NOTE** Interest incurred for investment purposes (including investment in business endeavors) is classified as "investment interest expense", and may be deductible, but is subject to special limitations. Any disallowed portion is carried over indefinitely and may be deductible in a later tax year.

Home office deductions

A home-based business can deduct some of the home expenses, generally limited to the net income of the business. To be entitled to a home office deduction, the owner must use the office *exclusively* and *regularly*:

- As the principal place of business. There are two ways to meet the "principle place of business" requirement: the statutory administrative/management activities test or the Supreme Court's comparative analysis test.

- As a place to meet or deal with patients, clients or customers in the normal course of business.

- In connection with the business if it is a separate structure that is not attached to the house.

Exclusive use means only for business. If the office is also used for personal activities, it does not meet the exclusive use test. However, this does not mean that an entire room must be completely business use, a portion of a room may qualify if used exclusively for business purposes.

Regular use means on a continuing basis. Occasional or incidental business use does not meet the regular use test even if the office is not used for personal purposes.

The expenses are either fully or partly deductible. If the company is losing money, some of the expenses are carried over until there is a profit.

Fully deductible	Expenses directly related to the business use of the home. These expenses may include business telephone and insurance costs, business supplies and equipment, and painting and repairs of areas used specifically for business.
Partly deductible	Expenses indirectly related to the business use of the home. These expenses include depreciation, utilities, repairs, maintenance, real estate taxes, insurance, rent, etc. To determine the deductible business expenses, multiply the total expense by the business percentage. The business percentage equals the area of the home used for business divided by the total area of the home. This area is expressed in square feet (SF). Thus, if the office has 100SF, the storage room is 50SF and the total house size is 2,000SF, the company can deduct 7½% of the house expenses (100+50÷2000=7.5%).

Travel expenses

Deductible travel expenses are ordinary and necessary expenses for travel away from home on business. This category does not include expenses that are for personal or vacation purposes. Examples of travel expenses include: airfare, meals and lodging, telephone expenses, etc. The fare paid for airplanes, trains, buses, taxis or other types of transportation is deductible. If the business trip is overnight or long enough to require rest, the cost of lodging is deductible. The cost of meals is also deductible, but only to the extent of 50% of the actual costs incurred.

NOTE — In lieu of maintaining substantiation of actual costs incurred for lodging, meals and incidentals, a taxpayer may use a standard "per diem" allowance. The IRS publishes annual tables providing these "per diem" amounts for various locations in the United States and abroad. Although the standard meal allowance relieves the burden of keeping records of actual meal expenses, records still must be kept to prove the time, place, and business purpose of the travel.

Equipment purchases and depreciation

Normally, equipment (or furniture, buildings, vehicles and similar assets that have useful lives of more than one year) can't be deducted as an expense in the year it is bought. There are two ways that these assets get deducted: depreciation and expensing.

Depreciation	A way of deducting the cost over several years. Each year, the company deducts the part of the original cost that *wears out* that year, based on the asset's estimated useful life. The useful life is defined by IRS rules. For example, if a machine costs $8,000 and has an 8-year useful life, the depreciation is $1,000 per year. There are depreciation methods, described in IRS publication 534, that produce even larger deductions.
Expensing	A company also can deduct the full cost of a limited amount of new assets every year. This expensing deduction is limited to a set amount each year and doesn't apply to real estate. Starting in 2003 the limit on new asset purchases qualifying for the expensing option is $100,000. Thus, a company could pay $4,000 for a new computer and deduct it right away. If the company loses money, there is a further limitation on this deduction; it must be carried over until the company shows a profit.

Employee expenses

Salaries, wages, and other forms of compensation to employees are generally deductible business expenses. There are four tests to determine whether payments to employees are deductible. The employees' pay must be:

- Paid or incurred for services performed on behalf of the business.
- Ordinary and necessary for the business.
- Reasonable in amount.

 NOTE The Internal Revenue Service looks closely at compensation paid to highly-paid employees, especially owners, partners, shareholders and officers to determine it meets the legal standard.

Medical benefits

Insurance premiums paid for health and accident insurance for employees are generally fully deductible, and employees don't have to pay tax on the benefits they receive. Employee group plans, however, must provide continuation coverage for specific time periods to employees and their beneficiaries if they quit, get fired, laid off, become disabled or die.

Sole proprietors, partners and more than 2% owners of "S" corporations can deduct the health insurance premiums paid to provide them, their spouse and dependent children with this medical coverage against ordinary income. This deduction is claimed on page 1 of their personal tax returns. "C" corporations can deduct 100% of the health insurance premiums paid on behalf of their shareholder-employees and their immediate families.

Retirement benefits

Contributions to qualified retirement plans are generally deductible by a business, and employees aren't immediately taxed on these contributions. Employees don't pay tax on the benefits until they receive them in the form of retirement benefits.

NOTE A qualified retirement plan must meet many strict requirements, including equitable coverage of employees, employees' entitlement to the money in their pension accounts and proper computing of contributions and benefits.

There are several different kinds of retirement plan, so a company owner should take the time to pick the right one. All companies can have either pension or profit-sharing plans. Proprietors and partners can have Keogh or HR-10 plans, designed for self-employed people and their employees. Small companies can have Simplified Employee Pension (SEP) or SIMPLE plan, both of which have very few administrative requirements.

Expenses of starting a business

The costs to get ready to do business are not immediately deductible. Instead, these costs are deducted or "amortized" over a period of time, in the same way that equipment is depreciated. If a new business makes the proper election, these costs can be deducted in equal amounts over 60 months from the start-up of operations. If the business doesn't get started or if it fails, these expenses are deductible in full at that time.

NOTE An election to amortize organization or start up costs must be included with the company's first tax return or no deduction will be allowed.

Nondeductible expenses - penalties/fines

Penalties or fines paid to a federal, state or local government agency for a violation of any law are not deductible. However, penalties paid for nonperformance of a contract or for late performance are generally deductible.

TAX COMPUTATION, CREDITS AND OTHER TAXES

Tax computation - general

The next step after calculating business gross income and allowable deductions, is to figure the net income or net loss. The step after that, figuring the tax, depends on the type of business organization.

For sole proprietorships, partnerships, LLCs or "S" corporations, the net income or loss is included in the owner's personal income tax returns, as one component of personal gross income. For "C" corporations, the corporation pays federal income taxes on its net income.

If you lose money in the business, the loss may be able to be carried back to offset net income in preceding years, resulting in a refund of prior year taxes paid. If any loss remains after the carry back, it can be carried forward to offset future income for the next 20 years.

Federal Tax Credits

Some business expenditures can produce tax credits. A tax credit is a direct reduction of tax liability. Two of the more common tax credits for small business owners are the jobs credit and the research credit.

Jobs Credit	The jobs credit is a percentage of wages paid to employees who are certified as members of a targeted group. Job credit wages are limited to $6,000 for each employee and $3,000 for each qualified summer youth employee.
Research Credit	The research credit is a percentage of expenses for research and experimental activities. The credit is 20 percent of the amount by which research expenses for the year exceed the average of a base period amount.

Proprietors, partners, LLCs and "S" corporation owners use the tax credits to offset federal income taxes on their personal income tax returns. A "C" corporation uses the tax credits on its federal income tax return.

 NOTE There are many other credits available, so consult CAAS and/or your professional advisor regarding availability.

State tax incentives

Connecticut also grants tax credits, but only to "C" and "S" corporations. These credits are direct reductions of the state tax liability. Listed below are some of the credit programs.

Connecticut "S" Corporations are limited to only a portion of the credit that would be allowed to them as a "C" Corporation. This percentage varies each year, and is the same percentage as the portion of Connecticut "S" Corporation income subject to Connecticut corporation taxation. See the discussion under "S" Corporations-State income taxes for further information.

Connecticut state tax incentives	
EDP Equipment Credit	This credit is allowed for the amount of personal property taxes paid to the local authorities on computer equipment.
Machinery and Equipment credit	A 5% or 10% credit (depending on size of corporation) is allowed for amounts spent for machines and equipment.
Research and Development credit	A tax credit is allowed based on a specified percentage (ranging from 1% to 10%) of research and development expenses spent for R&D performed in Connecticut.
Work Education	This credit is 10% of wages paid to a public high school student enrolled in a cooperative work education program.
Neighborhood Assistance Program	Allows a state tax credit of up to 60% of donations to approved child day care programs, employment and training programs, and programs for low-income people.
Manufacturing Facilities in Distressed Municipalities and Enterprise Zones	This credit is equal to 25% (50% for a qualifying facility in an enterprise zone) of the Connecticut tax allocable to approved manufacturing facilities.
Contributions to Low and Moderate Income Housing Projects	A 100% credit is granted to corporations that donate to approved housing programs.

Some other programs for which tax credits are granted are expenditures for air pollution abatement or industrial waste facilities, wages incurred for apprenticeships in machine tool and metal trades, expenditures for day care facilities and expenses for employee training. Contact the State of Connecticut Department of Revenue Services for further details on any of these credits.

ESTIMATED TAXES

Both the IRS and Connecticut operate on a *pay-as-you-go* basis, and require taxpayers to make advance tax payments during the year. The objective is to get taxpayers to prepay either their current year's tax bill or an amount equal to last year's tax bill, whichever is less. How a business prepays taxes depends on the type.

■   Sole Proprietors, Partners, SMLLC and LLC Members and "S" Corporation Shareholders have to make estimated tax payments if the total of their personal income tax and self-employment tax exceeds their total federal tax withheld and credits by more than $1,000.

These are paid with IRS Form 1040-ES, Estimated Tax for Individuals. Taxpayers make their estimated tax payments four times a year.

■ "C" corporations also make estimated tax payments if the tax for the year is expected to be $1000 or more. These tax payments may either be deposited at a bank, which transmits them to the IRS or transmitted electronically. They are due on the 15th day of the fourth, sixth, ninth and twelfth months of the corporation's fiscal year.

The following table summarizes the IRS estimated payment schedule for individual taxpayers and calendar year corporations.

Due dates for income tax estimates		
Installment	**Proprietor, SMLLC, LLC, Part, LP, LLP**	**"C" Corporation**
1	April 15th	April 15th
2	June 15th	June 15th
3	September 15th	September 15th
4	January 15th (following year)	December 15th

There is an underpayment penalty if the required estimated tax payments are not made by the due date. However, there are exceptions to reduce or eliminate the underpayment penalty, and an explanation of these rules can be found in IRS Publication 334 or the annual Connecticut income tax booklet.

TAX TRAPS FOR BUSINESS OWNERS

Hobby loss rule

A tax pitfall to sole proprietors is the "hobby loss" rule, which disallows losses from activities that are hobbies rather than profit-making endeavors. The targets for this rule are taxpayers who have businesses, such as horse farms, orchards and crafts production where the owner has no profit motive and is just trying to get a tax writeoff for a personal interest. The tax law presumes, in general, that if an activity makes a profit for three years out of five, it is not a hobby. There are two exceptions. One exception is for taxpayers who lose money in the first few years of operations. They can elect to postpone the three-year test until after their fifth year in business, by filing IRS Form 5213. This election operates as an *all or nothing* requirement. If the taxpayer passes the three-year test, any losses incurred during the five years are deductible. Otherwise, none of them are.

Another exception is made for a taxpayers who , despite having ongoing losses, prove the business was not a hobby. Factors that enter into this proof include the time and effort devoted to the business, the business-like manner in which the business is conducted, the expertise of the taxpayer, and the nature of the activity.

 NOTE However, it is up to the taxpayer to prove the profit motive behind the activity. This proof can include computerized accounting records, time sheets, promotional materials, diaries and correspondence.

Alternative minimum tax (AMT)

This tax was originally designed to ensure that businesses that receive special exemptions, deductions and credits pay at least some minimum amount of tax. The alternative minimum tax potentially applies in some way to all businesses. Sole Proprietors, Partners, LLC members and "S" Corporation shareholders are subject to the "AMT" on their personal income tax returns. "C" corporations are directly subject to the corporate AMT.

In effect, the alternative minimum tax takes back special benefits that business owners receive. Every company must compute this AMT before filing its tax return. In their tax planning, company managers should remember that the AMT may reduce the benefits of jobs credit programs and other special tax benefits.

Doing business in more than one state

If a corporation does business only in Connecticut, all of its income is taxed by the State of Connecticut. But, if it is also doing business in other states, a portion of the profits may be taxable in those other states. Multi-state corporations must *apportion* their income among the states in which they operate. The general formula for this is found in the state tax returns and considers the locations of sales, employees wages and corporation property. These rules vary from state to state.

If a corporation sells in other states or has employees or property located outside Connecticut, it may be subject to taxation in those other states, and should contact a tax advisor to check on state tax filing requirements. Once again, the specific state laws of the state in which you operate must be consulted in detail.

Interest and penalties

Both the IRS and Connecticut charge penalties and interest for taxpayers that do not follow the tax filing and payment requirements. Among the many reasons that penalties may apply are:

- Underpaying estimated taxes.
- Late tax returns.
- Late payment of the balance of tax owed.
- Failing to file returns.
- Substantially understating income tax liability.
- Negligence.

> **NOTE** IRS penalties can go up to 25% of the tax due. Connecticut penalties are generally 10% of the tax due. The interest rate for late payment of IRS taxes is usually one or two percentage points over the Prime Rate. The rate for Connecticut is much higher: 1¼% per month or 15% per year.

The combined penalties and interest can easily double the tax to taxpayers who are careless about their tax obligations and should be avoided whenever possible.

Examination of Returns

Both the Internal Revenue Service and the Connecticut Department of Revenue Services conduct examinations of a limited number of tax returns each year. These exams can be done by mail, at the Government's offices, or at the taxpayer's place of business or CPA's offices. At the start of an examination, the government employee assigned to your return will notify you of the records to provide.

A taxpayer can have someone else, such as a CPA or Attorney, represent them at the examination. The representative needs a written Power of Attorney, authorizing them to represent the taxpayer. Federal and state agencies each use different forms for this purpose. For many companies, it is common for professional representatives to handle audits, because of the potential for both additional taxes and penalties and because of their knowledge of extremely complex tax laws.

Statute of limitations

The statute of limitation defines the period in which the IRS and Connecticut may assess additional tax and a taxpayer may request a refund of overpaid taxes. Generally, this period is three years from the return's due date or the date the return is filed, or two years from the date the tax was paid. If a return is never filed or is found to be fraudulent, this period remains open indefinitely. Both the IRS and the State of Connecticut have administrative appeal procedures in case of a disagreement.

Information returns

Many small companies fail to file information returns for payments they make during the year, and thereby expose themselves to penalties. The IRS refers to these information returns as Form 1099. These must be given to payees during January every year, and usually filed with the IRS by February 28. The table below lists many of the types of payment that must be reported and the minimum amount for each type. If the limit is zero, all payments must be reported.

Levels for sending Forms 1099	
Type of payment	**Minimum**
Rents	$600
Royalties	10
Other Income	600
Federal Income Tax Withheld	0
Fishing Boat Proceeds	0
Medical and Health Care Payments	600
Nonemployee Compensation	600
Dividends or Interest (paid by banks or finance companies)	10
Excess golden parachute payments	0
Gross proceeds paid to an attorney	0

The most commonly omitted 1099 form for small companies is the one for nonemployee compensation. This applies to subcontractors, consultants, CPAs, other unincorporated payees who receive $600 or more. The other is payments to attorneys. Not included in these reportable payments are payments for the purchase of goods or merchandise. Reportable payments generally only include payments for services. The penalty for failing to file a Form 1099 is $50 per failure - one penalty for not providing the Form to the payee, and another penalty for not filing a copy of the Form with the IRS. Therefore, the actual penalty is $100 per overlooked form.

CONCLUSION

All companies, or their owners, must pay income taxes on the profits they earn. The way the company is taxed depends on which type of entity was selected.

Most normal business expenses can be written off on the company's tax return, reducing the amount of tax paid. Some, however, are only partially deductible and some, like equipment, must be written off over several years. A thorough knowledge of all of the tax laws applicable to business in general and to your particular form of organization is absolutely critical to ensuring compliance with all tax filing and payment requirements, and to make sure you take full advantage of any available tax incentives.

INTRODUCTION

Small businesses pay many other taxes besides income taxes. The income tax gets more publicity than other business taxes, but the other taxes can cost more. One of the most costly, payroll taxes, was discussed in the Paying Employees chapter. This chapter covers other taxes, such as: sales and use, excise, and property.

The sales tax has long been the mainstay of Connecticut's revenue picture and will remain so for many years. Yet, it is widely misunderstood by owners of small companies. Many of these owners do not learn that their sales are taxable until an auditor reviews the company's books and records.

This chapter discusses the Connecticut sales and use tax and what things generally are taxable. It also tells how to find out if something is taxable, and discusses the audit and enforcement process. It also briefly describes state and federal excise taxes as well as property taxes.

ORGANIZATION OF CHAPTER

This chapter discusses the following topics:

- Connecticut sales and use tax.
- State and federal excise taxes.
- Property taxes.

CONNECTICUT SALES AND USE TAX

The sales tax is the first tax a small business encounters because the state places a tax collection responsibility on every business. This tax covers equipment and services that are needed in order to start in business. It also covers services and products a business sells. Some business transactions are exempt from sales tax. It is important before starting the business to know what tax benefits the state allows and what the tax responsibilities are.

Of all of Connecticut's taxes, the sales and use tax is one of the largest revenue generators for the state. As one of the largest, the state aggressively seeks to assure that businesses are properly meeting their sales and use tax obligations. They do this by imposing high rates of interest and stiff penalties for not complying with the rules. Therefore, it is important to understand this tax well.

What follows is only a brief explanation of the sales and use tax. However, it should provide adequate knowledge and guidance to steer the new business owner in the right direction. The Department of Revenue Services publishes a detailed list of instructions (Form 0-88) which may also be helpful. First, we will look at who and what is subject to the tax. We will then look at a number of the exemptions allowed by the state. Finally, the material covers reporting procedures, forms and the state's audit procedures.

Registering to collect sales tax

For general business registration, Connecticut uses an all-purpose form, REG-1, which covers both income tax and sales tax. When you file this form with the Department of Revenue Services, you are assigned a registration number, which is used for all reporting and correspondence. If your business won't collect sales tax or file a separate income tax return, it does not have to register.

Who is subject to the tax

The sales tax is imposed for the privilege of making sales within Connecticut. The sales tax, although imposed on the business, is paid to the retailer by the consumer. It is the consumer who is liable to the retailer for the tax. The retailer in turn is liable to the state and is acting as an agent of the state when collecting the sales tax from its customers. Therefore, it is extremely important to pay the tax when due the state and not retain it in the business.

 All businesses, regardless of legal form, are required to collect Connecticut sales tax from their customers on all <u>taxable</u> sales.

What is taxable

Connecticut's sales tax law is written so that everything's taxable unless there is a specific exemption. The sales tax is imposed on retail sales of tangible personal property, the sale of a wide range of services and the leasing or rental of tangible personal property (not real property.) It also is charged on hotel, inn and motel room rentals for less then 30 consecutive days.

Taxable Property

Only the sale or leasing of tangible personal property is subject to taxation. Therefore, the sale or leasing of buildings or land is not subject to the sales tax. However, not all tangible personal property is subject to tax. There are many exemptions, discussed later under *exempt property transactions*.

Taxable Services

Connecticut charges sales tax on many services. The list below shows examples of common taxable services.This is not an exhaustive list of all the taxable services; there are hundreds of taxable services and the number changes daily.

Further, there are uncertainties in many categories of taxable services because of a few words of description can change a service's taxability. As a result there often are disagreements between taxpayers and the state about interpretations of the law. We strongly recommend that owners of service-oriented companies consult with a tax advisor or call the Department of Revenue Services before starting-up to find out whether their services will be taxable.

Examples of taxable services
1. Computer and data processing services. (Taxed at lower rate)
2. Painting and lettering services.
3. Private investigation and protection services.
4. Services to industrial, commercial or income producing real property.
5. Business analysis, management consulting and public relations services.
6. Motor vehicle repair services.
7. Credit information and reporting services.
8. Employment agencies providing personnel services.
9. Landscaping and horticulture services.
10. Maintenance and janitorial services.
11. Exterminating services.
12. Lobbying or consulting services.
13. Repair or maintenance service including any contract of warranty or service.
14. Photographic studio services.
15. Renovation services such as paving, painting, wallpapering, roofing, siding.
16. Advertising or public relation services.

Tax rate

The sales tax is figured as a percentage of gross receipts (sales price) from sales. The current general tax rate is 6%, but the rate can be higher or lower depending on the property or service sold; for example, hotel rooms are taxed at 12%, hospital rooms at 5.75%. In addition, when sales and use tax is eliminated on services, it is often done by a process of phasing out, reducing the rate until it reaches 0% and the service is no longer taxable.

When and where is the sale taxable

When and where the Connecticut tax applies depends upon whether the sale is property or a service. The table below shows the difference.

Taxable property	Tangible personal property is taxed at the time the transfer of title occurs. Title must pass in Connecticut in order for the sale to be taxed in Connecticut.
Taxable services	A service is taxed at the time it is performed. The tax on services generally occurs where the benefit of the service is realized and not necessarily where it is performed. The service must generally be received by the purchaser in Connecticut in order to be taxed in Connecticut.

Who and what is exempt from tax

Not all sales of tangible personal property and services are subject to the tax. There are numerous exceptions. It is beyond the scope of this chapter to cover all of the exceptions. Only the major exceptions will be covered to give a flavor of the depth and breadth of the exemptions. The list below gives two categories of exemption: exempt customers and exempt property.

Classification	Example
Exempt customer *Customers who don't have to pay sales tax on anything they buy if it is for the customer's exempt business*	United States government. Connecticut or any city or town in Connecticut. Nonprofit charitable hospitals. Charitable and religious organizations. Service centers for the elderly. Low and moderate income housing facilities.
Exempt sale *Products or services that aren't taxable at all, regardless of customer*	Purchases for resale. Clothing costing less than $50. Prescription medicine and medical equipment. Groceries - food items. Component parts used to assemble manufacturing machinery. Manufacturing and printing machinery. Safety apparel.

Exemption Certificates

Of the exemptions listed above, three deserve further explanation: Resale Exemption, Machinery Exemption, and Charitable and Religious Organization Exemption. To get these exemptions, the purchaser must give the seller an exemption certificate. It is not enough for the seller to rely on the name of the purchaser, or the apparent destination of the sale. The seller must have the necessary certificate on file to prove the exemption. Otherwise, a tax auditor can demand that the seller pay the tax anyway.

There is a different certificate for each situation:

- *Resale*: Resale Certificate.
- *Machinery, Tools and Materials*: Manufacturing Exemption Certificate.
- *Charitable and Religious Organizations*: Charitable/Religious Exemption Certificate.

The exemption certificate is an important bit of self-protection for the seller. In general, having one means that the purchaser will not have to pay the sales tax if it is later determined that a sale was taxable. Purchasers do not have to file their certificates with the state. The seller *must* keep a copy of all exemption certificates to prove that sales were tax-free. You can get a copy of these on the web at: www.drs.state.ct.us/forms/forms.html.

 NOTE The only requirement is that the seller accept the exemption certificate in good faith. If so, the seller will generally be relieved of liability. Good faith is having a reasonable belief that a resale certificate is valid.

Employees versus Independent contractors

If an employee performs a taxable service for an employer for a salary, the service isn't taxable. If an independent contractor performs a service for a fee, the service may be taxable if the service is a type that is taxable. For example, if a consultant provides a taxable service, such as advertising or public relations, as an independent contractor for a fee, the service is subject to tax. If the same person is hired as an employee for a salary, the service isn't taxable.

Use tax and out of state purchases

A use tax is really a sales tax charged in two situations: out-of-state purchases and in-state purchases on which no sales tax was charged. The use tax rate is the same as the sales tax rate and the tax is paid with the same form as the sales tax.

Most small businesses encounter the use tax on out-of-state purchases. As a rule, if an out-of-state transaction would have been taxable in Connecticut, it is subject to use tax. For example, if a company buys $1,000 worth of supplies in Massachusetts for use in Connecticut, it must pay Connecticut use tax on the purchase. If the Massachusetts vendor charges $50 Massachusetts sales tax, Connecticut allows a credit for the Massachusetts sales tax already paid and as a result the company must only pay a $10 Connecticut use tax. If the company makes a mail order purchase and the seller charges no sales tax, the buyer must pay the full Connecticut use tax on the purchase.

> **NOTE** Even if the purchase takes place in Connecticut, there may still be a use tax on it. For example, if a company buys something for resale, which is an exempt sale, but then uses the item in the business instead of reselling it, it has to pay a use tax.

Procedures and forms

Connecticut charges a high rate of interest and penalties for not meeting sales and use tax obligations. The tax law dictates the time for paying taxes, the forms and the due dates.

When the Tax Is Due to the State

In general, the tax must be reported in the period when the property is sold or when the service is provided, not when it is paid for. Thus, if a company makes a sale in March and receives payment in April, the sales tax must be reported in the March quarter, not the June quarter. If the customer doesn't pay, or returns the merchandise, the state refunds the tax paid, or allows a credit on the next sales tax payment. The seller must be able to prove that the account was uncollectible.

An exception to this general rule allows service providers that use the cash basis of reporting on their income tax returns to pay the sales tax on the cash basis, when they get paid, rather than when they provide the service. Companies that use the accrual method for income taxes must still pay the tax when the service is provided.

Forms to File and Paying Tax

The same form, OS-114 applies to all sales and use tax payments. The return and payment are due on the last day of the month after the reporting period. For example, if the tax period ends in June, the tax must be paid by the end of July. The reporting period can be either annual, quarterly or monthly:

- **Annual**: Taxpayers whose total tax liability for the 12-month period ending on the preceding September 30th was less than $1,000.

- **Quarterly**: New taxpayers or taxpayers whose total tax liability for the 12-month period ended on the preceding September 30th was less than $4,000.

- **Monthly**: All other taxpayers.

The following table illustrates the payment rules.

Example - Sales tax payment dates		
Threshold	**Reporting Period**	**Due Date**
Taxpayer whose annual tax liability is less than $1,000	January-December	January 31 of next year
New Taxpayer	January, February, March	April 30
Tax liability was less than $4,000 for the 12 months ending on the preceding September 30	January, February, March	April 30
Tax liability was $4,000 or more for the 12 months ending on the preceding September 30	January	February 28

The state will determine when, and if, the reporting period for your company should be changed and will notify you.

An extension to file the return may be granted in some situations, such as illness or personal hardship. However, this does not extend the time to pay the tax. A return must be filed even if no tax is due or no sales were made during the reporting period.

Penalty and Interest
The state charges interest for late filing. The rate is 1% of the tax due per month (12% annually) from the original due date of the return to the date of payment. The penalty for failure to pay tax when due is 15% of the tax due or $50, whichever is greater. In addition, civil and criminal penalties may be imposed for sales and use tax violations.

Audits

Connecticut generally has 3 years from the time the business files its tax return to perform an audit and assess additional taxes. If no return is filed the audit time period is unlimited; the state auditors can audit as far back as they want.

The audits are done by professional auditors from the Connecticut Department of Revenue Services (DRS). If the taxpayer disagrees with the DRS auditor, the DRS has an administrative appeal procedure. If that fails, the taxpayer can still go to court to resolve the dispute.

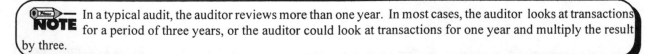

NOTE In a typical audit, the auditor reviews more than one year. In most cases, the auditor looks at transactions for a period of three years, or the auditor could look at transactions for one year and multiply the result by three.

The auditor generally looks at three areas: fixed asset purchases, recurring expenditures, and gross receipts. There are different approaches to each area:

Fixed Asset Purchases

Under the first category the auditor looks at the company's tangible personal property purchases during the audit period to determine if Connecticut sales or use tax was paid. The auditor normally wants to see the invoice for each fixed asset purchase. One focus is on out-of-state vendor purchases to determine that the taxpayer paid a Connecticut use tax. Another is on items that may have been purchased with a resale or manufacturing exemption certificate and used for something else.

Recurring Expenditures

These are the company's administrative or overhead expenses, such as office supplies, repairs, etc. The auditor normally does not look at all at expenditures for the whole audit period but instead selects a sample period, such as 1 to 6 months, and looks at expenditures during that period. Based on the error rate in this sample method, the auditor figures a tax for the entire period. For example, if the auditor finds that 5% of the expenditures in the sample period didn't get taxed properly, the company will be charged an extra tax on 5% of the expenditures during the entire audit period.

Gross Receipts

The third target area in an audit is the company's sales. The auditor first checks to see that the sales reported on the sales tax returns equals the sales reported on the company's books and records and the Federal income tax return. If the books or income tax return's sales are more than those reported on sales tax returns, the auditor asks for an explanation for the difference. If the difference can't be explained, the company may be charged sales tax on the difference.

Next, the auditor looks at sales to see if the tax was figured correctly, collected and paid on time. Here, too, the auditor uses a sample approach and figures a tax assessment based on the findings for a small part of the company's sales. The emphasis is generally on exempt sales and out-of-state sales.

To prepare for a sales tax audit, or to prevent problems in case there is an audit, company personnel should follow a five step process:

1.   Review all fixed asset invoices to be sure tax was paid when appropriate.

2.   Reconcile sales reported on the books and Federal income tax return with that shown on sales tax returns.

3.   Review supplies and other recurring expenditure invoices for sales tax applicability.

4.   Keep a three-ring binder or file folder of exemption certificates received. Be sure there is an exemption certificate to support every exempt sale or that a "blanket" exemption certificate that covers purchases over a period of time is kept. Don't take a customer's word that a sale is exempt. Either get a certificate or collect the sales tax.

5.   When making an out-of-state purchase from a vendor who doesn't collect Connecticut sales tax, if the purchase would be taxable in Connecticut, report the purchase and pay the appropriate amount of Connecticut use tax on it.

STATE AND FEDERAL EXCISE TAXES

Both Connecticut and the Federal government charge excise taxes. An excise tax is a special form of tax. Tax rates are not listed since they are continuously changing and vary greatly.

CONNECTICUT EXCISE TAXES

Alcoholic beverages

Each distributor of alcoholic beverages must pay a Connecticut excise tax on all sales of alcoholic beverages. Alcoholic beverages include spirits, wine, beer and liquor. The tax is generally imposed on a per barrel or per gallon basis. The tax is paid monthly with the filing of a return to the state.

Cigarette and tobacco products

A Connecticut stamp tax is imposed on all cigarettes held in-state for sale. The tax is paid by purchasing stamps from the state then sticking them on to the cigarette packages. The tax is on a per cigarette basis. An excise tax is also imposed on other tobacco products such as cigars, smoking tobacco, and chewing tobacco. The tax is imposed based on the wholesale sales price. These taxes are paid monthly with the filing of a return to the state.

Admission

A Connecticut excise tax applies to admission charges to commercial amusement or entertainment places and on dues or initiation fees to private clubs.

Motor fuels, gasoline and special fuels

Distributors must pay a Connecticut excise tax on each gallon of fuel sold. Fuel includes gasoline, gasohol, and diesel. The rate of tax depends on the type of fuel sold. Some sales of fuel are exempt from tax. For example, fuel sold which will be used exclusively for heating purposes is exempt from the tax. The tax is paid monthly with the filing of a return to the state.

Motor carrier

A Connecticut motor carrier road tax applies to private motor carriers operating on Connecticut highways. The tax is based on the amount of fuel used by a motor carrier in its operation in the state and the tax rate is the same as the motor fuels rate. The tax is paid quarterly with the filing of a return to the state.

Petroleum

A Connecticut excise tax is imposed on the distribution of petroleum products in the state. The tax only applies to the first in-state use of the petroleum product. The tax is based on the quarterly gross earnings and is paid quarterly with the filing of a return to the state.

FEDERAL EXCISE TAXES

The federal government also charges excise taxes on many business activities. Federal excise taxes include:

- Environmental taxes.
- Communication and air transportation taxes.
- Fuel taxes.

- Luxury tax.
- Retail tax.
- Manufacturers tax.
- Other miscellaneous taxes.

If the company is doing business in any of these areas, it may have to pay excise taxes using IRS Form 720. Contact a tax advisor, the Internal Revenue Service or the DRS to get more information. Publication 510, obtained from the IRS, discusses specific details about federal excise taxes. It also explains IRS Form 720, the Quarterly Federal Excise Tax Return.

PROPERTY TAXES

Depending on the type of business, property taxes can be a large tax liability. It is important to have a basic understanding of how Connecticut taxes property owners.

Taxable property

There are no state property taxes. Instead, property taxes are assessed by local governments. In Connecticut, the town or city is the taxing unit for assessing and collecting property taxes. In general, all real estate and personal property in Connecticut is taxable unless it is specifically exempt from tax. There are many exemptions and it is not practical to explain all of them in detail here.

Exemptions

Exemptions generally include inventories of manufacturers and mercantile operations and acquisitions of new manufacturing machinery and equipment. Partial exemptions may be allowed for manufacturing facilities and equipment operating in an enterprise zone. The property owned by various organizations are also exempt, such as the property owned by nonprofit charitable, educational, religious and scientific organizations, as discussed in the Starting a Not-for-profit Organization chapter.

Rate of tax

Property is assessed at a uniform percentage throughout Connecticut, currently 70%, of the market value. The tax rate is determined by the local tax district and, as a result, varies from town to town. For real estate, the town uses a periodic appraisal to figure the assessment. For business equipment, the town uses the company's cost. The taxable basis of equipment is adjusted downward for older equipment. Appeals from assessments may be made to the town's Board of Tax Review during a specified period each year.

Form to file

All business property owners have to file a return on or before November 1st of each year listing all taxable personal property they own or lease on the assessment date, October 1st. The towns charge interest if the tax isn't paid on time.

Audits

Many towns hire outside auditors to help them with taxpayer compliance. The town and the auditor first look for companies that aren't filing property tax returns. Then, they visit companies to check the declared valuations against property on hand. They are allowed to look at the company books and tax returns in order to check on valuations. Property owners can appeal valuations.

CONCLUSION

At least annually, it's a good idea to review the company's sales, excise and property tax situation. The following is a checklist of things to look for:

- Review the possibility of sales and use tax exemptions for the business and customers.

- Invoices should be reviewed for sales and use tax applicability.

- Review the possibility of hiring an employee as opposed to an independent contractor.

- Consider Federal and state excise tax responsibilities.

- Review with municipality personnel the types of property that may be exempt from property taxes.

- If property has recently been revalued by the municipality, review the assessed value to determine its reasonableness in light of local conditions.

- Companies that are located in enterprise zones may be eligible for property tax abatements, exemption from sales and use taxes as well as a variety of other state and local incentives. Consult your Chamber of Commerce to see if your business is located in an enterprise zone.

Chapter 13
Starting a Not-For-Profit Organization

INTRODUCTION

Not-for-profit organizations face big challenges in their efforts to house the homeless, help welfare recipients learn work skills and gain employment, provide caring environments the terminally ill, nurture preschool children, educate the public and fulfill other worthwhile goals.

Organization leaders must develop active, efficient service organizations and complete many financial tasks in order to set up their organizations. These tasks include applying for federal tax-exempt status, registering as not-for-profit enterprises in Connecticut, filing annual information returns, developing Boards of Directors and maintaining effective financial controls.

ORGANIZATION OF CHAPTER

This chapter discusses the following topics:

■ Benefits of tax-exempt status.
■ Eligibility for tax-exempt status.
■ Starting a not-for-profit organization.
■ Qualifying for tax-exempt status.
■ Obtaining not-for-profit benefits.
■ Reports due by tax-exempt organizations.

BENEFITS OF TAX-EXEMPT STATUS

The not-for-profit world is characterized by scarce resources and an unending demand for those resources. The not-for-profit status provides several advantages that allow the organization to make better use of its funds. Below are some of the benefits:

■ Exemption from federal and state income taxes.
■ Property tax and sales and use tax exemptions.
■ Exemption from Federal unemployment taxes.
■ Discounted prices on office equipment.
■ Preferred postal rates.
■ In some cases tax deductions for donors, which helps in fund-raising.

To claim these benefits, the organization must qualify for not-for-profit status, undergo special government scrutiny and provide special reports to government agencies.

ELIGIBILITY FOR TAX-EXEMPT STATUS

The Internal Revenue Service grants tax-exempt status to two types of organizations. Their names come from the Internal Revenue Code sections that establish them:

■ Section 501(c)(3) organizations.
■ Other Section 501(c) organizations.

Section 501(c)(3) organizations

The category includes organizations that benefit the general public. It includes organizations formed for religious, charitable, literary, educational, or scientific purposes, product safety testing, promoting amateur athletics, or preventing cruelty to animals.

An organization must receive one-third of its support from the general public or government to qualify as a publicly-supported tax-exempt organization. However, an organization can still be tax-exempt if receives over 10% of its support from the public or government and it is also organized and operated so as to attract continuous government and public support.

> **NOTE** If an organization doesn't meet these public support tests, it is classified as a private foundation, which still receives not-for-profit status, but is subject to strict deduction limitations, pays tax on its investment income and must make mandatory annual distributions.

Other Section 501(c) organizations

Many other organizations can receive the benefits of tax-exempt status, other than the receipt of deductible charitable contributions. These organizations include employee associations, labor organizations, chambers of commerce, and social clubs.

STARTING A NOT-FOR-PROFIT ORGANIZATION

The first step in starting a not-for-profit organization is to create an organizational document. This document, known as a charter, constitution or articles of incorporation, is important for all types of business groups, but it is especially important for not-for-profit organizations because the Internal Revenue Service uses it to test their eligibility for tax-exempt status. An organizational document is usually prepared by an attorney, and to pass Internal Revenue Service scrutiny and help ensure that an organization is granted tax-exempt status, it must do these things:

- **Mission** - Clearly and briefly define a mission. The mission is a statement of the actions the organization will take to carry out its goals. Besides helping with IRS approval, a clear mission can make it easier to move community members to action and to raise funds.

- **Limits of Power** - Limit the purposes and powers of the organization to tax-exempt purposes. It cannot allow the organization, except for a minor part of its activities, to do things that are not related to its exempt purposes.

- **Use of funds** - Prohibit the organization's net earnings from being used to benefit private individuals.

- **Legislation** - Prohibit the organization from influencing legislation or campaigning for or against candidates for public office. It can elect to come under provisions allowing limited lobbying expenditures.

- **Dissolution** - Require that if it goes out of business the assets be distributed to another exempt organization or transferred to a federal, state or local government for a public purpose.

A helpful publication in determining tax-exempt status is Internal Revenue Service Publication 557, "Tax-Exempt Status for Your Organization." This publication is a detailed review of the many types and qualifications of tax-exempt organizations.

Once the organizational document has been created, the organization must incorporate as a non-stock, not-for-profit corporation by registering with the Connecticut Secretary of State and paying the necessary fees.

For an organization to become a not-for-profit organization, it must first qualify as one. Later, it must file special reports with the IRS, and sometimes with Connecticut. A summary of the application forms and reports appears in the following table.

IRS not-for-profit forms and publications	
Form number and name	**Explanation**
Application forms:	
1023, 1024 Tax exemption applications	Application for exemption from income tax, under Sections 501(c)(3) or 501(a) or 120.
SS-4 Application for federal employer identification number (FEIN)	Registers organization with the IRS. Even if the organization doesn't have employees, it needs this ID number.
Annual Information Returns:	
990 and Schedule A Returns of Organization Exempt from Income Tax	Reports financial information including Statement of Revenue and Expenses and Balance Sheet for past fiscal year. Includes information on program activities, contributions to the organization and the names of board members. Schedule A includes supplemental information on the sources of financial support necessary to maintain tax-exempt public charity status.
990EZ	Short version of Form 990 for organizations with gross receipts under $100,000 and total assets under $250,000.
990-T Exempt organization business income tax return	Filing of financial information if gross unrelated business income is $1,000 or more. Must be filed on or before the regular due date for Form 990.
2758, 7004 Application for extension of time to file	Requests extension of deadline for filing annual returns. See form's instructions for which version to use. A total of six months extension is available.
Other IRS forms:	
1128 Application for change in accounting period	Must be submitted and approved by IRS before any changes in accounting period can be made.
5768 Election/revocation of election by an eligible section 501(c)(3) organization	To elect to expend a limited but more than "insubstantial" amount of money on lobbying.

Connecticut not-for-profit forms	
Form number and name	**Explanation**
Application forms:	
CPC-63 Registration statement	Registration with Connecticut Department of Consumer Protection Public Charities Unit.
CPC-54 Exempt verification status	Verification of exempt status also filed with the Public Charities Unit.
Annual information return:	
CPC-60 Annual report face sheet	Accompanied by IRS Form 990. If gross revenues exceed $200,000, a complete set of audited financial statements is sent to the State.

QUALIFYING FOR TAX-EXEMPT STATUS

In order to qualify for tax-exempt status, an organization must file applications with both the federal government and Connecticut. This is a several-step process starting with requesting exempt status, receiving a provisional exempt status, operating provisionally and receiving a final exempt status. The entire process takes about five years from start to finish.

Federal qualification

To be exempt from federal tax, an organization must file an application along with a $500 fee to the Internal Revenue Service. Depending on the type of organization, it files either Form 1023 or Form 1024.

Form 1023

Form 1023 is the initial application for exemption under **Section 501(c)(3)** of the Internal Revenue Code. This form should be filed within fifteen months from the end of the month in which the organization was formed. The organization will also have to include its Articles of Incorporation and its Bylaws, along with selected financial information and information about its founders. If tax-exempt status is granted, it is retroactive to the date the not-for-profit organization was formed.

Once the Internal Revenue Service receives Form 1023, it issues a definitive or an advance ruling regarding the organization's status as a public charity or private foundation. Private foundations must meet more stringent standards than public charities; e.g. private foundations are required to distribute annual income and may possibly be required to pay excise taxes.

If an organization receives an advance ruling, it is permitted to operate as a public charity for five years. At the end of that time, the organization must submit information indicating that it has met the public support test during the five years of the advance ruling period. If this information does not indicate that the organization met the public support test, the organization will have to pay excise taxes as if it were a private foundation.

Form 1024

Form 1024 is the application for exemption under **Section 501(a)**. It is used to obtain exempt status for other organizations such as civic leagues, social and recreational clubs and employees' associations.

> **NOTE** The IRS **determination letter** is the evidence that the organization's not-for-profit status has been approved. It is a valuable document that must be attached to many applications and certificates, so make plenty of backup copies.

Connecticut qualification

To be exempt from Connecticut corporation tax, an organization must send a copy of the 501(c) ruling received from the Internal Revenue Service stating that it is exempt from federal tax. Connecticut will automatically exempt the organization from the state corporation income tax and no annual tax return will be due to the state.

OBTAINING NOT-FOR-PROFIT BENEFITS

Receiving the benefit of not-for-profit status usually requires small additional steps. Only the income tax exemption is automatic, which comes with the filing of federal tax-exempt forms.

Sales tax exemption on purchases

An organization that has been granted exemption from federal tax can get an exemption from sales tax on purchases in Connecticut, as long as the items purchased are to be used for the purpose of the organization. The organization must provide the seller with a form CERT-119, *Certificate for Purchases of Tangible Personal Property and Services by Qualifying Exempt Organizations*, with a copy of the first page of its IRS determination letter. For exempt meals and lodging, CERT-112 is used.

Sales tax exemption on sales

Small not-for-profit groups such as accredited schools, little leagues, scouts and parent teacher organizations are not required to register with the Department of Revenue Service to collect sales tax on items sold if the items are sold for $20 or less and the purpose is to raise funds for youth activities. Other organizations would have to collect sales tax on taxable items sold to raise funds, unless the activity qualifies as an "occasional" or casual sale.

Funds solicitation

The Connecticut Solicitation of Charitable Funds Act requires charitable organizations to register before they can solicit funds. An organization registers by filing Registration Form CPC-63 with the state's Public Charities Unit and paying a $20 registration fee. Registration is a one-time task; there is no annual renewal.

Some organizations are exempt from registration. There are six categories:
1. Religious corporations, institutions, or societies.
2. Parent-teacher organizations and educational institutions,.
3. Non-profit hospitals.
4. Government agencies.
5. Solicitors of funds for the above organizations.
6. Charitable organizations that do not pay anyone to solicit contributions, and receive under $50,000 annual contributions of money, credit, property, financial assistance, etc. The $50,000 limit does not include membership dues.

An organization that falls within one of these six categories must verify its exemption from registration by filing Form CPC-54, Exempt Status Verification. There is no filing fee and no other form need be filed in the future if the organization qualifies as exempt, although the Department of Consumer Protection can require continued proof of exemption.

Federal unemployment taxes

Tax-exempt organizations are exempt from paying federal unemployment taxes. When the organization files its SS-4 to obtain a federal identification number and identifies itself as being not-for-profit, the government automatically will not send the annual unemployment form.

Discounts on purchases

Many businesses maintain special discounted price schedules for their not-for-profit customers. These price schedules are not often publicized, so it is a good idea to ask when making a purchase. Mail-order firms that sell computer hardware and software normally maintain separate telephone sales lines for not-for-profit organizations.

The Connecticut State Agency for Federal Surplus Property allows qualified not-for-profit organizations to receive surplus furniture and office equipment at no charge from the surplus office. To take advantage of this benefit, contact them at:

> Connecticut State Agency for Federal Surplus Property
> 165 Capital Ave., Room 420
> Hartford, CT 06106
> Phone: 860-713-5159
> Fax: 860-713-7476

Preferred postal rates

The United States Post Office maintains a special discounted price schedule for not-for-profit organizations to use in their mailings. To apply for these rates, the organization must file PS Form 3624, available at your local post office. Attached to the form must be a copy of the organization's articles of incorporation or charter describing the organization's primary purpose, and also of not-for-profit status, such as a copy of the IRS determination letter. Additional documents may be required; a more thorough list and instructions can be found at: http://pe.usps.gov.

Property tax exemptions

In Connecticut, town tax collectors are allowed to exempt a portion of the real estate and business equipment of not-for-profit organizations. The exemption applies to property that the organization owns or that it rents. Tax collectors normally require the organization to file an application and prove that it is tax-exempt.

REPORTS DUE BY TAX-EXEMPT ORGANIZATIONS

An organization may have to file annual informational returns with both the federal government and Connecticut depending on the type of organization, its annual gross receipts and its total assets at year end.

Federal Reports

Not-for-profit organizations may have to file Internal Revenue Service Form 990, Return of an Organization Exempt from Income Tax, or Form 990EZ, Short Form Return of Organization Exempt From Income Tax. An organization can use Form 990EZ instead of Form 990 if its gross receipts for the year were less than $100,000 and its total assets at the end of the year were less than $250,000. Some types of organizations such as schools, religious organizations or state institutions are not required to file at all. Also, an organization whose annual gross receipts are normally less than $25,000 does not have to file.

If an organization is required to file Form 990 or 990EZ, it is due 5½ months after the end of the organization's tax year. Form 990 and 990EZ's Schedule A, includes information about activities of charitable organizations that claim "public charity" status.

Late filing or failing to file, without a good reason, can cost an organization a penalty of $10 per day up to a maximum of $5,000. Even incomplete filings can cost penalties. The Internal Revenue Service can reject an incomplete Form 990 or 990EZ and charge the same penalty as if the form had never been filed.

The due dates for filing Forms 990 and 990EZ can be extended by filing Form 2758 with the Internal Revenue Service by the due date of the return. By filing successive Forms 2758 for three months each, the time for filing a Form 990 or 990EZ can be extended to a maximum of six months.
Every organization with gross unrelated business income of $1,000 or more must file Form 990-T, Exempt Organization Business Income Tax Return, by the fifteenth day of the fifth month after the close of the not-for-profit organization's year. 'Unrelated trade or business' is any trade or business which is *not substantially related* to the organization's exempt purpose. This is discussed in detail in IRS Code Section 513(a). The due date of Form 990-T can be automatically extended six months

by filing Form 7004, provided the organization is formed as a corporation. If it is formed as a trust, Form 2758 must be used.

Tax-exempt organizations must make a copy of its three most recent annual information returns and its Form 1023 or Form 1024 available for public inspection. If they don't comply with this requirement of public inspection they face a $10 per day (maximum of $5,000 per annual return) penalty.

Like their taxable counterparts, tax-exempt organizations must withhold and deposit payroll taxes for employees and file quarterly payroll tax returns. These are the federal income tax and the social security taxes withheld and reported on Form 941.

Connecticut Reports

Tax-exempt organizations must also withhold and deposit Connecticut income tax on employees' wages. The amounts are reported quarterly on Form CT-941. Most tax-exempts are also subject to Connecticut unemployment tax, paid quarterly with Form UC-5A. Religious organizations are exempt.

An organization does not have to file a state form comparable to the Federal Form 990 with Connecticut. However, if it is registered with the state to solicit funds, it must file Form CPC-60, Annual Report Face Sheet and a copy of its Internal Revenue Service Form 990 or 990EZ within five months after the end of its tax year. If the organization collects more than $200,000 in gross revenue, not including government grants and fees, it has to have an annual audit performed by a Certified Public Accountant. The audit report can be either an accountant's report on the Internal Revenue Service Form 990 or a standard accountant's audited financial statement. There is a $25 filing fee for the CPC-60. The organization can get a three month filing extension from the Public Charities Unit by writing a letter to the unit.

Information about the Connecticut Solicitation of Charitable Funds Act and filing forms can be obtained from the state agency that oversees the law:

> Public Charities Unit
> Department of Consumer Protection
> c/o Office of the Attorney General
> 55 Elm Street
> Hartford, Connecticut 06106
> Telephone: (860) 808-5030

CONCLUSION

Tax-exempt organizations receive many benefits, such as exemption from federal tax, relief from Federal unemployment taxation and property and sales tax exemptions. Many organizations find it time-consuming to become tax-exempt, and the process does contain some traps for the unwary. The annual state and federal reporting requirements are very different from those for profit-making businesses.

This discussion was intended as an overview, not to cover all exempt organization issues. Organizations that seek tax-exempt status will find it worthwhile to seek professional guidance.

Thanks for reading this book!

We hope it's helped you take the right steps toward starting your own business. Refer to it often and don't be afraid to ask for help. We'd like to ask two more things of you:

✔ Refer someone else to the book, which is our contribution toward business in Connecticut. It's how we in CAAS help businesses in Connecticut and also how we finance our operating expenses.

✔ Help CAAS with your financial support. We're all unpaid volunteers, but we have operating expenses to pay. Your charitable contribution helps economically disadvantaged people receive the help they need to navigate today's complex financial environment. The person just coming off welfare into that first job, the divorcee trying to sort out the pieces, the homemaker starting up a home-based business to augment the family income, an affordable housing group setting up a budget for a house renovation, a group of entry-level workers setting up a day care co-op so they can seek employment. We're here for all of them.

Copy this page and mail it in with your check
Or... order and pay online! Logon to www.purtill.com.

Community Accounting Aid Services, Inc.
1800 Asylum Avenue, 4th Floor
West Hartford, CT 06117
(860) 570-9113

Please send me a copy of *Starting a Small Business in Connecticut*.

Name: _____

Address: _____

City: _____ State: _____ Zip: _____

Daytime Telephone: _____

Price	$ 28.95
Shipping and handling	2.50
Connecticut sales tax (deduct for out-of-state shipments)	1.89
Total	$ 33.34

Please count me in as a contributor to CAAS's work with economically disadvantaged people.

I enclose my contribution $ _____

Total enclosed $ _____

Please make your check or money order payable to Community Accounting Aid Services.

Thank you!